Hugh Mackay was born in 1938 and educated at Sydney Grammar School, the University of Sydney and Macquarie University. He was elected a Fellow of the Australian Psychological Society in 1985.

He is a social researcher, novelist, columnist for the *Weekend Australian* and bestselling author of two other books in the field of social psychology: *Reinventing Australia* (1993) and *Generations* (1997).

Other Books by Hugh Mackay

NON-FICTION
Reinventing Australia
Generations

FICTION
Little Lies
House Guest

THE GOOD LISTENER

Better relationships through
better communication

HUGH MACKAY

MACMILLAN
Pan Macmillan Australia

First published as *Why Don't People Listen?* in Pan in 1994
by Pan Macmillan Publishers Australia
This Macmillan edition published 1998 by Pan Macmillan Australia Pty Limited,
St Martins Tower, 31 Market Street, Sydney

National Library of Australia
cataloguing-in-publication data:

Mackay, Hugh.
[Why don't people listen?]
The good listener.

ISBN 0 7329 0931 7.

1. Interpersonal communication. 2. Interpersonal relations. 3. Interpersonal relations.
4. Communication. I. Title. II. Title: Why don't people listen?

302.2

Typeset in 12/14 point Garamond by Midland Typesetters Pty, Maryborough, Victoria
Printed in Australia by McPherson's Printing Group

Contents

Preface

Communication is probably one of your favourite subjects—and so it should be. After all, we humans are 'herd animals'. We belong in communities. We thrive on relationships. We need to communicate.

But communication has had a tough time during the last quarter of the 20th century. The relentless changes of the past twenty years have had the effect of breaking down many of our traditional groups and isolating us from each other. Our personal relationships have often been the casualties of social, economic and technological change.

This has been a time of redefinition of everything from gender roles to social class. We are adapting to new patterns of marriage and divorce, a new sense of cultural identity, and the constant introduction of new technology which inevitably reshapes the way we live.

While we have been struggling to keep up with the changes, it has been easy to forget that the most precious resource we have for coping with life in unstable and uncertain times is the resource of our personal relationships. The thing we most need is each other.

If the time has come to start putting more emphasis on the quality of our relationships, and giving more attention to the life of our 'herds'—families, work-groups, friends, neighbours—then the time has certainly come to take more care with our communication.

Hence this book.

Preface to the Second Edition

The warm response to *Why Don't People Listen?* from students, teachers, managers, communication professionals and general readers has been gratifying, but there has been one recurring problem with the book: its title.

When I settled on *Why Don't People Listen?*, I believed that was the most commonly asked question about communication. I still believe that, but I have discovered that, as a book title, it has one serious flaw: people can't easily remember it. Perhaps because it is too 'wordy'; perhaps because it focuses on the negative; perhaps because questions don't work well as book titles ... for whatever reason, I'm frequently confronted by people who tell me they love the book, but who are struggling to recall its exact title.

So ... here is a new edition, in a larger format, with a new name: *The Good Listener*. I now wish, of course, that I had settled on that as the title back in 1994, instead of confining it to a sub-heading in Chapter 5.

This second edition has been lightly edited, to correct some minor errors and to smooth some rough edges in the writing. Essentially, though, it is the same book.

Acknowledgements

My introduction to communication theory came from the late Dr Peter Kenny, when we worked together in 1962 in the audience research department of the Australian Broadcasting Commission. Peter urged me to explore the extraordinary body of mass communication research which was then being published in the USA (most notably, the work of the late Joseph Klapper who subsequently became my friend and mentor).

I gradually developed a broader interest in the process of human communication in any setting, partly under the influence of the work of Carl Rogers (the American psychotherapist and founder of the school of client-centred therapy). After Peter Kenny moved into the academic world, he continued to stimulate and challenge my ideas about communication both in the mass media and in the context of personal relationships.

In 1975, I established The Centre for Communication Studies (in Bathurst, NSW) as an educational offshoot of my communication research and consulting business. My aim was to conduct seminars and workshops on the application of communication theory to management and I was fortunate to have the support of Dr Robert Wilson who was at that time the director of training at CSR

Limited. Following some research into the training needs of CSR managers, Robert had concluded that a high priority was to improve managers' understanding of the communication process.

With Robert's encouragement, I developed an educational program which led to a close and productive association with the management community of CSR. The program was modified for wider use and I subsequently conducted more than 300 communication workshops for managers from a variety of industrial, commercial, marketing, educational and government organisations. In every case, I learned as much as I taught.

In 1979, I was invited by the editor of *The National Times*, Evan Whitton, to write a weekly column on 'Persuasion' with a particular emphasis on the communication process in politics, business and the media. One of those columns attracted the attention of Caroline Jones who was then running her hugely successful morning radio program for the ABC (*City Extra* on Sydney's 2BL). Caroline invited me onto the program to discuss the subject of that column—listening—and that discussion led to a fortnightly interview in which we would explore a communication issue followed by talk-back conversation with listeners. She encouraged me to present my ideas about communication in a more permanent form and, with her support and collaboration, I produced the *Better Communication* series of audio tapes, with Caroline as co-presenter. *Why Don't People Listen?* is a further step in the development of that material.

The author and the publishers would like to thank the following for permission to reproduce material in this book:

Extracts from 'Negotiation and Mediation' by P. Carnevale and D. Pruitt reproduced, with permission, from the *Annual Review of Psychology*, volume 43, 1992, by Annual Reviews Inc.

Extracts from *What Is This Thing Called Science?* by A. F. Chalmers, 1982, reproduced, with permission, from University of Queensland Press.

Extracts from *The Wind In The Willows* by K. Grahame, 1980, reproduced, with permission, from Reed Consumer Books.

Extracts from *Amusing Ourselves To Death* by N. Postman, 1986, reproduced, with permission, from William Heinemann Ltd.

Extracts from *On Becoming A Person* by C. Rogers, 1967, reproduced, with permission, from Constable Publishers.

Extracts from *The E-Mail From Bill [Gates]* by J. Seabrook, 10 January 1994 reprinted by permission © John Seabrook. Originally in *The New Yorker*.

Extracts from *C. J. Jung Speaking: Interviews and Encounters*, by W. McGuire and RFC Hulk1 (eds), 1980, reproduced, with permission, from Thames and Hudson Ltd.

Extracts from *Organisational Change By Choice*, by D. Dunphy, 1981, reproduced, with permission, from McGraw-Hill Book Company.

Extracts from *The Men We Never Knew* by D. R. Kingma, 1992, reproduced, with permission, from Conan Press, Berkeley, California.

Extracts from *The Psychology of Communication* by G. A. Miller, 1967, reproduced, with permission, from HarperCollins Publishers/Inc. for Basic Books Inc.

The publishers would welcome any information about the following material:
Irrational Man by W. Barrett, 1961
Steps To An Ecology Of Mind by G. Bateson, 1987
Influence: Science and Practice by R. Cialdini, 1985

and tender their apologies if any infringement of copyright has occurred.

Meet the family ...

Most of us learn about communication from our families. We learn it as part of the broader lessons our parents teach us about how we should treat each other and what degree of responsibility we should accept for each other.

Of course, such things are rarely spoken about, because they don't need to be made explicit. The lessons are obvious from the way our families behave.

Family life isn't all sweetness and light. In fact, when you're in the middle of one, a family can feel anything but sweet. All families are unhappy families, sometimes, and that is probably just as well. After all, the family is not only the place where we learn about tolerance, forgiveness and unconditional love; it is also where we learn about adversity, conflict and compromise.

If families are functioning properly, the big pay-off for society is that children will have already learned many of these lessons before they are let loose on the community. That is presumably one of the things we mean when we say that the family is the social unit.

A family figures prominently in the pages of this book, and I'd like to introduce them to you.

Bill is in his early forties. He grew up on a farm, but had his heart set on the city from an early age. He works in a department of the public service. He was married to **Judith** and they had one daughter, **Kelly**. The marriage ended in divorce when Kelly was seven. She stayed with her mother until, nine years later, Judith remarried and went to live in the USA with her new husband. At that point, Kelly came to live with Bill who, by then, had married **Margaret** and had a son, **Michael**, now seven.

Margaret is in her early thirties. She had to be persuaded to marry Bill, partly because he is ten years older than she is, and partly because her closest friend had married a man with children from a previous marriage, and she wasn't keen on putting herself through the kind of difficulties they'd had to face. The fact that Kelly was living with Judith at the time weighed in Bill's favour, but the arrival of Kelly on the scene all these years later has greatly complicated the life of the household.

Margaret's own parents are divorced and she has a difficult relationship with her father, **Cole**, who is a fading celebrity in the media. Cole was never in favour of her marriage to Bill, and still makes his feelings known—though he is devoted to his grandson, Michael.

Rather against Bill's wishes, Margaret has recently returned to full-time work as an account executive in an advertising agency. She is stimulated by the job, and excited by her prospects for promotion.

We join the family as Michael answers a telephone call from his mother . . .

CHAPTER 1

The Injection Myth

'*Michael? Listen to me. What's that noise in the background? Well, go and turn it down. I'll hang on . . . Are you there? Listen. Something's come up at work and I'm going to be a bit later than usual. I'll tell you about it when I get home. Is Dad home yet? Well, when he comes in, tell him I'll be about an hour late, and he should go ahead with the dinner. We're having sausages and they're in the fridge. You could get them out for him. Tell him you should all go ahead and eat if I'm not home in time. Now, where's Kelly? Is she home yet? Good. Will you tell her I'm going to be a little bit late home, and she should get on with her homework now. It will be too late after netball. If I'm not home in time, Dad can take her to training. Michael, are you listening? Put Kelly on . . . Well, tell her to turn off the TV and get on with her homework. I'll see you soon. Don't forget to tell Dad about the dinner. Oh, and you can have your bath now, Michael. Michael?*'

Margaret replaces the receiver in its cradle, runs a brush through her hair, grabs her briefcase and dashes to the lift. She's waited too long for this moment: a meeting, at last, with the Grey Eminence himself, to be told about her new responsibilities. All the signs point to a big promotion. Bill won't know what to *say. He never does. Kelly might actually smile, though.*

An hour later, snug in her warm car in heavy traffic, Margaret is brimming with the desire to tell her family about her new job. Every time the traffic stops, she hugs herself. She can't help it. She sings. She smiles at everyone. She plans the presents she will buy the family with next month's increased pay cheque. She resists using the car phone to call her husband. She wants to see his face when she tells him. Sometimes she thinks he believes in her more than she believes in herself. No, that's an unworthy thought. No one believes in her more than she does ... right now, anyway.

It isn't just the money; not at all. The extra will be useful, of course, but it's mainly the recognition. The feeling that it's all worth the effort. Juggling the family and the job ... all the pain of trying to settle Kelly into the family after Bill's ex remarried and went overseas. Hard for Kelly. Hard for Bill. Hard for Michael to accept an older sister—half-sister—moving in like that, ruling the roost. Everyone trying too hard at first, except Kelly herself. Hard for Margaret, too: who'd be a second wife?

The Grey Eminence hadn't let her down. What an unbelievably pompous man. How does he manage to talk without moving his top lip? His shoes were dirty, too. Why do men in that position think they can get away with being so patronising? Because they can, of course. Because we're all so insecure, we hang on every word. We're grateful for every little crumb he throws us. But this is more than a crumb.

Margaret turns into her driveway, locks the car and

runs into the house. 'Hello. I'm home.' No answer. 'Hello! It's me.' Silence.

Empty kitchen. No sign of the sausages. No sign of Bill. No TV. Puzzled, she goes to Michael's room. His school bag is on the floor, unopened. His pyjamas peep out from under his pillow, announcing No Bath. Kelly's room is too frightful to contemplate, but the jeans on the floor suggest that she has changed for netball, so that's something.

In the main bedroom, Bill's briefcase is on the bed and his jacket has been thrown over the chair.

Likely explanations abound, the most likely being confirmed by a note on the kitchen bench which Margaret has missed on her first breathless swing through the house.

'Gone to McDonald's. Then to drop Kelly at netball. Come and find us—or we'll see you when we get back. Love. W.'

W! After years of trying to get Bill to call himself William, all she's achieved is that he signs notes 'W' instead of 'B'.

Come and find us, indeed.

Margaret goes to the refrigerator, takes out the sausages, pours herself a drink and begins composing her speech of welcome. Its main theme will be along the lines that no one around here ever listens properly to me. I make myself perfectly clear, but it's like talking to a fish-shop window: you all sit there with glazed expressions and open mouths, and nothing I say seems to make any impression at all. It's not as if you're not capable of listening to me, but it just seems to go in one ear and out the other. Why do I waste my breath? If I've told you once, I've told you a hundred times: I

*shouldn't have to be here for this house to run smoothly.
I'll say it again: I shouldn't have to be here for this
house to run smoothly. You all know what has to be
done. Michael was supposed to have his bath. Kelly was
supposed to do her homework **before** netball. Bill was
supposed to cook a few simple sausages. Is that too hard?
But no, you all slink off to McDonald's with nothing
done. Typical. It's as if I'd never spoken.*

*And when Bill and Michael arrive home, chirping and
cheerful, that is pretty much the message which greets
them. In the surly silences which follow, there is no
opening for the news about Margaret's promotion: that
will have to wait for a phone conversation from work the
next day.*

Margaret is far from being alone in feeling that much of
what she says seems to fall on deaf ears. One of the most
common complaints about personal relationships is that
we are not taken seriously enough; that other people are
not paying enough attention to what we say; that we are
not understood.

There is no mystery about all the reasons why people
don't seem to be listening carefully enough to what we
say. The following chapters of this book will explain that
without too much trouble. The *real* mystery is why, when
we are so keen to communicate, we so consistently fail to
take into account what our experience should have taught
us at a very early age: the fact that, generally speaking,
people only pay close attention to things which directly
concern them—things which are relevant to their own
situation, their own needs, their own interests—and, even
when they do listen, they will be listening to everything
in their own way.

People are not blank slates on which we write our messages. People are a pulsating bundle of attitudes, values, prejudices, experience, feelings, thoughts, sensations and aspirations. They are active, not passive, even when they are listening. Is it any wonder that, unless we make sure the relevance of our message is obvious to the audience, there is every chance that they won't really listen at all (even if they are nodding and grunting encouragingly) or that, if they do, their own concerns might still get in the way?

Margaret is packing a picnic for her and the children to take to the park for Saturday lunch. Bill has had to bring some work home from the office, and he is sorting out some papers on the dining-room table.

'I think we'll take the dog,' says Margaret. 'Michael and Kelly are going to ride their bikes, so I'll walk instead of taking the car. At least the dog will get some exercise ... and so will I.'

Bill looks up from his papers and smiles vaguely. 'Good idea.'

'We'll go to Beauchamp Park ... it's a bit closer and it's safer for the kids to ride. We won't be long. Kelly has to be back in time to get ready for Rebecca's party. See you later.'

Bill looks up again. 'Where are the kids?'

'They're getting their helmets on.'

'Don't forget to take the cricket bat and stumps. Michael would love a few hits. Kelly can bowl if you're not up to it.'

'Fair go. I'll be looking after Bruce.'

'Are you taking the dog?'

*'I just **said** I was taking the dog.'*

'*I'd better clear my stuff off the back seat of the car. Just a tick.*'

'*Bill . . . we're not taking the car. We're walking. I just said we were walking.*'

'*Walking? But it's too far to walk. We've never walked there before. It would be all right for the kids riding, but it's too far for you and Bruce to walk.*'

'*Beauchamp Park? Too far? We always walk there. Almost always.*'

'*Beauchamp Park? But you said you were going to Lily-dale Park.*'

'*Goodbye, Bill. If we're not back by dark, ring your mother. She'll tell you what to do next.*'

Margaret's parting shot may have been a bit unnecessary, but she made her point. Bill wasn't listening properly, and why wasn't he? Because his mind was already on his work and he thought she was making a routine announcement. He didn't catch any of the details because there didn't seem to be any need for him to do so. He really did think she had said they were going to Lilydale Park, because that's where they usually go and that was where he was expecting them to go. It seemed to have nothing to do with him, though, either way.

In fact, the whole conversation only began to have relevance to Bill when he thought he would have to clear the back seat of the car to make room for the dog. If that point hadn't come up, the whole message would have been lost on him.

But was the message important to Bill? Yes, he needed to know where his family was going in case he had to contact them unexpectedly, or in case they were late home and he wanted to go and meet them, or in case he decided to abandon his work and go to the park himself. But Margaret didn't take into account Bill's mind-set (pre-occupation with his work; expectation about her going to the usual park) and so she neglected to identify the real point of the message *for Bill*. She said what she was doing: she failed to say what it had to do with him, or what he should do about it.

If Margaret really wanted Bill to listen, how might she have handled it?

'Bill, I've changed our plans for the picnic and I'd better tell you where you can find us if you need to. Bill?'

'Oh, yes ... Where? I might come, later on.'

'We're going to Beauchamp Park instead of Lilydale Park, because it's a bit closer and I'm going to walk the dog there instead of driving. The kids are going to ride their bikes. Come and join us if you get sick of working. So where would you like us to have the picnic? ... Just so you'll know where we'll be. Where would be the best spot?'

'Oh ... what about near the azalea garden. Well away from the swings, if you're taking Bruce. Little kids get scared of him. I think I will come later. I might bring the bat and ball.'

Of course, Margaret is perfectly capable of choosing the best spot herself, but if she really wants to communicate about this, she will have to take definite steps to make sure Bill's mind is focused on the subject. Asking him to suggest a spot would be one good way of getting him to see the relevance of the message to him.

Conversations like that generally take the first direction rather than the second, simply because we seem to be so reluctant to accept the fact that people are *not* blank slates. We cling to the idea that messages are powerful, audiences are passive, and all we have to do is say what we want to say and let the communication process take care of itself.

Margaret is a classic case in point. She has been operating on the assumption that saying it will make it happen; that getting the message *in* is the critical part of the process; that words have a magic power of their own, before which all resistance crumbles.

The curious thing is that Margaret is an intelligent woman who has had years of experience in dealing with other people. She is well educated. She has fallen in love once or twice. She has borne a child and adjusted to the rigours of a blended family. She has a good job, and is doing well at it. She manages her money sensibly and runs the household efficiently. People like her. She is a good citizen, a good neighbour. She cries in sad movies and bops to old songs on the radio. She thinks a lot. She feels things intensely. She even writes some secret poetry.

And yet ... when it comes to communication, she often fails. Not that it cripples her personal or professional life: she gets by, with lots of misunderstandings, lots of wasted effort, lots of repeated messages and lots of frustration. But, for someone who is so competent in so many other ways, and who so desperately *wants* to be a good communicator, it is amazing that she has not yet realised her fundamental and recurring error.

Margaret, like millions of other people, has fallen for the 'injection' myth. This myth has spawned a whole theory about how communication works and, because it is such a seductive theory, many people cling to it throughout their lives.

The 'injection' myth treats messages rather like drugs

which act on other people's minds. It assumes that messages have inherent power (their 'meaning'). In order to be effective communicators—the theory goes—we first have to craft our messages as carefully as we can, so as to maximise our 'impact' on the listener.

Having created our message, we now choose a medium for injecting it into the mind of the other person. The medium we choose is the equivalent of a hypodermic syringe or even a gun: we load our message—like a drug or a bullet—into the medium and then inject it via the eye or the ear—or preferably both. At that point, we've done all we can. The drug, entering the mind of the other person, will now do its magic work. It will cause that person to think what we want them to think, to feel what we want them to feel or, if it's a really powerful message, it might even get them to do what we want them to do.

If only the injection myth were true! Wouldn't communication be easy if all we had to do was inject messages into each other's minds and then sit back and wait for them to work. Parents would have perfectly obedient children. Misunderstandings would never arise in marriage. Marketers would have consumers rushing to buy every product cleverly advertised on TV. Politicians would be believed. Preachers would convert all those who listen. Teachers would have classrooms full of knowledgeable and biddable students . . .

But wait a minute. Isn't this a picture of total communication chaos? If messages were so effective, how would we cope with all the contradictory and competitive messages? If message-drugs were so powerful, wouldn't we be in a state of constant indecision and conflict, under their influence? If all we had to do, in order to communicate, was to inject messages into each other, wouldn't we become slaves to the power of language, instead of its masters?

In any case, don't parents find that they can express themselves with great clarity and yet still fail to communicate? Don't politicians find that the vast majority of voters are unmoved by what is said in election campaigns and continue to vote as they habitually vote, for reasons which are often unrelated to specific election policies? Don't even the most loving couples find that misunderstandings occur out of the blue—sometimes at the very moment when they most desperately want harmony? Don't teachers learn that a student's ability to replay information is not necessarily a sign that the mysterious thing called education is actually taking place? And don't 80 per cent of new products fail, in spite of all the skill of advertisers?

The truth is that if we approach communication as if it were a process of injection, we will have entirely missed the point. We will have failed to notice that you can't separate communication from the idea of a relationship between two or more people and that a relationship is an extraordinarily complicated thing. We will have failed, in particular, to see how each party to a communication encounter is an *active* party: listening or not listening; merely hearing or actively interpreting; rearranging, distorting, filtering and ultimately accepting or rejecting what is being said.

Committed injectionists, like Margaret, persist with their view because it offers an easy way out: it relieves them of the need to take the complexity of a relationship into account, or to acknowledge that other people might have views and dispositions quite different from—and even resistant to—their own. Intellectually, they know that different people have different points of view and different values but, if they cling to the injection view of communication, they can delude themselves into believing that the power of the message will finally win the day. The injection myth feeds our vanity and fuels our self-centredness. It seems to give us the whip hand. It puts the power of language itself at our disposal (and haven't we been told that the pen is mightier than the sword?).

Even non-verbal messages are regarded by injectionists as having the inherent power to communicate:

'I had a terrible row with Bill once. It was a misunderstanding over something quite trivial, but it just seemed to drag on and on. I made it very clear that I was desperate for him to drop the subject and just take me in his arms and cuddle me, but he couldn't seem to get the message at all. He seemed to think that I needed space to be alone, to recover from our argument. It wasn't like that at all. Sometimes I really can't understand why he can't pick up the most obvious signals I send him.'

Because the signals we send to other people—whether in speech, in writing, in facial expressions, in gestures or even in our body posture—seem so clear to us (in the sense that they express exactly how we are feeling or what we are thinking), it often amazes us when other people don't pick up those signals and read into them the meaning which, to us, is so clearly there to be read.

Although it is true that so-called 'body language' often sends the most effective messages of all (see Chapter 7), those messages still have to be interpreted by the person who receives them. A shrug doesn't signify the same thing to everyone, in all circumstances; a kiss can be used to express meanings ranging from sexual desire to friendship, respect, hypocrisy or betrayal; a wink may be interpreted as darkly conspiratorial or light-hearted and cheeky.

Like all other messages, the messages of 'body language' do not contain meaning, but only express it.

It is easy to see why the injection myth has such a powerful hold on us: after all, this is the way we *want* communication to work. We *want* people to automatically understand what we are saying, whenever we try to express what's on our minds. We *want* people to resolve their conflicts with us by simply accepting our point of view. We *want* people to absorb what we are saying to them without being distracted by their own opinions on the subject, or even by their feelings towards us.

When Margaret came home from her meeting with the Grey Eminence, she was so utterly focused on her own need to tell her news, there and then, that she couldn't see beyond that need: she didn't begin to appreciate how the rest of her family might have interpreted her phone call to Michael.

Even when she rang Michael, her messages were all couched in her own terms, stated from her point of view, and based on the assumption that her family were, in effect, blank slates waiting for her instructions and wishes to be written upon them. It had never occurred to Margaret that this approach was bound to reinforce the very thing to which she was so violently objecting: she *said* that the rest of the family should be able to get along without her constant presence, but her own approach to communication made it clear that she still wanted everything done her way, after all. She was prepared to berate her family for their lack of initiative or independence, and yet she continually sent them messages which encouraged them to remain dependent upon her.

Did she give any thought to how her phone message might actually be received? Did she anticipate the likely— or possible—reactions of her family to the news that she might be up to an hour late getting home? Did she pause to think how the message might be expressed from their point of view, rather than from hers? No, she didn't, because injectionists don't. If you go along with the myth of the powerful message, you don't need to waste time with all that 'sensitivity' stuff.

(But all is not lost: Margaret, as we shall see, is capable of learning from her mistakes ... just like the rest of us. Give her time.)

What actually happened, on the receiving end of Margaret's call, was this:

Michael is having a running battle with Kelly over who is getting favoured treatment. Kelly envies Michael the fact that he is living with both his parents, whereas she only sees her mother on her occasional visits from America where she now lives with her new husband—a man with whom Kelly has no sense of affinity at all. Kelly is devoted to her own father, and strongly resents his remarriage. She knows Margaret is trying hard to make up for the absence of Kelly's mother, but that only seems to make it worse. Even though she sometimes wishes that Bill and Margaret's marriage would fall apart, she resents any sign that Margaret is anything less than a perfect wife. Coming home late from work is an example of the kind of thing Kelly believes that Margaret shouldn't do.

Kelly and Michael don't spend much time in each other's company, and that suits both of them. Each of them is quite pleased to have the other as scapegoat, and as something to complain about to their friends.

After Margaret's call, Michael goes straight to the family room and tells Kelly that Margaret will be late home, that Dad is going to get the dinner and that Kelly should turn off the TV and do her homework before netball practice.

'Shut up, will you. I'm watching something.'

'Yes, but Mum said you should turn it off and do your homework.'

Kelly throws a cushion at him. 'Shut **up**, will you. Can't you see I'm in the middle of a program?'

Michael ducks and retreats, storing the details of this encounter to tell his mother.

Bill comes in the back door, whistling cheerfully, and plants a kiss on Michael's head.

'Hi, Dad. Mum just rang to say she will be late home and you should go ahead with the dinner. It's sausages. Yuk. Can we go to McDonald's?'

'Not tonight, Mike. If Mum says it's sausages, sausages it is. Where's Kelly?'

Bill goes into the family room and gives his daughter a hug. 'How was your day?'

'Don't **ask** me that. I've told you. I hate being cross-examined about my day, every day.'

Undeterred, Bill starts to whistle again as he goes into the bedroom to remove his coat and tie.

Kelly calls from the family room, 'Can we have McDonald's? Margaret is going to be late ... again. And I've got netball.'

'Oh, I forgot about netball. What time do you have to be there?'

'Seven.'

*Suddenly, Bill is irritated. He's sure his daughter should be doing her homework instead of watching TV, and he can't bring himself to say so for the hundredth time. He can't face the thought of cooking sausages and vegetables with a deadline on him. And why **is** Margaret late again? Even though there is no reason to suspect anything untoward, these late nights are happening more frequently, and without warning. Surely ... well, surely Margaret wouldn't be getting sucked into that advertising agency crowd ... drinks after work, gossip, everyone calling everyone else 'darling', blokes included. Hell.*

'Let's go to McDonald's,' Bill calls from the bedroom to shouts of assent from both his offspring. 'You'd better get ready for netball first, Kelly.'

Kelly snaps the TV off and springs to her room.

'Aren't you supposed to be having your bath, Michael?'

'Dad. What do you think I am? I'm not going to McDonald's in my pyjamas.'

Bill feeds the dog, scribbles a quick note to Margaret (adding an ironic 'W' to express his feelings about a dangerous tendency towards pretentiousness in his wife), compliments himself on remembering to take a jumper for Michael, and heads for the car with the children. Nothing to it, he thinks; I haven't even made a mess in the kitchen. I wonder if she'll tell me why she was late.

Had Margaret tried to imagine the scene at home before she made her call to Michael, she might have sent a quite different message and achieved a quite different result. But she was distracted by the matters on her own mind. She didn't stop to think that no one else in the family knew this was such a big moment for her. It never occurred to her that a meeting with the GE could be confused with a routine bit of working back (even though she had not bothered to mention that she was going to an important meeting). Not that it mattered either way; her messages seemed to her to be perfectly clear.

Injectionists dwell at the centre of power: at least, that's how they feel. The idea that the communication process could involve a complex, vibrant web of subtle interconnections—that communication could be about much more than person A sending a message to person B—is foreign to the injectionist. The idea that messages need the fertile ground of a functioning relationship in order to blossom and flourish would challenge everything the injection theory stands for. The idea that listeners might actually have the power of interpretation—bringing their own meanings to a conversation—would explode the myth itself.

But the myth persists. We so easily fall into the trap of thinking that *we* made ourselves clear; what's wrong with those people who didn't understand us? *We* gave a good presentation; why was the audience so unresponsive? *We* created a powerful advertising campaign; why were consumers so impervious to it? *We* presented an invincible election manifesto; why were the voters so stupid?

It is said of Oscar Wilde that, on the opening night of one of his plays, a friend asked him how the play had gone. Wilde is supposed to have replied, 'The play was a success, the audience was a failure'. Blaming the audience for our failure to communicate with them is the last refuge of the frustrated injectionist.

'I put a completely clear notice on the board,' says the perplexed sports teacher, 'but people have been coming up to me all day, asking me to explain what's going on. Can't they read?'

'You send out a memo about something,' says a weary manager, 'and it sinks without trace. Sometimes I send the same memo around twice, just to see if it will get some reaction. I don't know what's wrong with some of these people . . . '

Nagging: sure sign of an injectionist

Criticising their listeners for not responding is one sure sign of the injectionist in our midst. Another sign is the tendency to nag—to keep repeating the same message over and over again in the face of its obvious failure to communicate.

Margaret's cry of despair, 'If I've told you once, I've told you a hundred times' is actually an extraordinary confession of her own failure to understand that there is more to communication than the sending and receiving of messages. A person who says, 'If I've told them once . . . ' is admitting to the continued use of a message which has proved itself to be ineffective. Blind faith in the injection myth is never revealed more starkly than in such a statement.

What Margaret is really saying is this: I have repeated this message on many occasions and, on each occasion, I notice that it has failed to achieve the response I was hoping for. But I have pressed on with it: 40, 50, 60 repetitions . . . no problem. Even though it hasn't worked so far, if I repeat it enough times, it might start to work.

A person who believes in 'injection' is quite prepared to keep repeating an ineffective message because, if you go along with the myth that there is some inherent power in the message, you could easily fall for the idea that this magic power builds up cumulatively. It didn't work the first time (or the first ten times), but, like a drug, it will gradually wear down the resistance of the listeners until they finally respond.

It is faith in the ultimate power of a repeated message that allows the nagger to keep nagging, even in the face of obvious failure. But even the analogy of the message-drug doesn't support the argument of the nagger. The wrong message does not become right with repetition: like the wrong drug, it is likely to produce either no response in the listener or, worse, a hostile response of resistance and ultimate rejection.

The behaviour of naggers shows us that belief in the injection myth is far from being a harmless belief. It seduces us into thinking that, because messages are powerful, we can increase their power by repeating them endlessly (as if messages will wear down a listener in the way that dripping water will wear away stone).

In spite of the overwhelming evidence that communication does not work like that, the injection theory still strikes many people as being the right approach. There is even some physiological support for it: after all, when I speak to you, my voice creates vibrations which activate your hearing mechanism and send messages to your brain. In that sense, I have injected the message into your brain. If I write you a letter, your eye sees the words on the page and sends those visual messages to the brain. There, too, a sort of injection of those visual messages takes place.

But we know there is much more to communication than seeing or hearing, because there is much more to communication than the exchange of messages. It is in that 'much more' that the secrets of effective communication are hidden.

The injection myth is based on a serious misinterpretation of how communication actually works. Its basic error is to confuse the physiology of seeing or hearing with the psychology of responding. The injection myth assumes that, as long as the message does something to the audience, communication will take place. In fact, communication occurs when *the audience does something with the message.* The more we look at the way communication works, the more we see that the real power is not in the message, but in the listener. The listener has the power to interpret the message and, in communication terms, that's the ultimate power.

Already, we've arrived at the First Law of Human Communication:

It's not what our message does to the listener, but what the listener does with our message, that determines our success as communicators.

It is tempting to look at some famous communicators in modern history—Hitler, Churchill, Kennedy—and assume that their messages were so powerful that they must be exceptions to the first law. In fact, such examples strongly support the proposition that messages only appear powerful because they strike a responsive chord in an audience whose 'chord' is waiting to be struck. It is the existing predispositions of the audience which give the message its apparent power: those predispositions breathe life into a message which might otherwise fall on apparently deaf ears.

Here is Carl Jung's account—given in a 1939 interview with H. R. Knickerbocker—of why Hitler seemed to have such a powerful effect on his German audiences:

It is because Hitler is the mirror of every German's unconscious, but of course he mirrors nothing from a non-German. He is the loudspeaker which magnifies the inaudible whispers of the German soul until they can be heard by the German's unconscious ear.

He is the first man to tell every German what he has been thinking and feeling all along in his unconscious about German fate ...

What about advertising and other forms of persuasive mass communication? Surely advertising is an example of the injection theory at work; surely advertising 'does things' to consumers? Not so: the billions of dollars which have to be spent each year on advertising are a testimony to its relative ineffectiveness, rather than its effectiveness.

In any case, effective advertising (like all other forms of communication) works by evoking responses which are already there. In *The Responsive Chord*, Tony Schwartz describes this as 'resonating' with the existing attitudes and dispositions of the consumer. Schwartz observes that 'a listener or viewer brings far more information to the communication event than a communicator can put into his program, commercial or message' and that the communicator's task is not to get a message across, but to 'evoke this stored information'.

It will help our understanding of communication if we think of messages as keys to unlock meaning. We need a theory of 'release', not a theory of 'injection'. When we speak of a powerful message, we are really referring to the power of the message to *evoke* a response, not to shoot a bullet of meaning into the mind of another person.

CHAPTER 2

Messages and Meanings

Why do we persist in thinking that messages are powerful and that the people we speak or write to are simply the passive recipients of our messages? One reason is that we have been conditioned to think that meanings are actually in the message, so that if we can get the message into the mind of our audience, the meaning will lodge there too. Another reason is that our meanings are so clear to us that it is hard for us to accept that they may not be so clear to those who interpret what we say. But, fundamentally, we keep falling for the injection myth because the things we want to communicate seem so interesting or important to us that it is hard for us to believe that they are not equally interesting or important to other people.

Margaret has been cleaning the kitchen floor. It is a wet day and the backyard is muddy. In the breaks between rain showers, Michael has been running outside to play. Each time he comes back inside, he is leaving muddy marks on the freshly scrubbed kitchen floor.

Margaret is becoming exasperated and finally says to Michael, 'Wipe your feet'. He pauses, looks at her and says, 'Yes, Mum' and runs back outside.

A minute or two later, he dashes inside again, fails to

wipe his feet again, and leaves more muddy marks on the kitchen floor.

Margaret grabs him as he rushes past, on his way to watch a favourite TV program.

'Hold it right there, young man,' she says. 'What did I just say to you?'

'What?' asks Michael, puzzled.

'What did I just say to you, when you raced outside a minute ago?'

'You said to wipe my feet, didn't you?'

'Yes ... and you said, "Yes, Mum". Do you remember?'

'Huh? Yes, I remember,' says Michael, impatient to break away from his mother's grip to see the start of his program.

'And what do you think I meant by that?' asks Margaret.

'By what?' says Michael, puzzled again.

'Listen! When I said, "Wipe your feet", what do you think I meant?' Michael looks quizzically at his mother, scarcely believing that she could really want him to explain such a simple message.

'Go on,' Margaret persists, 'what do you think I meant?'

'You meant that you wanted me to wipe my feet on the mat, so I wouldn't leave any muddy marks on the floor ... because you were washing the floor and you wanted to keep it clean. Can I go and watch TV now?'

Michael rushes off and Margaret mutters grimly to herself, 'It just goes in one ear and out the other. I should make **him** wash the floor ... '

Margaret has not yet learned the difference between the

message and the meaning. Like most injectionists, she is inclined to think that, if people hear what we say and understand what we mean, then we have communicated with them.

When Margaret asks her son, 'What did I just say to you?' she is falling for the trap of assuming that seeing or hearing a message is the main thing in communication: if you want to know whether you've 'got through' you look for traces of the message-drug in the brain of the listener. Teachers make that assumption every time they pride themselves on a student's ability to play back, parrot-fashion, what the teacher said. Advertisers do it when they regard 'advertising recall scores' as an indication of the effectiveness of their campaigns. And parents—like Margaret—do it whenever they interpret a child's ability to recall a message or repeat an instruction as a sufficient sign that the child has *engaged with* the message.

Finding traces of our message in the mind of the listener can fool us into believing that communication has taken place, but that's a very dangerous delusion. Michael—like all of us—is exposed to thousands of messages every day, and he doesn't attach any meaning to most of them. Getting Michael to acknowledge that he heard his mother say 'wipe your feet' tells Margaret nothing beyond the fact that Michael's brain and central nervous system are in working order: he is capable of hearing sounds and recalling them on demand.

Margaret's second line of inquiry, 'What did you think I meant by that?' gets her a little closer to finding out what she needs to know, but not close enough. The fact that Michael can guess what his mother meant is a very different thing from Michael himself having given the message any meaning of his own. (Remember the First Law: It's not what our message does to the listener, but what the listener does with our message . . .)

What Margaret really needs to find out is not whether Michael knows what their exchange meant to her, but whether it meant anything to him.

In the circumstances—given that Michael was on his way inside to watch a TV program—it is most likely that he attached no meaning at all to the message. But suppose he did: suppose that the message had some particular relevance for Michael, at that moment. What meaning might he have associated with those words? Of course, what Margaret *wanted* him to think was something like this:

My mother works very hard. She is trying to run this household as well as holding down her new job, and it is very tough for her to keep the place tidy when she has so little time and energy. The least I can do is wipe my feet so I don't double the work load involved in keeping the kitchen floor clean.

Hmm. For a seven-year-old, that's an unlikely interpretation of the message because it is not relevant to Michael's train of thought at the time. When people interpret a message, they are putting their own meaning into it. They are interpreting it in their own terms. To rephrase the First Law of Communication: it is not a matter of what meaning the message puts into their minds; it is a question of what is already in their minds—in the form of stored experience and potential responses—which they can draw on to make sense of messages which are relevant to them. Messages can't evoke what isn't there.

If Michael did see some relevance in his mother's message—if he found that it resonated in some way with what he had learned from his previous experience—he might interpret it like this:

My mother is an incorrigible nagger, and this is just the latest piece of evidence. If it's not one thing, it's another. Wipe your feet, blow your nose, clean your teeth, pick up your clothes, go to bed, get up, pack your bag, unpack your bag, take your elbows off the table ... I have only been on the planet for seven years and this woman has never been off my back. I can't remember a time when she wasn't issuing instructions of one kind or another.

That would be a pretty free translation, but a vague idea along those lines could well have formed in Michael's mind as his only *psychological* response to his mother's message.

If Margaret had known what was going on in her son's mind, she would have been understandably furious. It is easy to imagine her objection: 'What I said could not possibly be interpreted as meaning that. Is the child stupid? Doesn't he understand the meaning of simple words? What is the world coming to if we are going to let people make up their own meanings for the things we say to them?'

The bad news for Margaret is that people *always* make up their own meanings for the things we say to them, because that's what interpretation is. Many of our misunderstandings about communication arise from confusion between three quite different things:

• the messages we send each other;

- the ideas in our minds which we are trying to express when we send those messages (our *intended* meanings); and
- the ideas in the minds of our listeners which they draw on to make their own sense of what we say to them (their *interpreted* meanings).

If you are speaking to a large audience, your message will have as many *interpreted* meanings as there are people in that audience. In practice, many of those meanings may turn out to be almost identical with each other (especially if it's a technical talk being given to a specialist audience), but there may be many shades of meaning in interpretation which will create the potential for communication difficulties.

Once we begin to realise that people put meaning into messages (rather than messages putting meaning into people) we also begin to understand where the real power lies.

The distinction between the message and its two meanings (mine and yours) is difficult to make in practice, because we grow up with the idea that language 'contains' meaning. We look in a dictionary and feel as if we are discovering the inherent meaning of words. We read something and, being unable to discuss it with its author, we try to work out what the author had in mind from the 'meaning' of the words themselves.

There is no escape from that: we often find ourselves in the position of having to guess at the meaning which is being expressed in a message without having the benefit of a discussion with its author. But if we understand the significance of the First Law of Communication, we will realise that we are actually using the message as a focus for some 'meaning' in us, rather than having meaning put into us by the message.

This is why different people can obtain such different impressions from the same message. It is also why people can read such different 'meanings' into works of art; why people who watch a movie can come away with such radically different perceptions of it; why statements which seem 'full of meaning' to one person can seem 'empty' to another. It is why public speakers are sometimes perplexed by being asked questions which sound as though they are a response to some other lecture altogether.

How right we are when we say, 'There are two sides to every story'!

The inconvenient truth is that language is nothing more than a system of symbols which we use to *express* meaning. Meaning is not *in* the language itself; meaning is in the minds of the people who use language in order to try to share their ideas with each other. Of course it *seems* as if meaning is in the words and the other symbols we use to communicate, because we so habitually use the same words to express particular meanings. When I say, 'The umbrella is black', you will have a fair idea of what I am describing—but only because we have both learned to use those particular symbols to express particular ideas or meanings. The meanings are not magically *in* the words. (In any case, as we shall see in Chapter 8, language is frequently used as a code to *conceal* meaning.)

So, rather than thinking of a message as a drug to be injected into the mind of the audience, try thinking of it as an empty vessel—just like a cup, or a bucket. When we create our message, it feels to us as if it 'contains' the meaning we want to convey. That is why the meaning of our own messages is so clear to us.

The heart of the communication problem is this: when I offer you a message which seems full of meaning to me, it appears to you only as an empty vessel. You see the cup, or the bucket: you do not see the meaning which I thought I had put into it. Writing in the *Australian Journal of Communication*, Robyn Penman refers to the profound mistake we make when we treat a conversation as if 'we put our thoughts into words ... and send it to another to take the thoughts back out'.

If we are going to communicate with each other, you will have to put your own meaning into the empty vessel of my message and then we shall have to check to see whether our two meanings have something in common— whether they overlap with each other. If they do, we are communicating. In fact, a good definition of communication is, simply, *the sharing of meaning*.

The 'meanings' of communication

One of the problems with the study of communication is that people mean so many different things by the word itself. Someone will say, 'Have you seen this communication from head office?', treating the word 'communication' as if it is interchangeable with the word 'message'. Someone else might say, 'we have had the phone connected, so now we are in communication with the outside world', as if 'communication' means the same thing as 'contact'. Sometimes we use the word to describe nothing more than the media we use for transferring information from one place to another, as in 'the communication industry'.

When people say 'We have a communication problem',

they sometimes mean 'We have a shortage of information'; sometimes, 'We have too much information but no way of interpreting it'; sometimes, 'We aren't being told what we really want to know'; sometimes, 'We have received different messages which seem to contradict each other'. (By the way, they hardly ever mean, '*I* am the communication problem'.)

Some people think that those who speak fluently are automatically good communicators; others notice that a person may say very little—and not say it very well—but may nevertheless communicate very effectively. It isn't surprising that 'communication' is interpreted in so many different ways. Like all processes which involve human beings and their emotions, the process of communication is complicated, unpredictable and difficult to control. It is tempting to pick on the bits we can control—the message, for example, or the medium through which the message is being sent—and focus all our attention on that, as though *that's* what communication really is. And because we spend so much time using the basic skills of communication—reading, writing, talking, listening—it's also tempting to confuse those with communication itself. But, as we all know, it is possible to have a conversation with someone which doesn't produce any communication, any shared meaning, at all.

Once we grasp the idea of 'shared meaning' or 'common ground' as being the essence of communication, we can appreciate how dangerous—and inappropriate—the old-fashioned 'injection' model really is. If the purpose of communication is to share something, then the idea of one person doing something to another is bizarre. Communication, like any other form of sharing, demands the participation of both of us.

If we are going to begin to understand the communication process, we need to know what happens at that critical moment when we are offered the empty vessel which
we call 'messages'. Most of the time, nothing much
happens except a simple, physical response which records
the message as an event in our brains. But that is not
communication: it is only a tiny step on the pathway to
communication.

We are bombarded with so many messages every day—
from the people we meet, the things we read, the sounds
we hear, the sights we see, the things we touch and smell,
the television we watch—that it would be impossible for
us to attach some meaning to every single message which
comes into the orbit of our experience.

Everything we perceive is, potentially, a message. The
world we live in is teeming with objects, events and information which we could, if we chose, treat as messages
crying out for meaning. But most of those messages will
remain meaningless to us.

If I walk into a room where a fluorescent light tube is
flickering, my brain will register the flickering tube as part
of the scene but, if I have gone to that room to find a
book on a bookshelf in there, I will attach no significance
(no 'meaning') to the fluorescent light and, at that time,
it will not register as a 'message' at all. But if I am an
electrician called to that building to check on faulty fluorescent light tubes so that they can be replaced, the flickering light will be a message to which I will attach
immediate significance ('meaning') as soon as I walk into
that room. The bookshelf, by contrast, will be psychologically invisible.

It is easy for us to ignore most messages which float
past our consciousness at any given moment. They may

stimulate our senses but the process may stop right there: if they have no particular relevance to us, we won't go to the trouble of giving them any meaning. The empty vessel, though observed, remains empty.

In practice, people agree with each other about the 'meaning' of most words they use. Over time, and within particular cultural groups, we learn to use words which will produce fairly straightforward, easily shared interpretations of their meaning. It is true that when we look in a dictionary, we find an account of meanings which are generally agreed upon by groups of people within a particular language system. But we also notice that every time a new edition of a dictionary is published, it contains thousands of alterations which reflect the fact that people have begun to use some words (like 'gay') in new and different ways, and to abandon others entirely. Although we may be able to agree about the way in which we will use individual words, the more we build those words into complex combinations (like sentences), the less we can rely on everyone else attaching the same meaning to the combination as we had in mind when we constructed it.

Bill is chatting to one of the young clerks in his office. He enjoys the opportunity to talk to some of the younger people in the department, partly because it sometimes gives him clues about how to handle his increasingly difficult relationship with Kelly.

They are discussing changing tastes in popular music. Bill mentions Margaret's enthusiasm for the pop songs of her adolescence. He describes how he sometimes finds her bopping to golden oldies on the radio.

A look, familiar to Bill, appears on the face of the clerk: eyebrows slightly raised; not quite smiling.

Bill smiles at himself. 'I suppose chaps your age don't use the word "bopping", do you?'

'Bill, chaps our age don't even use the word "chaps".'

Our use of words is constantly evolving and, as part of that process, we use old words in new ways. In particular, slang provides many colourful cases: words like 'unreal', 'radical' or 'cool' come and go in the lexicon of young people, as they search for fresh ways of charting the timeless terrain of the human psyche.

There is no need to go as far as Humpty Dumpty in Lewis Carroll's *Through the Looking-Glass*: acknowledging that language and meaning are different things does not give us licence to say that we can randomly make any word mean anything we like. The possibility of communicating with other people depends upon being part of a community of agreed meanings—rather like parties to an unwritten contract to let certain words stand for certain meanings, at least for the time being.

But, even within a community of agreed meanings, we need to recognise that we use language to say what *we* mean: the sounds we make are devoid of any meaning of their own, or that meaning would be self-evident.

We could, if we chose, use the word 'black' to describe anything which we now call 'white'. It just so happens that, historically, language has evolved in a way which makes that seem like a silly idea. But, if we were devising a secret code (that is, establishing a closed community of agreed meanings), we could certainly play tricks like that. There is nothing *inherent* in the sounds we make or the shapes we write which either determines their meaning or prevents us from using them to mean something unconventional. (The word 'cool', for example, is often used in colloquial language to convey an idea which has nothing whatever to do with temperature. In the world of fashion, hot merchandise can still be cool.)

We don't need to feel despondent or helpless about all this, but we do have to take it into account whenever we want to communicate with other people. We have to recognise the legitimacy of their interpretations. It is the meanings which they give to our messages which have to be explored and understood if we want to establish whether we are on common ground.

The house is in its usual early-morning state of turmoil. Kelly and Michael are arguing over their right to use the bathroom first. Bill is standing in the middle of the kitchen reading the paper. Margaret is in the process of throwing some breakfast together for herself, before she leaves for an early meeting at the agency.

Margaret calls to Kelly, 'Have you put your lunch box in your bag?'

Kelly's answer comes from the bathroom.

'Yes, Margaret.' Even though the words are muffled by a mouthful of toothpaste, there's a distinct note of exasperation.

Margaret looks in the fridge and sees Kelly's lunch box is still sitting there, not yet packed in her school bag.

She looks at Bill and rolls her eyes. He raises his eyebrows, not sure of what is going on, but not wanting to be drawn into it.

Margaret says, through clenched teeth, 'I ask her that every single morning, and she always says she has done it. But she never has. Am I going mad, or what?'

Margaret is not going mad. Kelly's interpretation of the meaning of her question just happens to be different from hers.

Margaret has been asking Kelly the very same question every morning for months, and Kelly has long since given up treating it as a question which literally 'means what it says'. She knows it is her stepmother's way of reminding her to pack her lunch box. That is the *point* of the question, as interpreted by Kelly. In the beginning, she used to give a literal answer (which was always 'no'), and then a tiresome little debate would follow. From Kelly's point of view, saying 'yes' has become the most painless way of acknowledging the reminder, without having to admit that the deed has not yet been done, and without having to endure a more explicit reminder.

The 'rolling stone' problem

You and I attend the same meeting but, when we talk about it afterwards, we find that we have quite different impressions of what went on. I am convinced that the other people at the meeting were enthusiastic about putting a particular idea into practice, but they wanted more time to think about the details. You are equally convinced that they were not enthusiastic about it at all, and that they had virtually decided to shelve the whole thing.

How could we have come away from the same meeting with such different interpretations of it? The answer is that the meeting itself—like any message—was meaningless: we had to put our own meanings into it. We drew on our own experience, our own attitudes, our own values (and, quite probably, our own aspirations and expectations) to reach our own conclusions about what happened.

In the same way, different religious groups will interpret the 'meaning' of scripture in ways which suit their own theological frameworks. Each of them is convinced that the other's interpretation is wrong, and their faith in the rightness of their own interpretation may lead them to believe that anyone who interprets the scriptures differently is deliberately distorting or obscuring the meaning. Once we have filled a message-vessel with meaning, it usually seems to us that the meaning was always there, or even that it is inherent.

For example, what does the proverb 'A rolling stone gathers no moss' mean? (By now, I hope that you are already resisting the way that question is phrased: I hope that you are conceding that the proverb itself doesn't mean anything; we mean things by it. All right, what do *you* mean by that proverb?)

Some people might want to offer a literal interpretation: when a stone rolls down a hill, the fact that it is moving makes it impossible for moss to form on it. But most of us assume that, in the case of proverbs, we are expected to give some more subtle, symbolic meaning to the words. Proverbs, in our culture, have the status of mini-fables with a kind of inbuilt moral.

So, metaphorically speaking, what meaning do you give to the proverb?

You might interpret it as saying that a person who keeps moving (a shiftless, restless kind of person) will never acquire any substantial material possessions. A similar interpretation would be that a person who never settles down will never prosper.

But you might interpret the proverb as saying that a person who keeps on the move and remains open to new ideas and experiences will never stagnate. Another way of expressing that interpretation would be to say that people who keep moving will not become dull.

It all depends on how you interpret the word 'moss'. The first interpretation of the proverb treats moss as a good thing, standing for wealth, or perhaps wisdom; the second interpretation regards moss as a negative thing, symbolising stagnation.

As in the case of religious prejudice, people who believe the proverb 'means' one thing would find it almost incredible that anyone could interpret it in another way.

The origins of that particular proverb suggest that, when it first came into common usage, 'moss' was a slang term for money—rather like 'dough' or 'bread' at later periods in the history of our language. But the original use of the word is irrelevant to those who want to use the proverb to express some other meaning.

In the same way, dictionary definitions of words are irrelevant to those who use old words to mean new things. Dictionaries are, after all, museums of meaning: they tell us how people have used words in the past to express certain meanings, but they cannot hold up the process of evolution in language.

In some subcultures, the statement that something 'fell off the back of a truck' no longer has any direct connection with things literally falling off the backs of trucks. When the term is used, it will often be intended to convey the idea that something was obtained by rather irregular—and possibly illegal—means. A confidential document, for example, may have been obtained deviously and may then be described as having 'fallen off the back of a truck'. If you are not part of the cultural group which associates that particular meaning with that set of words, you might interpret the statement more literally and completely fail to share the intended meaning.

You can have endless fun with the 'meaning' of proverbs, cliches and other colloquial sayings. What might we make of Margaret's frequent threat to the children that she is going to 'read the riot act' (or should that be 'Riot Act'?)? Since she is obviously not going to do any such thing, the meaning of the threat is in Margaret, not in those words.

A news magazine ran a cover story about the former Australian prime minister, Paul Keating, about eighteen months after he took office. 'Is Paul cut out to be the PM after all?' asked the banner headline on the story. One reader assumed that the story must be suggesting that, contrary to earlier expectations, Mr Keating *is* cut out to be PM. The 'after all', to that reader, suggested that previous doubts had been swept aside and the prime minister had now established his credentials.

But another reader interpreted the headline quite differently. The second reader's view was that the key phrase, 'after all', clearly implied that, on reflection, it now appeared that Mr Keating was not suitable to hold the office of prime minister.

Take your pick. You won't find the answer to that difference of opinion by further study of the headline: you would certainly have to read the article before you could confidently interpret those words (and the journalist responsible for the headline would presumably be astonished—and possibly irritated—by the suggestion that anyone could have read any meaning into those words other than the meaning originally intended).

Margaret is getting ready to go to Michael's school for a

parent–teacher interview. She is not looking forward to it. She finds these encounters a bit awkward. Although Michael is doing quite nicely at school, she doesn't really like his teacher much. The teacher often seems to adopt a tone which feels patronising to Margaret, although Bill says she imagines a lot of it. Also, Margaret hates sitting on those silly little chairs. She suspects that the teacher quite likes making the parents feel uncomfortable. Bill thinks she overreacts.

Bill is on the phone. Margaret backs up to him, pointing to her zipper. As Bill zips up her dress, she hears him say, 'Sorry, Geoff, I can't make it. Marg has to go to a parent–teacher thing at the school, and I'm going to babysit the kids'.

Margaret spins around to face him with a look of amazement.

Bill raises his eyebrows. 'Got to go, mate. Ask me some other time. Hope you can get someone else.' He looks at Margaret, knowing he's erred, searching for a clue. 'Did I say something wrong?'

'Bill, you can't babysit your own kids. They're your kids. When you're at home with the children, you're not babysitting. You're just staying home with the children. Babysitters are people we pay to come and look after the kids when we go out. Do you know what I'm talking about?'

He doesn't, and his face says he doesn't.

'Just now, talking to Geoff, I heard you say you were going to babysit the kids. Isn't that what you said?'

'Yeah. I might've. I was just explaining to Geoff why I couldn't go around to his place for cards. That's all. What does it matter what I said? **He** *knew what I meant. Anyway, what's got into you? Was it the word 'baby' that*

you objected to? I know they're not babies . . . it's just a manner of speaking. You used to say it yourself when we used to get Jane around to look after them, before Kelly was old enough.'

'Bill. Listen to me. I don't care if you call them orang-outangs or water buffalo. What I object to is the idea that if I'm at home with the kids when you go out, that's normal. You never say that **I'm** babysitting the kids, because you know it would sound stupid. But if I go out, suddenly you're not just a father at home with his kids, you're **baby-sitting**. It's your attitude that I'm objecting to. It's the point of view that's wrong. Can't you see what I'm saying? Everything you do around the house is such a big deal for you. Even being at home with your own children has to have a special label. Babysitting! What next?'

'But all I meant was that I couldn't play cards because I had to stay home and look after the kids, because you were going out. What's wrong with that? Isn't that babysitting?'

'Bill. I'll say it one more time. You can't babysit your own kids. You're their father, right? Their father can't be their babysitter. I have to run.'

And as Margaret rushes out the door, Bill faces an evening which feels to him exactly like babysitting.

The word 'babysit' can be used by Bill to mean one thing—general childminding duties—and by Margaret to mean something much more specific, and definitely unrelated to parenting. Worse, its use by Bill to refer to minding his own children offends Margaret because she sees it as a symptom of the deeper problem that Bill seems unable to grasp what she means whenever she talks about coparenting. (Bill has a similar problem, she notices, with another of

Margaret's favourite expressions, 'gender equity'.)

Words which we think of as having particular and special meanings often pass into common usage as symbols for quite different things. When philosophers refer to 'begging the question', they are referring to something which we might normally call a 'circular argument': trying to prove a conclusion by putting forward an argument which already assumes that the conclusion is true (for example, trying to prove that 'God is a creator' by pointing to the world as evidence of 'God's creation'.) But, in everyday speech, that technical term has been hijacked to stand for the idea that some question seems begging to be asked. A politician answers a journalist's question and the journalist, dissatisfied with the answer, says, 'But that begs the question, "What about the right of all workers to a decent basic wage?".'

'That's not "begging the question",' says the philosopher. 'But the question *was* begging to be asked,' says the journalist. And never the twain shall meet.

(The word 'disinterested' has gone the same way. A good, useful word, many of us thought, which expressed a meaning quite distinct from 'un-interested'. If I am disinterested, according to that traditional view, I am certainly not *un*interested, but I am remaining detached from any judgment.)

But there is no point in the purists getting upset when the evolutionary flow of usage gradually changes the way in which words are used to express meaning. Even those of us who thought that 'anythink' was a perversion of 'anything', used only by those without a decent education, now find well-educated people adding the final 'k' as if it is an extra refinement of speech. And it's hard to find anyone who still thinks that the opposite of an introvert is an extravert: usage has taken Jung's term and represented it as 'extrovert'. In such cases, the words change but our meanings don't. In other cases, the words stay the same, but the meanings change ... all of which suggests that, in English at least, we simply have to go with the flow. (Or am I going over the top ... a statement which, in this context, has nothing whatever to do with going over the top of anything at all.)

Dare I suggest that there's something of a two-edged sword about all this? And does that imply that it cuts both ways? (I'll leave you to work that one out, along with the problem of how to keep a straight face when someone says they did something 'in one foul sweep' or that they were 'sparking on all fours' ... creating a picture for me of an electric baby.)

'Understand me, not my message'

Sometimes—especially when we are communicating with people we know well—the difference between messages and meanings seems to disappear. We use familiar language and we understand each other easily. Where misunderstandings occur, they can easily be cleared up.

But even in well-established relationships, there is sometimes such a big gap between what someone is saying and what they apparently mean by what they are saying that we are immediately on the alert.

Margaret and Bill are having some friends around for a barbecue on a Saturday evening. The day has been very busy. Michael has to be taken to a football game in the morning, and Kelly to netball in the afternoon. In between, Bill was trying to clean up the barbecue area and Margaret was doing a little shopping and straightening the house. There is a fair amount of tension in the air, especially when Michael starts absentmindedly kicking a pile of leaves around the barbecue area after his father has carefully swept them up.

The time for the guests' arrival is approaching and Margaret is about to get into the shower. She is rummaging through her wardrobe and suddenly says, with great irritation, 'I haven't got a thing to wear'.

Bill's own patience has worn rather thin and, at that moment, he has discovered that the pants he wanted to wear have a stain on them which neither he nor Margaret had noticed the last time he wore them.

Bill doesn't respond immediately to Margaret's outburst. He has been down this kind of road before. He realises that he will be in trouble if he makes the mistake of responding to her remark as though she literally means what she says. The situation won't be helped by a response like, 'What is the wardrobe full of, then, if it isn't things to wear?' In lighter moments, he might get away with a remark like that, but not now.

Margaret continues fuming and rummaging and Bill wonders what she is really trying to say. He feels sympathetic because he can see that she is genuinely upset, but he is also a bit puzzled because he does think that Margaret spends rather a lot on clothes. She certainly has a better selection to choose from than he does.

He ventures a response: 'I'd be happy to go shopping with you next week if you think you need some new casual clothes.'

'What do you mean "next week"? The Simpsons will be here in thirty minutes, and I haven't got anything to *wear* **now**. *We are not going to go shopping in the next half hour, are we? Why don't you talk sense?'*

'Sorry, I was only trying to help. Anyway, you look terrific just as you are.'

Margaret is clearly displeased by that remark and stalks into the bathroom in high dudgeon—or as much dudgeon as she can muster in her underwear.

Obviously the meaning which Margaret was trying to express was quite different from what might normally be associated with the words, 'I haven't got a thing to wear'. The literal truth is that she had many things to wear, so the meaning of her remark is certainly not to be found in the words themselves.

When emotions are running high, we often say something which is not only different from the literal truth, but is, in fact, the very opposite of the literal truth. In choosing such an obviously 'wrong' message to express our meaning we add great intensity to the encounter by forcing the listener to look beyond the words.

Perhaps all Margaret needed was some reassurance that, whatever she wore, Bill would think she looked wonderful. (Perhaps one of the guests was particularly glamorous; perhaps she had taken Bill's eye on more than one previous occasion; perhaps Margaret was not looking forward to the prospect of seeing her husband flirting with another woman.)

Bill might have done better to keep quiet. This was one of those overheated situations where Margaret was stating the very opposite of the truth in order to capture Bill's attention. She certainly achieved that. But her use of the 'wrong' words should also have alerted Bill to the fact that she wanted him to understand *her*, not her statement.

When we hear people saying what seems to be the opposite of the truth, we generally interpret it to mean something else. 'It's not the money, it's the principle of the thing' often makes more sense if we interpret it as meaning that it is, in fact, the money. 'With the greatest respect ... ' often precedes a statement which makes it clear that there is a distinct lack of respect involved. 'I don't want to contradict you' can almost always be interpreted as meaning that I want, very badly, to contradict you and I am indeed about to do so.

Statements like 'I want to go to bed and stay there forever' or 'This hurts me more than it hurts you' (when it obviously doesn't), or assertions by people trying to extricate themselves from a relationship that 'I will always love you as a friend', demand very careful interpretation.

In such cases, the hidden message usually turns out to be: 'Understand *me* ... don't worry too much about the words.'

Under some conditions, people who say the very opposite of what they know to be literally true are not telling lies. They are merely demonstrating that meaning is in how we *use* words, not in the words themselves.

The more we explore the gap between messages and meanings and the more we try to understand the process by which people give meaning to each other's messages, the more we come back to the First Law of Human Communication: *It's not what our message does to the listener but what the listener does with our message that determines our success as communicators.*

Once we have begun to live with the First Law for a while, we come to realise that the most useful discipline in communication is to avoid asking the question we always *want* to ask: 'What will my message do to this person?'. Instead, we shall have to get into the habit of asking a more realistic, but more awkward, question: 'What will this person do with my message?'

People who are prepared to accept that core discipline sometimes find that it transforms their lives by altering their whole approach to personal relationships.

CHAPTER 3

The Power of the Cage

*B*ill's childhood is spent on a farm. From an early age he knows that the life of a farmer is not for him. He hankers after the city, a broad education and a career which is not constrained by the vagaries of commodity prices and the weather.

His two older sisters both marry farmers and stay in the district. As a high school pupil, Bill senses the strong pressure he is under to get some agricultural qualifications and come home to take over the running of the family farm. His father makes his feelings known to Bill at every available opportunity. Conversation around the dinner table often focuses on farming matters and on the need for Bill to become more familiar with the work of the farm.

Gradually he finds the courage to begin asserting his own views on the subject. He realises that his father is scarcely listening to him whenever he mentions his wish to study for an Economics or Arts degree rather than Agriculture, but he chips away at the subject and gradually becomes more confident in discussing his ambition to move permanently to the city.

In private discussions with his mother, Bill is more frank. He confides in her his deep dislike of the rural life and his difficulty in trying to tell his father how strongly he really feels about it. His mother confirms his impression that his father is not really listening to Bill's point of view because he is so firmly set on the idea of his son taking over the family farm, as he had from his own father.

In Bill's last year of high school, when he is beginning to plan his move away to university the following year, his father shocks everyone by making an offer for the neighbouring property. He explains that he wants to be sure the business will be substantial enough to support both of them when Bill returns from university.

'I've got a few years left in me, you know, and young Billy is going to want to make a decent living for himself. Before you know where you are, he'll have a wife and kids running around the place . . . and we need a more secure operation for the longer term. And Galbally is prepared to sell at the right price. I think he's quite keen to get out, frankly. Makes sense all round.'

Bill is paralysed by the sense of an overpowering obligation to fulfil his father's wishes, yet he is as determined as ever to leave home and establish his own career in the city. The big smoke, his father calls it, as if it were a fantasyland where Bill might want to go for some adolescent fun, but where no right-minded person would want to settle permanently.

Bill's conversations with his mother become more urgent and despairing. She, too, is stunned by her husband's decision to buy the neighbouring farm and she is as perplexed as Bill by the evidence which suggests that his clear statements about his own ambitions have failed to draw any response from his father. It is as though he can only hear what he wants to hear; as though Bill's opinions simply don't exist. It's not even as if he is regarding Bill as needing to get the city out of his system before *he comes to his senses and returns home. In his father's mind, Bill will go to university, will study Agriculture, will come home and gradually take over the running of the farm. That is simply how it will be.*

When the time comes for Bill to enrol in his university course, he settles on Economics and explains his decision to his father. The reaction is a surprise to Bill: his father takes it in his stride, and even compliments Bill on his decision. He participates in all the discussions about Bill's application to live in a university college, and shows every sign of support.

Bill's studies proceed well and he comes home for most of his university vacations. His father continues to show more than polite interest in his studies and mentions that a lot of the local lads are getting an Economics degree under their belt before moving on to Agriculture. That's when the penny drops. Bill realises that his father has interpreted his decision to study Economics as a sign that he is, after all, going to come home to the farm, but that he is going to qualify himself more thoroughly first.

Bill writes his father a letter in which he spells out his plans and makes it clear, yet again, that agriculture has no place in his thinking about the future. He says he is sorry. He acknowledges that his father will be disappointed. He explains his desire to build his own career, based on his own interests.

There is no response to the letter. When Bill phones his mother, she says that her husband read it cursorily, put it aside, and has not even mentioned it to her. She found it on the desk in his office.

Bill worries that his father might actually be losing his grip. Is he so determined that Bill should take over the farm that he really can't grasp the point of what Bill is saying?

When Bill graduates, he takes a job in the public service which is, to him, like a dream come true. He is able to apply his new-found knowledge and skills, and the prospects for promotion seem excellent. Two of his university friends have secured jobs in the same department and, at last, Bill feels that he is really on his way.

His father is shattered. He sells the Galbally property quickly and cheaply and becomes cranky and withdrawn. His wife reasons with him. Hadn't Bill made his intentions clear, right from the start? What is so surprising about what has happened? Isn't this what Bill had always said would happen? Why hasn't he been able to accept that Bill meant what he said?

Her husband refuses to discuss it. For months, he virtually ignores news from Bill and shows no interest in his wife's reports of Bill's progress in his new job. All he will say, over and over again, is, 'The public service. The public service. I never thought a member of my family would join the public service,' as though the **real** disappointment is in Bill's choice of a public service career, rather than his failure to come home to the farm.

Towards the end of that year, he has to take his wife to the city for some medical tests. They spend some time with Bill, visit his office, have a meal in his flat, meet his friends. They see a young man who is clearly contented, ambitious, successful and popular. Bill asks some questions about the farm and shows an intelligent interest in what is going on. But he takes care to mention that it all seems very remote from his new life and that he is sure he has made the right decision.

On the way home from their visit, Bill's father says to

his wife, 'You never know with young Billy. He might still decide to take up farming one day, but we'd better not bank on it.'

It is easy to accept that we are the products of our experience, but not so easy to acknowledge that we are also prisoners of our experience. This is only another way of saying that we are limited by what we have learned from all our yesterdays in trying to make sense of what is happening to us today. Our discoveries, learnings and decisions gradually evolve into a recognisable pattern (sometimes called a 'world view') which we use as a framework—or a template—for making our own sense of the world.

We badly need that framework. If we were not capable of creating patterns of meaning out of our experience and our memories, we would never learn from them and every new experience would be a mystery to us. Imagine trying to cross a busy road if you did not have the ability to store, organise and learn from all your previous experiences of crossing busy roads. The challenge of getting from one side to another without being knocked over would seem impossibly daunting. (For young children who have not yet acquired the ability to construct reliable and trustworthy frameworks from their experience, the challenge *is* too daunting.)

It is as though we are engaged in a lifelong process of constructing personal 'cages' around ourselves. The bars of our cages are all the things that life has taught us: our knowledge, our attitudes, our values, our beliefs, our convictions. As the cage becomes stronger and more complex, we feel increasingly comfortable inside it and increasingly confident in our ability to cope with the world beyond the cage.

The cage therefore plays a crucial role in our mental health because, being a framework constructed out of the 'bars' of our own experience, it gives us a clear sense of personal identity and a deep sense of personal security.

Where we have been, and what we have learned from the journey, defines who we are.

You may not like the image of a cage to describe the mechanism by which you store your life's experiences and incorporate them into your view of the world. Perhaps you prefer the image of a cocoon: a place created out of the strands of 'meaning' which you have acquired from your own experience and which you have gradually woven into a familiar and comfortable shape.

But remember that this cage is not like a prison or a dungeon: inside the cage, it feels like a bright, airy, comfortable place. It's where we belong; where we can be ourselves. The cage is a self-protective device which we have willingly and actively constructed because it serves the very important purpose of organising our experience for us.

To put it in communication terms, the cage is our storehouse of 'meaning': it is the resource we need for making sense of the things people say to us.

In either case—cage or cocoon—we are looking at the most powerful element in the communication process. The cage is not simply a source of comfort and security: it also acts as a filter or an insulator in the process of interpretation. Because we look at the world through the bars of the cage, the bars impose their own pattern on what we see: our values and beliefs affect the way we perceive and interpret what's out there. From inside the cage, the cage itself is part of what we see.

To fully appreciate the way the cage imposes its own pattern on our view of the world, we only have to observe how a literal, physical cage affects the view of those inside it. Monkeys at the zoo don't see the tourists: what they see are the tourists *through the bars of the cage*. A garden viewed through a lattice screen is patterned by the screen: the screen is part of the view of the garden. Any scene viewed through a window is framed by the window. An event filmed for a TV news bulletin is filtered by the camera lens which can only focus on some of the story (and it is then filtered even more through the editing process). A street seen through the slats of a venetian blind is striped by the blind.

So it is with the invisible, psychological bars of our personal cages. Once we have made up our minds about something—once our experience has taught us something—we will tend to look at the world through the filter of the expectations created by that conviction, conclusion or predisposition.

In *The Extended Phenotype*, Richard Dawkins recounts the story of an African pygmy who was taken out of the forest for the first time in his life by a friend—the British author Colin Turnbull. Together they climbed a mountain and gazed over the plains. The pygmy, Kenge, spotted some buffalo grazing below them, several miles away. He asked Turnbull, 'What insects are those?' After a moment's astonished reflection, Turnbull realised that forest vision is so limited that Kenge had never had to learn to make an allowance for distance when judging size. When Turnbull told him that they were buffalo, Kenge roared with disbelieving laughter.

Kenge was caged by his own experience, as we all are. Our cages may be distorted by our sense of belonging to one social class rather than another, or by our prejudices on the subject of race, religion, politics or gender. A woman who believes that all men are male chauvinist pigs, for example, will be as incapable of identifying sensitivity in a well-meaning man as Kenge was of identifying buffalo on the distant plains.

Our reactions to watching politicians on television often show how hard it is for us to see what is actually there, without being influenced by our own conditioning and our own prejudices. Supporters of Paul Keating, for example, regard an outburst of colourful language as a sign that the man is human, that he is a welcome breath of fresh air in an otherwise boring forum, and that he is giving the opposition no more than they deserve.

His opponents, watching the very same outburst, may turn away from the TV set in disgust. They see his language as a sign of vulgarity, as evidence of a street-bully mentality, and as an unacceptable way for a prime minister to behave.

The language itself is neither one thing nor the other: our judgments depend on what is in us, rather than what is in the prime minister's words. Even the most formally delivered policy speech will be similarly judged: 'Isn't he wonderful' or 'Isn't he a phony', depending on your point of view. When political passions are involved, our capacity to make impartial judgments is severely impaired. Our adversarial parliamentary system thrives on strong cages.

Not surprisingly, when we look at things from a particular viewpoint, we see them from that point of view. Our interpretation of events tends to confirm the perspective from which they are observed.

In his 1711 *Essay on Criticism*, Alexander Pope gave us

a couplet which has endured as an apt and economical description of the power of the cage:

All seems infected that th' infected spy,
As all looks yellow to the jaundic'd eye.

The viewer is indeed part of the view!

People with strong beliefs find that their beliefs are further strengthened by what they see happening around them: the beliefs are themselves filters which colour or pattern (or perhaps distort) the view of what is going on. As soon as we begin to store and organise our conclusions about the world, we create an in-built tendency to look at the world in a way which will reinforce those conclusions. (For further discussion of the process of *reinforcement*, see Chapter 4.)

One of the most obvious ways in which the cage distorts our view of the world is in our personal assessments of each other. Prejudice about personal appearance—earrings on men, a blue hair rinse on women, jeans, double-breasted suits, crew cuts, stubble—can strongly influence our responses to each other and may cause us to react in a particular way to messages which, if they had come from someone who looked different, might have produced a quite different reaction in us.

Hans and Michael Eysenck's book, *Mindwatching*, describes some research into the relationship between status and appearance. Several groups of students were introduced to a man who was sometimes described as 'Mr England, a student from Cambridge' and sometimes as 'Professor England from Cambridge'. When the students were asked to estimate the man's height, 'Professor

England' was judged to be twelve centimetres taller than 'Mr England'. *Mindwatching* also reports the results of a survey of salaries being paid to men who had recently graduated from the University of Pittsburgh. It turned out that the tallest students received an average starting salary at least 12 per cent higher than their shorter colleagues.

The statement 'I don't like the look of him' is a sign that the cage is likely to work against whatever that person says. It is a common experience in meetings for people who are regarded as attractive and likeable to find that their points of view are more easily accepted than those who are regarded as unattractive or 'difficult'. In fact, there is a good deal of research evidence to support the proposition that people's attitudes towards physical attractiveness are so positive that they can get in the way of objectivity and fairness (or even reasonableness) in making judgments about other people.

For example, American research by G. R. Adams has shown that good-looking people are often judged to be more talented, kind, honest and intelligent than others—and that these judgments are made quite automatically and unconsciously.

A study of voting patterns in the 1974 Canadian federal elections suggested that physically attractive candidates received more than twice the votes given to unattractive candidates. Again, follow-up research (Efran & Patterson) revealed that voters were not only unconscious of their bias towards more attractive candidates but strenuously denied that their vote would be influenced by physical appearance.

The same kind of evidence emerges from research into the American judicial process. Several studies have shown a close relationship between defendants' physical appearance and their presumed guilt or innocence. A 1980 study by J. E. Stewart attempted to quantify this relationship. Pennsylvania researchers made personal judgments about the relative handsomeness of 74 male defendants at the start of their criminal trials. After those trials were over, the researchers checked their ratings of physical appearance against the results of the cases and found that, although many of the handsome men had been convicted, they received significantly lighter sentences than less attractive men. On the evidence of those subjective judgments, handsome defendants were twice as likely to avoid gaol as unattractive defendants.

It would be very hard to draw the conclusion from such evidence that people's experience has taught them that good-looking people are more honest, less violent or, in any other way, preferable to unattractive people. Rather, the evidence suggests that one of the most automatic of the filtering effects of the cage is to attach positive attributes to people whom we find beautiful, and negative attributes to those we find ugly. In communication terms, this creates a serious complication, because it means that physical appearance is a visual 'message' to which we attach all kinds of meanings which surround and influence the meaning which another person may be trying to share with us. (For further discussion about the relationship between the messenger and the message, see Chapter 7.)

'I won't hear a word against her,' says a loyal friend, using the cage as a quite explicit and deliberate defence against unwelcome information which might upset an existing framework of beliefs if it were accepted. People who are devoted to the memory of a political or religious leader, a sporting or cultural hero, or even a much-loved relative, may discount unpalatable facts which come to light after the person's death. To accept such facts would be to threaten the carefully constructed shape of the cage of that memory, and denial is much easier than revision. Indeed, so powerful is the effect of the cage in creating expectations that contradictory information is often interpreted so thoroughly that it scarcely seems to be contradictory at all. ('You hear people say the most awful things about him, but that is just because they are jealous of his achievements . . . famous people are always being attacked in that way.')

Even before we interpret what we see or hear, the cage filters our view of the world, focusing our attention on what is most relevant to our needs at the time. Imagine three people standing on a crowded footpath at lunchtime in a busy city, waiting to cross the road. One of them is heading for a sandwich bar to buy some lunch; the second is hurrying to meet a friend for a lunch-hour shopping expedition; the third, a car buff, is watching the passing traffic.

All three people are seeing the same streetscape, but they are not looking at it in the same way. Their eyes are scanning the same field of vision but, from inside their respective cages, different features of the streetscape attract their particular attention.

The first is focusing on the sandwich shop and evaluating the length of the queue. The second is glancing at a clock which tells her that she is running late for the appointment with her friend; the third has caught sight of an exotic car which is the apple of his eye. Ask the person heading for the sandwich shop what the time was, and he won't even have noticed that the clock was there, let alone what time it was telling, although his eyes actually saw it.

Ask the person hurrying to meet her friend what make of car was passing in the street, and she probably won't even be able to tell you what colour it was, though her eyes actually saw it. Ask the car buff what kind of shop was on the other side of the road and he probably won't have a clue, even though his eyes actually saw it.

We see what is there, but we observe it in terms of the perspective which our cage gives us. We effectively filter out those messages in our environment which are not relevant to our existing needs, interests or points of view. The power of the cage explains why it is possible for three people to attend the same meeting and then to give three quite different accounts of what happened and what was decided.

'But people will see you,' says Gloria, a character in Elmore Leonard's novel, *Pronto*, when a gunman describes to her how he intends to shoot his victim in a crowded restaurant.

'Yeah, what? Ask them, they all see something different. One or two witnesses, they can identify you. A lot of people there, you got no problem.'

Sometimes, the power of the cage produces an effect which looks like simple mishearing or misreading. I once checked into a hotel and, on the registration card, wrote in the name of my organisation: The Centre for Communication Studies. When it came time to check out, I found that the name had been printed on my bill as 'Centrefold Communication'. Clearly, the woman on the checkout desk had glanced at those words and made her own sense of them (assuming, perhaps, that I was some kind of talent scout).

Similarly, children often interpret messages which are beyond them in ways which make those messages seem sensible. A class in a Catholic primary school was being told, for the first time, about the approach of Ash Wednesday, and one of the children reported to her parents that they were going to celebrate Asphalt Wednesday. Simple distortions like that reveal how our capacity to interpret messages is limited by the framework within which we are operating—a framework which can only be built from the experience we have had so far.

One of the most obvious effects of the cage is to make messages seem simpler or more 'sensible' than they really are, so that we can absorb them without difficulty.

When messages appear to be misunderstood or misinterpreted, it is hard for us to realise that this is not always due to the ignorance, stupidity or inattention of the listener: what seems, from inside our cage, to be a *mis*interpretation is often nothing more than an interpretation made from within the cage of the other person.

No one *tries* to misunderstand or misinterpret: we simply interpret according to the framework within which we are operating, because the framework creates the filter through which we make sense of what is being said.

Michael comes through the back door, panting and flushed. He finds his mother in the family room and throws himself at her.

'Mr Jansen is a silly old bugger,' he sobs into Margaret's shoulder.

'Michael, what an appalling thing to say. Where on earth did you hear such an awful thing?'

'Well, he is. Everyone knows he is. And he just threw a rock at me.'

'Michael. What were you doing? Were you and Terry teasing Mr Jansen again?'

'We were just playing. We weren't doing anything wrong. You can ask Terry. And that dirty old . . . '

'Michael!'

' . . . well he shouted something at us and threw a lump of dirt out of his garden. He's a loony. Even Dad says that.'

'I've told you about Mr Jansen before. He's a very sad old man. His wife has died, and he's lonely. And he had a very hard time in the war.'

Michael is rapidly losing interest. He has heard about Mr Jansen's war too many times, when his mother has tried to defend or explain the eccentricities of their irascible neighbour.

'Is that what made him into a loony?' Michael asks, partly to get the spotlight off Mr Jansen and back onto him. The sympathy isn't flowing quite as freely as he expected. He's wondering whose side his mother is on.

'Mr Jansen is not a loony. And he is not a silly old bugger . . . and that is a word we don't use in this family.'

'Kelly does.'

'We'll talk about that another time. Now, I want you to understand, once and for all, that Mr Jansen may seem a bit strange but he can't help it. He's perfectly harmless and he would never do anything to hurt you. Just because he's working in his garden, he might look a bit grubby, but he is not always like that. You've seen him looking perfectly normal.'

'I'm scared of him. I hate having him living next door to us. He is a loony, and he does bad stuff. And he **always** looks dirty to me.'

'Michael, can't you understand what I'm telling you? Mr Jansen is a sad person and he has had a difficult life. We have to try and understand people like that. He can't help it. He's not bad, or mean, or dangerous.'

'Yes he is. Why did he chuck a lump of dirt at me if he isn't a loony?'

Just then, Bill comes in from the garden to see what is going on. Michael runs to him, tears breaking out again. 'Mr Jansen is a dirty old bugger and a dangerous loony. Mum says it's all because he was in the war. That's what made him so dangerous.'

'Michael,' says Margaret sternly, 'didn't you listen to anything I said?'

'But that **is** what you said,' says Michael and runs off before his parents can restrain him.

When Margaret's little lecture about Mr Jansen contradicts Michael's own experience in the street, how is he going to react to what his mother is saying? He has already incorporated his own experience into his own cage and that has given him the framework within which he will interpret his mother's messages.

Michael has an opinion—an attitude—which gives him a perspective on everything he is being told. He *knows* that Mr Jansen is a loony, and everything he sees and hears tends to confirm that existing point of view. Nothing Margaret might say is likely to change his mind: on the contrary, his personal, psychological comfort depends upon *not* changing his mind, since his own attitude is the result of his own hard-won experience.

In such circumstances, Michael behaves like most of us: he seizes on selected statements made by his mother

('Mr Jansen can't help it' or 'He may seem a bit strange') to confirm what he already believes.

Think again about the episode at the beginning of Chapter 1 when Margaret rang Michael, asking him to pass on instructions about the dinner to Bill. Once we understand how the cage works, the whole story makes more sense: from inside Michael's cage, the message that his mother will be home late is important, and he realises that it must be relayed to his father. But he attaches no importance to the need to get the sausages out of the refrigerator, nor to the need to have a bath before dinner, because both of these things contradict what Michael now interprets as the main point of his mother's message, namely an opportunity to get his father to take them to McDonald's. When Bill arrives home, Michael relays the message—as filtered through the bars of his own cage—including his own additional suggestion about McDonald's.

From inside Bill's cage, the situation which greets him when he arrives home is rather irritating. He is annoyed that Margaret will be late home and he is not attracted to the prospect of cooking sausages. Michael's suggestion of McDonald's strikes a responsive chord and, although he initially rejects it, he does incorporate it into the range of possibilities for the evening. Once he realises that Kelly's netball is an issue, a trip to McDonald's looks like the best solution to the problem of feeding the children and getting to netball on time.

From inside Margaret's cage, however, things look very different indeed. She interprets the whole episode not only in terms of her running battle with the family over trying to get them to take more responsibility for domestic matters, but also in terms of her great excitement about her new job. What she really *needs* is for the family to be at home together, having dinner, when she sweeps in with her big news. That is an attractive prospect, so the fact that her preconceived picture of how it would all happen is shattered by Bill's decision to take the children to McDonald's irritates her more than it might otherwise have done. She has constructed a little cage of expectation: she has approached the situation with a particular mind-set, based on her desire to tell the family her news, in her own way, and so her disappointment comes out as irritation and even anger.

The problem of expectation

Michael's class are being taken on a bushwalk by their teacher. She explains to them that, during the walk, they are to observe the various plants, insects, animals and birds in the bush so that when they return to their classroom, they can make a list of what they have seen.

*At the end of the excursion, Michael writes 'no kangaroos' as the sole record of his observations. The teacher acknowledges that neither he nor any of the other children had observed any kangaroos in the bush, and she sympathises with Michael in his disappointment. But she urges him to think about what **else** he might have seen during the walk, and to record that on his sheet.*

'But I was only looking for kangaroos,' he replies.

Just like the TV news camera, we perceive only part of what is there, selecting those messages which are most likely to fit comfortably with the pattern of our existing attitudes and values, and looking for things which fulfil our expectations. Just like the TV news editor, we then filter those messages even more carefully, adding our own meanings, holding onto some parts of the message and letting others go.

We don't only perceive and interpret selectively; we remember and forget selectively, as well.

The cage is one of our most powerful psychological weapons. It gives us the ability to shape the world to our liking. In communication, it allows us to deal with messages in a way which confirms what we already thought or what we had expected to hear—even when that was not the intention of the speaker. It explains our tendency to see what we want to see and hear what we want to hear.

The cage, in its various ways, affects our perceptions, our expectations and our judgments. We arrange our view of the world (and interpret the messages we receive) so that we can remain comfortable within the secure cage of our own prejudices, beliefs and predispositions.

In *Mindwatching*, Hans and Michael Eysenck quote an experiment conducted by researchers at the University of Washington who were testing some of the ways in which our recollection of events can be distorted by expectations created within us. People were shown a number of different films of traffic accidents and were then asked to answer questions about each accident. Those who were asked the question, 'About how fast were the cars going when they smashed into each other?' gave higher estimates of the cars' speed than those who were asked the same question, only with the word 'smashed' replaced by such words as 'collided', 'bumped', 'contacted' or 'hit'. The experimenters reported that estimates of the speed of cars involved in the accidents were almost ten miles per hour higher when the question used the word 'smashed' rather than 'contacted'.

Even though the participants in that experiment had seen the film for themselves, the way in which they were subsequently invited to describe it affected the descriptions they gave.

Michael and Kelly sometimes travel home after school on the same bus. One afternoon, there is a commotion on the bus. One of Michael's classmates has upset a girl from another school and the driver is loudly remonstrating with him: 'I've banned kids from this bus for less than that. You've caused trouble before. I've a good mind to report you to the school and have you banned from the bus. Now give her back her pencils and apologise for what you said. Go on ... I'm waiting. I'm not joking ...'

Walking home from the bus stop, Michael is in a state of high excitement. 'That's the end of Paul. Did you hear what the bus driver said? He's going to be banned. Yeah! I knew that would happen. He's in trouble at school, too. Serves him right.'

Kelly is intrigued. 'What has Paul done to you to make you so down on him?'

'He's always picking on me. He laughs if I get something wrong. And he always makes fun of me at sport, whenever I drop a ball or do anything ... I'm really sick of him.'

'He won't be banned from the bus, you know. The driver was just saying that. He was just threatening him to get him to give that girl her things back.'

'Yes, he will. The driver said so. He said he wasn't joking. He said he had banned other kids for less than that, and he was going to report Paul to the school. He's a goner.'

Kelly, uncaged on the subject of Paul but not wanting Michael to be too pleased with himself, chooses to place a cautious interpretation on the bus driver's remarks. Michael, caged by his own hostility to Paul, will not be convinced that anything less than a big fuss is going to happen. When subsequent events suggest that Kelly was right, and the offending boy continues to appear on the school bus, Michael is undeterred: the case against Paul is incorporated into his generally negative view of the boy, and he regards him as being under permanent threat of banning. In Michael's mind, it is only a matter of time.

The bars of Michael's cage are arranged in a pattern which says 'Paul is a nasty kid; he has been found out by those in authority; he will get his just desserts'. From now on Michael is actually less distressed by Paul's teasing because he sees him as a marked man who won't get away with being nasty for much longer. In fact, every perceived misdeed adds fuel to the comforting fire of Michael's prejudice.

It is the power of the cage which gave some justification to the remark by Josef Goebbels, Adolf Hitler's chief propagandist, that whoever tells the world first is believed. There's something in that: the first information we receive about a particular subject becomes part of the filter through which we perceive subsequent information. Our response to new information is a relatively uncaged response: from then on, however, we have a framework for making sense of additional messages.

'Your son has been killed,' comes the shocking news from the combat zone. The grieving parents incorporate that appalling message into their cages as they learn how to come to terms with a new, central fact of their lives.

A few months later, another message comes: 'We have a letter from your son.'

'But our son is dead.'

'Apparently not. We have a letter from him.'

'But our son is dead.'

'Captured, not killed.'

Then begins the process—almost equally painful—of demolishing the bars of a cage built in tragic error. The joy of learning that their son is actually alive is tempered by the emotional trauma of having to rethink, to rebuild, to reorientate. The news that their son is alive may be, in its own way, almost as hard to absorb as the news that their son is dead. In both cases, serious cage-work is called for.

In his British TV series on madness, Jonathan Miller refers to an experiment in which a doctor admitted a group of sane people to a mental hospital, identifying each of them as having some particular mental illness. Not surprisingly, they were regarded by the staff of the institution as exhibiting symptoms which were associated with the specified illnesses. Having had a mind-set created by the diagnosis on admission, the staff were looking for signs which confirmed it. The cage did its usual work: the behaviour of perfectly normal people came to be seen as evidence of whatever mental illness they were alleged to be suffering from. Once the label 'sick' had been attached to them by a qualified medical practitioner, the hospital staff saw everything through the filter thus created.

The powerful filter of professional prejudice

An inscription on the facade of the Social Science

Research building at the University of Chicago reads: 'If you cannot measure, your knowledge is meagre and unsatisfactory'. No doubt, many of its inhabitants, imprisoned in their modern laboratories, scrutinise the world through the bars of the integers, failing to realise that the method they endeavour to follow is not only necessarily barren and unfruitful, but also is not the method to which the success of physics is to be attributed.

You don't need to understand scientific method in order to see the point of this quote from *What is this thing called science?* by Alan Chalmers. It captures the idea of the cage in an almost literal way. Chalmers conjures up a picture of a group of scientists who have become so obsessed with the idea of measuring everything that they see the world—even the world of human emotions and relationships—through the filter of their own obsession with measurement. Being 'numbers' people, they can't admit the possibility that other kinds of data (non-statistical, qualitative data, for example) may be equally valid in the search for scientific explanations of human behaviour. No; to them, the need to measure everything is so powerful that it blocks out the possibility of accepting alternative points of view.

The French have a term—*déformation professionelle*—to refer to the peculiar potency of the cage of someone who has received highly specialised education and training. In his book *Irrational Man*, William Barrett speaks of this 'deformity' which professional people—and other highly educated people—must overcome if they are going to be able to communicate with others who are not similarly caged:

Doctors and engineers tend to see things from the

viewpoint of their own specialty, and usually show a very marked blind spot to whatever falls outside this particular province. The more specialised a vision, the sharper its focus; but also the more nearly total the blind spot toward all things that lie on the periphery of this focus.

This is why computer experts often seem to have trouble communicating with those outside their specialty. It is why lawyers tend to speak in 'legalese' and then wonder why their clients have so much trouble understanding what is going on. It is why people steeped in particular religious traditions and cultures often develop a form of religious jargon which makes perfect sense to those with similar religious cages, but no sense at all to those coming from a different religious (or non-religious) cultural background.

From inside the cage of the specialist, everything seems perfectly clear—so much so that it is sometimes difficult even for specialists to understand that other people might be having trouble understanding or interpreting what they are saying.

(For further discussion of the excluding effect of specialised language, see Chapter 8: 'What about your own cage?')

Architects see things in terms of form and function; accountants in terms of financial value; psychologists in terms of mental and emotional phenomena; environmentalists in terms of ecology; doctors in terms of health risks; and so on.

The 'professional deformity' of the highly educated specialist, however, is just one example of how the cage works for all of us. We all have the same problem as the scientist obsessed with numbers or the entrepreneur obsessed with commercial opportunities: our experience, our point of view, our predispositions—whatever they are—have taught us to see the world in ways which encourage us to make our own sense of what is going on.

The religious person interprets things within a religious framework; the atheist interprets *the very same things* within a non-religious framework. One says, 'See, the world is so complex, it must have been created by a divine intelligence. We will never penetrate its mysteries.' The other says, 'See, the world is so complex, it must be part of a vast cosmic accident and we will ultimately unravel its complexity through the study of astronomy, thermodynamics, or mathematics.' Each view of the cosmos filters out the possibility that the other may be right. The cage does its self-protective work.

All prejudice works in that way. A militant feminist, for example, might miss the whole point of a lecture, simply because the lecturer said 'he' when the feminist thought he should have said 'he or she': the prejudice about gender-free language, in that case, has effectively filtered out whatever else was being said.

The economist, similarly, may become so preoccupied with the economic consequences of a particular policy that the human consequences may be entirely overlooked.

Once we are imprisoned within the prejudices associated with a particular profession, discipline or school of thought, it becomes correspondingly harder for us to attend to messages which don't mesh with the particular framework of that prejudice.

Mind-sets of all kinds can have the same effect. A person who has decided that he is widely disliked will begin to interpret the innocent actions of others as if they are signs of hostility. A paranoid person is convinced that people really are persecuting him . . . the view from inside the cage of paranoia offers a perspective which makes that interpretation come more easily than the alternative interpretations.

The insecurity of a shaky cage

People who have not been able to build strong cages around themselves often feel insecure and anxious. While we admire a certain amount of open-mindedness in each other, we know that as we mature (that is, as we become more experienced) we are bound to reach some conclusions; to make up our minds about some important questions—at least for the time being; to rank our priorities and to settle on some core values. These are the very things that act as bars in our cages, and a cage which lacks sufficient rigidity or a sufficient number of bars makes us feel vulnerable, confused, indecisive or disorientated.

This is not to praise rigidity in itself: far from it! People who are so rigid that they are unwilling to think new thoughts and lack even the capacity to learn from new experiences have allowed their cages to imprison them utterly. Healthy cages are dynamic rather than static; they are evolving rather than stultifying. A soundly constructed cage will have some flexibility, but it will also have enough rigidity to give us the confidence to make sense of what is happening to us by relating it to a stable framework acquired from prior experience. Some rigidity is an essential part of the learning process: sooner or later, we have to reach a point where we know—or believe—*something*, even if we simultaneously acknowledge that there may be room for doubt, for development or for the revelations of new experience.

The phrase 'the innocence of childhood' implies an openness, a vulnerability which is associated with an unformed cage. In a child, such innocence is enchanting; in a mature adult, it is a worry. Yet there are times when, for various reasons, our cages seem to crumple or to be so damaged by attacks upon them that they are no longer comfortable places to be and we are forced to think about repairs or even rebuilding.

Take the case of a bitter divorce ...

In the early days of their relationship, Margaret experiences deep misgivings about Bill's ability to come to terms with the breakdown of his first marriage. She knows he is an intelligent and mature man, but she is puzzled by what seem to be almost infantile aspects of his behaviour. For a start, he can't stop talking about the ways in which he believes his wife has wronged him: over and over, endlessly repetitive, tiresome and ... well, boring.

Then there's the problem of revenge. Everything— ***everything****—seems to be weighed up in terms of its likely effect on Judith. Why can't he just forget all that property wrangling? Why can't they just start afresh? Why can't he just walk away from their house and their computer? Their computer! You would think that Bill was being divorced from the computer, the way he goes on about it. Just when it looks as though everything is going to be settled, he gets all worked up about the computer again. And Judith obviously knows how badly he seems to want it, so that's one thing she is never going to give up on. Their daughter, Kelly, the furniture, the dog, the beach*

*house . . . all settled. But the computer? Months of tur-
bulence over the wretched computer. Visits to the house
to make sure it's still there; endless phone calls; legal bills
which would have paid for a new computer three times
over, at least.*

*Even when they go out for dinner with new friends,
Bill seizes the first opportunity to talk about the ways
Judith has found to torture him. 'Why can't these things
be handled in a civilised way?' is his favourite line. Before
long, the computer pops up as a perfect example of how
irrational and stupid and mean and bitchy Judith is being.
The faces of their friends make it clear that they are wondering whether Judith could possibly be more irrational
or stupid than Bill himself appears to be over the
computer.*

*It is as though Bill has lost his sense of proportion; as
though his normal value system isn't functioning; as
though he can't see what his behaviour looks like to everyone else.*

*Then one morning, he snaps out of it. He goes to a
store and orders a new computer. He rings Judith and
tells her he has lost interest in the whole subject of property. She can have whatever she likes. He is calling his
lawyer to tell him to wrap everything up quickly. He's
sick of the whole thing. Bingo. Just like that. Margaret is
greatly relieved. She feels as though this is the real Bill.
Back from the crazies.*

*The very next day, a delivery van pulls up outside Bill's
flat. Judith has sent around the computer.*

During periods of sustained stress or trauma, the cage may
cease to function in its normal way. When the world no
longer works in the way we expect and our interpretations

of events no longer seem to make sense, we may begin to experience the peculiar sense of insecurity which results from a seriously damaged cage.

Divorce, bereavement, retrenchment, a life-threatening illness ... many things can trigger a collapse of our value system or a loss of clarity in our world view. At such times, the comfort and security of the cage are threatened by the need to rethink our priorities, to reassess our values or to rebuild our confidence.

In the short term, such periods have some of the vulnerability of childhood about them. We are more 'innocent' because we have lost confidence in our own reference points. We are not sure of who we are, what we stand for, or even what we want. That loss of the sense of identity and certainty which is normally provided by the cage means that we may be more open than at other times to the blandishments of new fashions, a new romance, new values, new religious perspectives.

We are most comfortable when our cages are functioning properly: when they become dysfunctional, we urgently seek replacement bars. Sometimes, we find that we have been too quick to build new cages and, when the crisis or the trauma has passed, we have to set about shedding the new material which we so enthusiastically incorporated into our wobbly cages to fortify them.

People who, almost unthinkingly, embrace a fanatical religious or political position—or fall dramatically in love with an inappropriate person—as an escape or relief from a trauma often find that, as life settles down again, they are rather embarrassed about their burst of enthusiasm. Their desire to replace a shaky cage with an exciting new one is understandable, but they are sometimes then faced with the slow and painful process of escaping from the 'emergency' cage and building yet another new structure out of the lessons learned from the trauma.

Falling in love 'on the rebound' is a familiar case in point: a broken heart can easily create a vacuum which, like a damaged cage, distorts our judgments about the suitability of alternative partners. A quick selection—made to fill the vacuum—sometimes leads to still greater heartache when the strength of the cage is gradually restored and we come to see the mistake we have made.

Adolescents often behave in ways which remind us that they are at a difficult stage in their life's work of cage construction. As the child-cage yields to an adult-cage, the transition can be confusing and painful for the adolescent, but also for the family and friends who are trying to cope with the instability and its consequences.

Our cages are sometimes built out of disappointment: *I have had no luck with the women in my life . . . women are hopeless . . . I actually hate women*; and misogyny becomes a perspective and an expectation in dealings with women.

Sometimes our cages are built out of pride: *I deserve better than this . . . I am not being treated as well as I should be . . . these people are worthless*; and a sense of superiority acts as a filter to denigrate and deride the attitudes and behaviour of other people (and to resist their messages).

Sometimes our humility, our guilt or even our sense of inferiority can cage us: *These people are different from me . . . they must be right and I must be wrong . . . I'm no good, really*; and a negative bias is built into our perception of the world as a place where we will not succeed.

The process of cage-building never ends. So it would be wrong to think of the cage as being a fixed, immutable frame of reference. New experience yields new insights and new perspectives, and the cage evolves and develops. It *feels* to us, on a day-to-day basis, as if the cage is fixed. We feel as if our beliefs are stable and our priorities are unchanging. It is therefore sometimes a shock to find, on being reminded of something we had said years ago, just how much our thinking has changed during the intervening time. But such changes often happen as a series of imperceptible shifts: they are more likely to be the result of minor adjustments, fine tuning and private reflection than of dramatic conversions or blinding flashes of inspiration.

What is true for ourselves is true also for others. In acknowledging that our own cages adapt—often quite subtly—to new experience, we must also acknowledge that other people's cages are in a state of constant evolution as well. It is particularly cruel to assume that another person's cage is a fixed and permanent structure: 'You have changed your mind' sounds like an accusation, as though cages should not be modified even in the light of new experience, and people who are challenged in that way often feel called upon to defend themselves.

Indeed, we are so committed to the idea of stable (and even rigid) cages in our culture that 'changing your mind' is regarded by some people as a sign of weakness or incompetence.

Tiny shifts, tiny adaptations, tiny adjustments are constantly being made to our cages. Sometimes these changes are apparent but, more often, they represent small accommodations which increase our level of psychological comfort without making us feel as though we have changed our minds in any significant way. (For a detailed discussion of how cages change, see Chapter 6: 'Changing People's Minds'.)

Although the cage evolves and adapts, its role in each moment of our lives is crucial because it is the power of the cage which enables people to 'do their own thing' with the messages they receive. However much our cages may change in fact, it is our tendency to resist change and to protect our cages *as they are now* that explains why the cage must always be taken into account when we want to communicate.

Recognition of the dominant influence of the cage leads to the Second Law of Human Communication:

Listeners generally interpret messages in ways which make them feel comfortable and secure.

The implication of the Second Law is clear: because we are at the mercy of the listener's cage, we need to explore and understand that cage before we can hope to communicate effectively. The ultimate key to success in communication lies in our ability to anticipate how other people will interpret what we are going to say. It is only when we have understood the mind-set of our audience that we are in a position to create a message which is designed *for them*.

In his book, *Influence: Science and Practice*, Robert Cialdini offers a rather graphic example of how one college student capitalised on her parents' mind-set:

Dear Mother and Dad,

Since I left for college I have been remiss in writing and I am sorry for my thoughtlessness in not having written before. I will bring you up to date now, but before you read on, please sit down. You are not to read any further unless you are sitting down, okay?

Well, then, I am getting along pretty well now. The skull fracture and the concussion I got when I jumped out the window of my dormitory when it caught fire shortly after my arrival here is pretty well healed now. I only spent two weeks in the hospital and now I can see almost normally and only get those sick headaches once a day. Fortunately, the fire in the dormitory, and my jump, was witnessed by an attendant at the gas station near the dorm, and he was the one who called the Fire Department and the ambulance. He also visited me in the hospital and since I had nowhere to live because of the burnt-out dormitory, he was kind enough to invite me to share his apartment with him. It's really a basement room, but it's kind of cute. He is a very fine boy, and we have fallen deeply in love and are planning to get married. We haven't set the exact date yet, but it will be before my pregnancy begins to show.

Yes, Mother and Dad, I am pregnant. I know how much you are looking forward to being grandparents and I know you will welcome the baby and give it the same love and devotion and tender care you gave me when I was a child. The reason for the delay in our marriage is that my boyfriend has a minor infection which prevents us from passing our premarital blood tests and I carelessly caught it from him. I know that you will welcome him into our family with open arms.

He is kind and, although not well educated, he is ambitious. Although he is of a different race and religion than ours, I know your often-expressed tolerance will not permit you to be bothered by that.

Now that I have brought you up to date, I want to tell you that there was no dormitory fire, I did not have a concussion or skull fracture, I was not in the hospital, I am not pregnant, I am not engaged, I am not infected, and there is no boyfriend. However, I am getting a 'D' in American History and an 'F' in Chemistry, and I want you to see those marks in their proper perspective.

Your loving daughter,
Sharon

CHAPTER 4

The Three Rs of Communication

Our cages lie squarely at the heart of every communication encounter. To switch the metaphor, they are like the traffic lights which control the flow of messages between us and others. Or perhaps you prefer the Chapter 3 analogy with TV news-gathering—thinking of messages as being selectively filmed through a filtered and hooded lens and then carefully edited before being screened as a 'program' in the mind.

Whichever metaphor you choose, the underlying point is the same: the mind-set of the audience determines whether communication is possible at all and it sets limits to the listener's capacity to respond to what we will say.

In fact, once we understand how cages are built, how they work, and how important they are to us, we have understood the secret of successful communication. Think of it in terms of the 'three Rs' of communication . . .

1 REINFORCEMENT

Because the cage is where we store the lessons we have learned from our experience, we naturally tend to protect it. Our cages define our identity and give us a much-needed sense of personal security, so attacks on them are bound to be resisted. The cage is a comfortable place to be: why would we welcome anything—such as an irritating or challenging message—which is likely to make us feel uncomfortable? (If we can't relax in the privacy of our own cages, where *can* we relax?)

Our preferred messages—the messages which capture our ready attention and interest—will be those that reinforce the existing shape and structure of our cage. Friends love retelling familiar stories and jokes which reinforce their shared values. Families love hearing their tribal folklore over and over again, because it reinforces the bars of their collective cage.

The faithful routinely attend services of religious worship, not to have their faith challenged or questioned, but to have it confirmed. People habitually watch their favourite TV programs for the familiarity and predictability of the formula. Rituals reassure us precisely because they are cage-affirming.

Even the rituals of violent *dis*agreement appeal to some people, because they love to exercise their convictions in vigorous jousting with people of a different persuasion. They know that they are not going to budge from their existing position: indeed, the whole purpose of repetitive disagreement (which often takes place between the best of friends) is that it creates opportunities for us to trot out the arguments which support our existing point of view.

It is easy to see why messages which fit with the existing shape of the cage are so welcome. Communication comes easily when a message supports what the other person already believes. But perhaps it is not so easy to appreciate that when you *attack* someone's cage you are just as likely to produce the reinforcement effect as if you had agreed with them.

When we are attacked, we defend. In the process of defending our existing point of view, we actually reinforce it. It is one of the great frustrations of the communication process that if you attack someone else's point of view, the most likely outcome is that you will reinforce the very view you wanted to change. The defensive capability of the cage is so powerful that attacks upon it tend to strengthen—rather than weaken—its bars.

This is not to suggest that cages are unshakable or utterly resistant to change. Under certain circumstances, cages can be modified, extensively rebuilt, or virtually demolished (and we explore how that might happen in Chapter 6: 'Changing People's Minds'). But the most likely effect of a disagreement is that both parties will go away from the argument believing *even more strongly* in the view they held all along.

Look at the experience of the early Christian church: under the influence of extreme persecution, did the faith of those early Christians waver? Have the Jews simply faded away in response to sustained hostility? Do Muslims who meet antagonism from non-Muslim communities find their conviction weakening? On the contrary, like most minorities who are persecuted, the faith of each of those groups is reinforced.

Religious, racial and cultural groups who have their beliefs, their customs or their values attacked by members of other groups usually find that their resolve is stiffened—partly because of the bracing effect of having to defend themselves, and partly because of the emotional lift which comes from the experience of group solidarity. People participating in protest marches and demonstrations, for example, are much more likely to be discouraged by indifference than by opposition.

Indeed, their protest gains momentum and passion when it is opposed.

If you want to see a graphic example of the cage in action, simply watch people having an argument. One person states a point of view and the other states a different point of view. The first person replies with a restatement, possibly expressed more strongly, and the second person does likewise. And so the argument proceeds with both of them becoming more and more vehement in the presentation of the points of view they brought to the argument. Are they prepared to give in? Are they stepping outside the comfort and security of their own cages so that they might better appreciate the opposite point of view? Is one of them showing some sign of gratitude to the other for having pointed out the flaws in the argument? Hardly. It is very unusual to hear people in the heat of an argument giving in to each other, or even acknowledging the possibility that they might *both* be right. Typically, the mere fact of engaging in an argument has a fortifying effect on our beliefs, convictions and points of view.

Cages attacked are cages defended, and cages defended are cages reinforced.

Kelly is showing signs of becoming sexually involved with her boyfriend, Damien, and Margaret and Bill are concerned. Bill refuses to broach the subject with Kelly; he says that he doesn't want their relationship to get heavy. He and Margaret have now talked about it so much that he becomes irritated whenever she raises it. Margaret realises that his irritation is itself a sign of Bill's uneasiness about what is going on, but she feels that something will have to be said to Kelly. Bill is obviously quite happy to leave it to her.

It is hard for Margaret to find an opportunity to sit and talk with Kelly about the situation. The attempts she has made so far have generally ended with Kelly storming out of the room under the impression that her stepmother is simply attacking her or criticising her taste in boys. Even Margaret's tendency to refer to Kelly's relationship with Damien as 'the situation' has created its own tension.

One Sunday afternoon, Margaret and Kelly find themselves at home together. Bill and Michael are kicking a football at the park, and Margaret's father is coming over for a drink later in the day. Kelly has finished her homework, Margaret has done most of the household chores and here they are, in a rare moment, sitting together in silence.

'Kelly, you know I am a bit worried about the situation with you and Damien . . . you know, getting too serious.'

'What do you mean, "the situation"?' Kelly stiffens and she looks everywhere but at Margaret.

'I know that you get upset whenever I mention this, but I am just saying this for your own good. I think you might find it helpful to hear what I have to say, without blocking me out as soon as I open my mouth. I really am thinking of you.'

'Well, it doesn't feel like that to me. I feel as if you are thinking of you. I know you don't like Damien much and you feel a bit embarrassed that he is spending so much time with our family. I feel as if you think your friends will judge you by my boyfriend, which is totally unfair.'

'Look, I know Damien is a nice fellow, and I know that you are very fond of each other, but . . . '

'It's the "but" that is always the problem. Why can't you just leave it at that? You think he is a nice fellow and

*you know we are fond of each other. All right. OK. Why do you have to say anything else? Why can't you just accept that that is how it is? He **is** a nice guy and we are fond of each other. Why does it have to be such a big deal?'*

'Kelly, there is more to it than that. Damien is a good deal older than you are, and boys sometimes want things to move along faster than girls are sometimes ready for . . . do you know what I am talking about?'

'That's the most sexist remark I have ever heard. You are dealing in some stereotype about how boys are sex-crazed maniacs, and girls are sweet, innocent little things who don't know what day it is. Where have you been all your life? Was that how it was with you and Dad? Did he leave Mum and go off in hot pursuit of you, while you were just standing around blinking innocently, or what?'

'Kelly! Don't talk about your father and me like that. You know that isn't fair. You know that your Mum and Dad were very unhappy together . . . '

'Why isn't it fair? You can talk about me and Damien as much as you like, but I can't talk about you and Dad. Who made up that rule?'

Margaret sighs. Kelly glances across at her and sees that her hands are tightly clenched.

'I'm sorry, Margaret. I didn't mean to snap at you like that. But this is very hard for me. I don't even want to talk about Damien. Why do I have to say anything about him? Isn't it obvious how I feel about him?'

'I know how you feel about him, Kelly. It's just that I don't want your relationship with him to move too fast. I don't want things to get out of hand, so you end up regretting the fact that you got too involved, too quickly.'

'You see ... it's what **you** want that we are **really** talking about. You don't want me to feel this way or that ... why can't we talk about what **I** feel, and what **I** want? Or perhaps you are going to pull the old stunt of telling me that I am too young to know what I want. Is that it?'

'Look, Kelly. I know how you feel. I know that you are very fond of Damien and I know that you want to see him as often as possible. But your Dad and I are worried that he might be distracting you from your school work, and you haven't been spending much time with your girlfriends ... and there are times when we just want to do things as a family, without necessarily having Damien ... '

'Is that all you can say? That I am fond of Damien? It is **much** more serious than that. If you think that's all there is to being in love with someone, I pity you. You sound as if you are afraid of people loving each other properly. I don't think you really know how I feel, at all. I don't think you are trying to see it from my point of view.'

'But, Kelly, I don't think you are seeing it from my point of view, either. I am trying to say something which is for your own good, but I feel as if you are just not prepared to listen to me.'

'I think we had better just agree to disagree. This isn't getting us anywhere.'

Margaret takes a deep breath, and tries again.

'Agreeing to disagree won't get us anywhere, either. I really do want to see if you can understand what I am trying to say. What do you **think** I am trying to say?'

'All right. Here goes. I think you are trying to say that you don't want me to have sex with Damien, because you *don't know if I'm on the pill. You also don't like him because of the ponytail and the earring he wears sometimes, and you think that people will disapprove of you because of him. You are probably also jealous of me because you can see that I am in love with him.'*

Margaret colours slightly, and concentrates very hard on the pattern in the carpet.

'Look, there is a bit of truth in what you say. You are only sixteen, after all, and it is much too early to talk about having a sexual relationship with someone. I admit that Damien's personal appearance is a bit of a shock, sometimes. I know he is basically a good fellow, and I can see that he is genuinely very fond of you, but . . . '

'Don't say but . . . '

'Sorry, I won't qualify it. I think he is a nice fellow and I realise that he is very fond of you and that you love him. That is all true.'

'At last we are getting somewhere. At least we can agree about that.'

Margaret moves across the room to sit beside Kelly on the couch.

'Do you understand why I am worried about you?'

Kelly crosses her legs and looks down.

'I suppose you think that I might get too involved with Damien and drop out of school. Is that right?'

Until that moment, the thought that Kelly might want to drop out of school had never crossed Margaret's mind.

'Oh no. I never imagined . . . It is just what I said before. Maybe you haven't been giving enough attention to your homework . . . keeping in touch with your own friends. Things like that.'

'But Damien is my own friend. The other girls know that.'

'Kelly, I just want you to know that I am a bit worried about the way your relationship with Damien is affecting your relationship with the rest of the family.'

'So that's it. It's not really me you're worried about. I knew it. You just think that I am not being a dutiful little stepdaughter, like I used to be. And so now you are blaming Damien.'

'It's not that simple, Kelly. What I said at the beginning is true. I am worried in case this relationship might be moving too quickly, and you might end up being sorry.'

'It's my life. Let me live it. Sometimes I think you and I live on different planets.'

Was that communication? What meanings did they share with each other? Did they reach common ground? Did either of them 'win' the argument? Did Kelly convince Margaret of anything (except, perhaps, that she was right to be worried about Kelly's deepening involvement with Damien)? Did Margaret convince Kelly of anything (except, perhaps, that she would be better off avoiding this topic in future)?

In many ways, that was a classic argument: each person came away from the encounter more than ever convinced of the rightness of her original—and continuing—position. Neither of them was expecting to give way, and neither of them did.

If any change occurred at all, it might have been a shift towards an even stronger commitment to their existing positions. Kelly would be even more inclined to defend her relationship with Damien; Margaret would be more than ever concerned about it; both of them would be feeling a little more defensive than they were before that encounter took place.

But some communication took place, nevertheless. Kelly certainly succeeded in making Margaret aware of the depth of her feelings about Damien and, in spite of her hostility and resentment, Kelly did experience a fleeting pang of sympathy for Margaret when she realised that she, too, was finding it hard to discuss the subject. In a curious way, Kelly and Margaret were momentarily closer to each other through the sharing of that discomfort.

In terms of Margaret's intentions, though, the encounter could hardly be judged a success. She failed to get Kelly to see things her way; she failed to express her feelings as she had wanted to (and she had become conscious of hearing herself slipping into the carping tone of voice which she had so disliked in her own mother). The fundamental problem, of course, was the cage: open communication between Kelly and Margaret was unlikely to occur when each of them was so absorbed by the need to focus on their own concerns. Each heard what the other was saying, but real listening (as we will define it in Chapter 5) was never a serious possibility.

It could have been handled differently, of course. In Chapter 5, we begin to see a change in Margaret which will open up the possibility of better communication between her and Kelly. But, for now, their conflict is simply doing what conflict generally does: reinforcing an entrenched position.

That outcome is so typical that it points to the Third Law of Human Communication:

When people's attitudes are attacked head-on, they are likely to defend those attitudes and, in the process, to reinforce them.

It is probably fair to suggest that 'reinforcement' is the single most important word in the whole vocabulary of communication theory. Because of the psychological significance of the cage to our mental health and our sense of well-being, the need for its reinforcement is one of the most basic of human needs. So we have to live with the reality that most messages will have a reinforcing effect— whether that effect is intended or not.

When our cages are attacked, we have three favourite defences: the *Yes, but* defence, in which we seem to acknowledge our opponent's argument but, instead of replying to it, we advance some other argument of our own; the *What would they know?* defence, in which we attack the messenger in the hope of destroying the message by association; and the *It couldn't happen to me* defence, which we employ when someone is trying to threaten us with dire consequences if we don't change our ways. (These three defences are discussed in detail in Chapter 6: 'Changing People's Minds'.)

So what are we going to do about the reinforcement effect, in practice? For a start, we may as well avoid having arguments with people whose opinions we seriously want to alter. There is nothing wrong with a good argument, of course, as long as we don't expect it to change anything. Arguments can be a very healthy form of self-expression (as described in Chapter 8), but they don't usually have much to do with communication, and they rarely result in people modifying their cages.

The reinforcement effect can be creatively harnessed, however. Take the case of a scout leader who was trying to motivate some of his colleagues at a training course. He wanted to encourage them to take their leadership responsibilities more seriously and to appreciate the impact of their personal example on the scouts in their charge. Instead of the normal 'motivation talk' which might have involved cajoling, inspiring or in some other way attempting to push his audience to think about their responsibilities, he adopted the unusual approach of suggesting to them that, when you think about it, the example of a scout leader really counts for nothing: at a camp, for example, the leader might as well sleep in and operate in a generally scruffy and inefficient fashion, because this will force the boys to look after themselves more diligently and independently. The lack of leadership, he suggested, will create opportunities for the scouts to take more initiative.

His talk was greeted with howls of protest. His audience strongly resented the suggestions he was making and argued persuasively for the opposite point of view. As the debate raged, they managed to convince themselves that their own leadership role was crucial and that, in particular, their example was one of the strongest influences on the attitudes and behaviour of the boys in their care.

That was a high-risk strategy (and he was a very unpopular speaker), but it was a good example of using the power of argument, not to change people's minds, but to deepen their existing convictions.

When we really need to communicate, we are most likely to succeed by expressing what we want to say in terms of the existing interests and attitudes of our audience. Knowing that the cage is powerful, we have to operate within the framework defined for us by the cage. Matching the message to the mind and mood of the audience is the best way of tapping into the reinforcement effect.

In 1972, the Australian Labor Party, under Gough Whitlam, won an election which brought to an end 23 years of government by the Liberal–Country Party coalition. One of the most influential factors in Labor's campaign was a slogan which said, 'It's time'.

That slogan was widely thought to have 'converted' a significant number of voters from the Coalition to Labor. In fact, its effectiveness was not based on the process of conversion at all: it was a classic case of the reinforcement effect. 'It's time' captured the existing feeling of most Australian voters at that time—a feeling that after 23 years the Coalition had lost its sense of direction and needed to be put out of its misery. 'It's time' was so successful precisely because it put into words what people were already thinking.

Parents sometimes use the reinforcement effect when they are trying to encourage their children to behave in a certain way. Instead of simply criticising the undesirable behaviour, they focus on some *other* aspect of the child's behaviour, praise that, and they try to show how it would be compatible with what the child is doing.

'A girl like you, who has worked so hard to earn all that pocket money, wouldn't want to spend any of it on sweets when you have almost got enough to buy the CD you want.' A bit heavy-handed, perhaps, but that's likely to be an effective strategy because it reinforces something which the child already feels: yes, she has worked hard to earn that pocket money; yes, she does want that CD; yes, it would be a bit silly to blow the budget when the goal is so close to being achieved.

Our cages are not neat and rational structures. They

contain widely disparate elements—including attitudes which, when considered objectively, are quite incompatible with each other and even contradictory. Effective communicators soon learn that it is better to reinforce a positive attitude than to attack a negative one. When a positive attitude is constantly reinforced, its significance becomes greater to the person who holds it and, over time, an attitude reinforced in that way may exert its own influence on other incompatible or negative attitudes. In other words, the reinforcement effect may be harnessed to change negative attitudes—not by attacking them, but by overshadowing them with a strongly reinforced positive attitude. People are more likely to make their own private adjustments to their cages in response to positive reinforcement than in response to overt attacks on attitudes which need 'correction'.

The world of advertising shows us how some attitudes can be changed (or made redundant) under the influence of positive reinforcement of other attitudes. How on earth did detergent manufacturers ever persuade large numbers of women to switch from hot-water washing to cold-water washing in the face of a strongly entrenched belief that hot water (and preferably boiling water) was essential to producing a clean wash? They did it by reinforcing some *other* attitudes which were compatible with cold-water washing: hot water sets stains; hot water shrinks; hot water damages delicate fabrics; hot water is expensive. By offering a cold-water detergent product as a solution to existing problems, they made it easy for consumers to experiment with the new cold-water products. Gradually, consumers' experience taught them that these detergents produced an efficient result, and the hot-water prejudice finally yielded to that experience. Had the manufacturers simply attacked the attitudes which favoured hot-water washing, their message would have been ignored or resisted.

Advertisers have always known that they will evoke their strongest response from consumers when they hold up a mirror to consumers' own preferences, values and dispositions. The classic 'reinforcement' advertising campaign has been the Australian campaign for Meadow Lea margarine, based on the slogan, 'You ought to be congratulated'. This slogan deliberately set out to reinforce positive feelings towards the Meadow Lea brand among people who were already using it (and, indeed, most effective advertising campaigns are clearly designed to preach to the converted).

Sometimes the most intelligent way to deal with the problem of reinforcement is to make sure that our message *won't* reinforce an existing attitude which might get in the way of communication. We may be able to do this by the careful choice of 'neutral' language which gives us safe passage through the minefield of existing attitudes.

Some years ago there was a sign on multilane highways in Australia which said, 'Slow vehicles use left lane'. For drivers with an aggressive and competitive mind-set (who regard the business of getting from point A to point B as incidental to their power struggles with other drivers along the way), the effect of that message was to encourage them to crowd into the right-hand lane, determined to avoid being identified as a 'slow vehicle'—a term which seemed to carry implications of incompetence or impotence.

Ultimately someone in authority understood the need to express the message in a way which would not reinforce that attitude. They didn't necessarily approve of the attitudes and values of the competitive driver, but they knew that if communication was to occur, they would have to take that set of attitudes into account. So a new sign was erected: 'Keep left unless overtaking'. The effect of the change of message on driver behaviour was dramatic, because the new sign did not imply anything negative about drivers in the left-hand lane and it did not stir the passions of drivers with a competitive mind-set.

When people appear not to be listening to us, the most likely explanation is that, although they are hearing what we say, they are interpreting it in their own way. To us, it looks as if they have not listened: to them, it's just another case of adapting the message to suit the cage.

In his hugely successful book, *The Lucky Country*, Donald Horne was intending to alert Australians to the fact that they had been 'lucky to get away with it' for so many years. He was suggesting that Australia had survived for too long on the basis of a series of lucky breaks and he was warning Australians that their luck would ultimately run out. But, the reinforcement effect being what it is, the very Australians who, as Horne suggested, had learned to rely on luck, interpreted the title of his book as reinforcing their faith in the fact that Australia was, indeed, lucky and that this was a matter for self-congratulation rather than concern. The phrase 'the lucky country', was used to support the view that Australia was blessed with good fortune and would continue to 'get away with it'. It is a phrase which, no doubt, came to haunt Donald Horne because it acquired a place in Australians' language and thought which was diametrically opposed to his own intentions in first using it.

Does the reinforcement effect mean that many of our attempts to communicate are simply futile? Yes.

Does the reinforcement effect mean that, even when we are trying to get people to change their mind about something, they are most likely to use our message to confirm what they already believe? Yes.

Does the reinforcement effect mean that, if listeners can't use a message to reinforce some part of their existing cage, the message may be ignored or rejected? Yes.

None of this should discourage us unduly, however: it should simply remind us that we are at the mercy of the listener's cage. The cage defines the framework within which we can communicate with another person. If we don't use the listener's cage as the reference point for our message, we are unlikely to be listened to.

Most fundamentally, though, our understanding of the cage reminds us that, if we want to engage the attention of the listener, we must start from where the listener is now. And that leads us to the second of the three Rs.

2 RELEVANCE

We have just seen that a likely explanation for people not appearing to have listened to us is that they may have distorted our message in some way so that it will provide welcome reinforcement of the cage. But there's an even more likely explanation: unless our message has obvious *relevance* to the needs, the interests or the situation of our audience, it will drift beyond the edge of their attention span.

In Chapter 1, we saw how Bill completely failed to grasp a clear and simple message from Margaret about a trip to Beauchamp Park, because the relevance of that message was not immediately obvious to him. Making your message relevant to your audience is the key to gaining their attention.

A mother cannot ignore the cry of her baby: it contains no words at all, but its sound is irresistibly relevant to her because it expresses the baby's need of her. The baby's cry is a message not only *for* its mother but *about* its mother.

Whether our message is ultimately going to be used to reinforce the existing attitudes of our audience or not, we won't even get to first base in communication unless the relevance of our message has triggered the attention and interest of the listener.

Bill has a big presentation to make to a group of senior people in his office. The section head, Christina, will be there—a woman notorious for her impatience and arrogance—and Bill has to outline his plans to improve the level of customer service in the operations of the section.

This is all new to Bill. When he joined the department, no one ever talked about customer service. In fact, no one ever talked about customers. Public servants didn't think like that. But what with 'user pays', corporatisation and the new broom at the top, customer service is all the go and Bill is learning the new language.

Margaret has coached him in his presentation, and she has had one of the artists in the advertising agency where she works prepare some graphics to illustrate the key points. Bill loathes overhead projectors, but Margaret has insisted that he must show his grasp of all the standard visual aids. Bill keeps assuring her that nothing much hinges on the presentation. His job isn't on the line. But

Margaret says things like 'Make every post a winner' and is encouraging him to take it all very seriously. She is certainly succeeding in making him nervous about his performance.

Bill and his colleagues file into the conference room where the section head and her three deputies are already installed. It is all very formal. Bill tries to break the ice with a witticism but the chilly silence tells him he is wasting his time. He plugs in his overhead projector, sets up his charts, and plunges in.

After ten minutes, Christina interrupts. 'When are you going to say something relevant to the matter in hand?'

'But this is all relevant,' says Bill, flabbergasted.

'I haven't heard a single thing about customer service yet.'

'But I'm setting the scene ... giving the background. I thought it might be helpful to run through a few of the statistics about customer contacts, just to show the dimensions of the problem.'

'We don't talk about problems, Bill. We talk about opportunities. I don't want all this statistical crap. I want to know what your plans are for making this section more responsive to customer needs. Sensitivity. That's the name of the game.'

Bill flounders a bit, sets aside most of what he was intending to say, and moves to some specific recommendations about new ways of making the section more accessible to the public.

After another few minutes, another interruption from the same quarter. 'Don't go into so much detail. Just give me the bare bones. What, precisely, are you recommending? Come to the point, Bill.'

Irritated, Bill moves rapidly to his last chart, drawn by

the agency, on which he has shown how the work-flow could be reorganised to cut response times dramatically. Almost dismissively, he takes Christina through it.

She leans forward enthusiastically. '**That's** what I've been waiting to see. You see that, you others?' Her deputies, who have been looking rather embarrassed on Bill's behalf, now begin to nod and smile.

'Forget all that other rubbish you were going on with. The director is going to love this. Response times are his baby. He's been making life hell for all of us, going on and on about it. If I can show him a chart like that, he'll be overjoyed. Are you sure your figures are right?'

'Absolutely.' Bill is smiling tentatively. 'But if it's response times you're interested in, I can prepare a few other things, as well. We could do a lot more with the phone-answering procedures, for a start. And the computer people say these estimates for mail responses are very conservative. I could probably come up with a much better picture than this. How much time do I have?'

'I'm seeing the director again in the morning. Can you finish it today?'

'No problem.'

'Get on with it, then. Oh, and well done.'

Back in his office, Bill is sweating profusely. He picks up the phone and rings Margaret.

'How did it go? Did you wow her? Was she impressed by the stats?'

'Well, no, actually. But that didn't seem to matter. Suddenly I'm the golden boy. I just happened to stumble on the only thing she was interested in. But it was touch and go there for a while.'

Many of our attempts at communication fail simply

because we haven't explored the cage of our listeners sufficiently to know what they are thinking about, what their frame of reference is, what will turn out to be relevant to their situation.

When Margaret talks to Kelly about her relationship with Damien, for instance, Kelly correctly complains that this is really a message about Margaret and *her* concerns, not a message about Kelly herself. It is always tempting to say what we want to say from our point of view, but everything we know about the cage tells us that unless we can present our message to our audience so it is clearly about *them*, we are unlikely to evoke more than polite interest, if that.

Most people's favourite subject is themselves. As long as they hear messages about themselves, they will be attentive. As long as the message has some implications for them, they will listen. As long as the message relates to their own circumstances, they will be involved.

People are gripped by bad news—stories of aircraft crashes and other disasters, for example—because they can see the potential relevance of those stories to their own situation. Even news of murder and mayhem, especially when there is an element of randomness about the choice of victim, has an irresistible fascination for us because we can see, all too easily, how we might have become involved ourselves.

Such stories also involve us because they tell us something about the extremes of human capacity and human experience: this is what *could* happen to me; this is what human beings like me *can* do.

The key word here is 'identification'. When we find ourselves identifying with a person in a news item, or a character in a film, a play or a novel, we are drawn into the story in a way which doesn't happen if we remain mere spectators to it. Identification is a powerful response precisely because it arises from our ability to connect what we are seeing or hearing with our own situation.

What Bill hit upon, almost too late, was the relevance of 'response times' to his section head—not because Christina herself was necessarily keen on improving the section's performance in dealing with its customers, but because she knew that her own position with the director would be enhanced if she could present a strong proposal on that subject.

Relevance is the 'hot button' in communication: it is the switch which activates involvement and interpretation; it is what transforms a message 'out there' into a message 'in here'.

In other words, relevance is that quality in a message which ensures that it will find a ready point of entry to the cage. That idea is captured in the Fourth Law of Human Communication:

> **People pay most attention to messages which are relevant to their own circumstances and point of view.**

One practical way of applying the Fourth Law is to ask yourself, 'What can the listener *do* about this?' Try to imagine the action which the audience might take if your communication with them is successful. This is not a universally suitable test, of course, because we often communicate to strengthen the bonds of friendship, to keep someone informed about things they need to know, or simply to share an idea with someone. In such cases, no immediate action may be called for.

But, in many situations—management, teaching, conversations between professional people and their clients, family discussions where the goal is to get something done—'action' is the ultimate test of relevance. Messages which cannot be acted upon are messages which can soon fade from our memory. If I don't have to *do* anything about what you are telling me, then I may feel that it doesn't warrant my close attention, and I may not even bother interpreting what you are saying.

One of our greatest frustrations in human relationships arises from the feeling that we are not being listened to. If we were more ruthless in applying the simple test of *relevance* before we opened our mouths, I suspect we could save millions of words, tons of energy, and a mountain of heartache. And we would never, never seem boring.

'Let me tell you about this wonderful movie I saw on TV ... ' may attract someone's attention if they happen to be interested in movies. But 'There was a scene in this movie I saw that really made me think of you' will have their attention, every time.

'Boys and girls, I want to tell you what our government is doing for education in this great state' will have the pupils' eyes glazing over in no time. 'Boys and girls, I want to explain to you why some of the things you do at school are going to change, and how you will benefit from the changes' raises the possibility, at least, that this might actually have something to do with *them*.

'The computer is down and there's nothing we can do about processing your transaction' is a statement about the bank and its problems; not a statement about the customer and hers. 'I realise you feel very irritated and impatient with us and I understand why. But let's see what can be done ... how quickly do you actually need the transaction to be processed?' may get us somewhere.

Talk to me about me and my concerns and you'll have my attention. Talk to me about you and your concerns and you'll have to work much harder to arouse my enthusiasm. So, if your message is about me and my interests or my dreams or my responsibilities or my problems, make sure you say so. If, on the other hand, your message has nothing much to do with me, ask yourself whether I am the right person to be talking to, after all.

3 RELATIONSHIP

The third of the three Rs of communication provides the answer to the question which has been lurking beneath our discussion of the first two. We know that messages will tend to be interpreted in ways which will reinforce the cage of the listener; we know that messages will probably be ignored unless they are expressed in a way which is relevant to the listener's attitudes, values or circumstances. But how do we *know* what will be relevant? How can we anticipate how the process of reinforcement might affect the way our message is being received? In short, how do we get inside the cage of the other person? Don't we have to communicate with them in order to do that?

One of the great conundrums of communication is that, in order to communicate effectively with you, I must first get to know you and understand the shape and structure of your cage, but I can't do that without communicating with you. That sounds like a paradox: I can't communicate with you until I've communicated with you.

It is true that I can't be confident of evoking responses from you until I know whether those responses are there, waiting to be evoked, and I can't discover that without evoking some other responses from you. (This is a bit like the classic educational paradox: you can't teach someone something unless they already know it—which is a cheeky and exaggerated way of saying that you can't draw an educational response from someone until they have acquired enough prior learning to be able to grasp the point of what you are saying. Aristotle observed that you can't discuss morality with someone who is devoid of any moral sense: the capacity for a response must first be there.)

In communication, the resolution of this apparent paradox is actually quite simple. In the early stages of a communication relationship, we have to be prepared to put more emphasis on building the relationship than on achieving particular communication goals. We have to try out messages to see if they happen to strike a responsive chord. We start to take little risks, looking for reactions. We read any early responses very carefully indeed, because they are giving us our first clues about the state of the other person's cage. In practice, communication begins with a discovery tour of each other's cages: the deeper sharing comes later.

Even the most routine and mundane conversational topics—such as the weather—provide those early opportunities to listen for the clues that will help us to learn how to communicate with another person. 'Getting to know you' is the essential prerequisite to confident and effective communication between us, and that's not a process which is helped by being rushed.

It's a bit like panning for gold: we have to work our

way through the whole routine before those tiny, precious specks begin to appear. In the case of communication, the 'specks of gold' are the promising early signs of the other person's responsiveness to us.

Communication is a journey, not a single, simple event. Communication is the process of gradually achieving a sense of being on common ground with another person. Communication is the slow—often difficult, sometimes painful—process of sharing ideas, thoughts, information with another person: sometimes stimulating them to contribute and sometimes asking them only to respond.

In order to get some insight into another person's cage, of course, we must be ready to offer some insight into our own. Before other people will be prepared to level with us (let alone make themselves feel vulnerable by revealing too much about themselves) we must show ourselves willing to level with them.

Communication—apart from the simplest information exchange—is something which evolves out of a continuing relationship with another person. Communication rarely happens as a one-off incident, or a brief encounter. Generally speaking, communication develops as a relationship develops. The better we know someone, the easier it is to communicate. (Think about the difference between writing a letter to a friend and writing a letter to a stranger.)

Communication is the outcome of the investment of time, effort and patience in the development of mutual understanding (including a mutually comprehensible language) between us and others.

In Chapter 7, we explore the effect on communication of the various media we use to send and receive messages:

in that chapter, we will return to the concept of communication as a relationship because we constantly need to remind ourselves that, in the end, the only really effective medium for human communication is the medium of personal relationships. All other media, from the telephone to television or a computer network, are mere approximations and substitutes for what happens when, face to face and over time, we begin to get to know each other well enough to be able to communicate.

Of course it is true, in a superficial sense, that communication can occur without a relationship existing. Yes, we can experience communication via a newspaper (just as we can obtain erotic stimulation from reading a book); yes, we can have a fleeting moment of successful communication with a total stranger (just as we can achieve sexual gratification from a one-night stand); yes, we can feel as if we are on the same wavelength as someone else with no prior relationship having been established (just as we can experience love at first sight).

But those cases do not alter the fundamental fact that, for most of us in most circumstances—at home, at school, at work, with friends—the quality of our communication with each other will be directly related to the amount of time and effort we are prepared to invest in our relationships with each other. Building a relationship is the necessary precursor to being able to communicate effectively, reliably and openly.

The fact that communication sometimes comes easily is a bonus. The contrary fact that most of us experience frequent communication failure and frustration should convince us that this is not an easy process. In fact, communication is one of the hardest things we do because, as the origin of the word itself suggests, it is all about being 'in community' with other people, and who ever said that was an easy state to achieve?

Bill is seething. He has been having a running argument, via an endless series of memos, with the manager of a branch office of his department. The new procedures for customer service are not being followed and the guidelines for customer inquiry response rates—set up after Bill's presentation to the head of his section—are being ignored.

The monthly return comes in from Croydon Bridge just as it always has, with no sign of recognition that there is supposed to have been a revolution. Other branch managers have all been making an obvious effort. Not this bloke.

Bill finds himself in a tricky position because, although he is responsible for the new procedures, he doesn't actually have any power in the line of management to the branch offices. As his boss keeps saying, it's all a matter of gentle persuasion. Suddenly he knows what it must feel like to be a consultant.

Part of the problem is that the person responsible for branch operations is on long-service leave—what a time to choose to go—and the stand-in is basically keeping the seat warm. No waves. No drama. That's his line. So it is being left up to Bill to do the best he can.

He's tried the phone, of course. No joy there. This bloke doesn't tend to return calls and, on the rare occasions when Bill can catch him, he sounds cordial enough but they never seem to make any progress. He says he has seen all the stuff Bill has sent him and, yes, he realises that changes have to be made, but doesn't Bill realise that these things take time, we are short of staff, there are a lot of other things going on as well, this is a bad time of year and, anyway, we haven't had any complaints about customer service from Branch Ops.

Somehow, Bill never seems to manage to sound quite as authoritative on the phone as he does on paper ... not that his memos are bearing any fruit either. It's a frustrating business, no doubt about it. What can you do, beyond a certain point?

Months pass. Bill getting nowhere with that particular branch manager. No animosity, but no real cooperation either.

The department's Christmas party looms. Bill is a reluctant starter. What's the point of standing around trying to think of something to say to people you never see from one year's end to the next, or else trying to act festive and jolly with people you see every day? No thanks. No way.

His colleagues persuade him. He is the golden boy of customer service, don't forget. The section head will be there, billing and cooing.

'That's what I mean,' says Bill. 'What a prospect. I prefer Christina when she's in battle dress. Anyway, I'll give it half an hour. After that, anyone is welcome to join me at the Gloucester for some more civilised rites.'

The conference room has been decorated for the occasion and people are spilling out into the passage and the reception area. Bill's heart is sinking, but he struggles to keep the right look on his face.

A breezy bloke he's never seen before puts a drink in his hand, smiles vaguely, and pushes off into the melee. Bill looks around for a familiar face, but his colleagues are nowhere to be seen. Sneaky bastards. Probably off to the Gloucester already. There's the section head in full party mode. Frightening.

Bill attaches himself to the nearest group and finds himself in the middle of a debate about the merits of soccer and **real** football. He treads warily, not sure which code they mean by 'real'. Why can't they talk about cricket, anyhow? It is the middle of summer, after all. Bill drifts away, glancing at his watch.

The breezy bloke is chatting to a couple of the receptionists. Hearts of gold. Been here for years. The best advertisement for customer service you could find. Naturals at it. Bill joins them. Blow me down, they're talking cricket. The appeal of the one-day game.

'I'm a bit of a purist myself,' says Bill, 'I'm still a sucker for the full-blown Test match. It's a thing you can't explain. You certainly can't explain it to the Americans. I've tried. Five days' play, and still no result. It's the art of it, isn't it? The science. Cat and mouse. I love it. What about you?' Bill raises his eyebrows at the other man.

'I'm with you. Can't beat the real thing. I was an absolute devotee of county cricket when I was in England for a while. Before I joined the department. I'm David, by the way.' He holds out his hand and they shake. 'But I can see why people go for the one-day game. You get a result. It is exciting. It's just that they should call it something else. Not cricket.'

'That's exactly what I say myself. A different game, a different name. Got any ideas?'

'I think it deserves the name it's already got. Pyjama cricket. Suits it.'

'Yeah. The best names usually come from the punters themselves. That's the thing about it. Like jumbo jets.

Boeing hate it, I gather. They wanted us to call them 747s. But you can't stop a good name sticking. Pyjama cricket, yeah. You're right. My name's Bill. Did I say that? Can I get you all another drink?'

'Actually, I wasn't going to hang around, myself. I'm not a great one for this kind of thing as a rule. I thought I might try to find a pub. Are you a local?'

Bill drains his glass. 'What are you girls doing?'

'We're waiting for the speeches. Can't miss them, Bill. Christina is going to give you a public pat on the head this year. You'll have to stick around.'

The visitor looks at Bill. Bill looks back. 'Where did you say you were from, David?'

'I didn't say. I run the branch at Croydon Bridge. A boy from the bush. What about you? What's this pat on the head you are going to get?'

Bill is stuck for words. The breezy bloke from the bush is, of course, the problem branch manager. He hadn't twigged. David is a fairly common name. Didn't recognise the voice. And David obviously hadn't recognised his either. Never spoken long enough for it to register.

'Look,' says Bill, biting the bullet, 'we've actually had a bit to do with each other, only the penny hasn't dropped until now. I'm the customer service person. All those memos . . . '

'Ah. Of course. Bill. How about that? I've never really talked to you properly about that, have I?'

The receptionists move away and Bill and David, heads together, begin to talk about the difficulties they have both been experiencing over the past few months—Bill's struggle to get support for his new procedures, and David being frustrated by the lack of interest from Branch Ops in some serious property maintenance problems which *have been distracting him and everyone else in his branch.*

As the party swirls around them, they discover a great deal of common ground, not only in their frustrations with the department but also in their family circumstances and personal histories. In particular, they are both having difficulty with teenage daughters and they both have rather tricky relationships with eccentric fathers-in-law. Bill confesses to having been brought up in the country— not far from Croydon Bridge—and hating it.

He offers to take David through some of the customer service material in his office and also to show him what the returns from other branches look like. They repair to Bill's office and, as the conversation proceeds, David begins to think there could be real advantages for him in adopting some of the ideas Bill is outlining. Good stuff. Neither man has any sense of connection between this encounter and their previous exchanges by memo and phone.

Bill invites David to join him and some of his colleagues at the Gloucester.

'But aren't you supposed to be staying for a paean of praise, or something?' David reminds him.

They endure the speeches together. Bill is indeed publicly acknowledged for his work on customer response procedures. A certain amoung of back-slapping takes place. Bill and David head for the lift as soon as they can.

At the Gloucester, the faces of Bill's colleagues register astonishment as he introduces 'David, from Croydon Bridge'.

The quality of our performance as communicators depends very heavily on the quality of our relationships with other people, and to complete the circle, the quality of those relationships depends very heavily on our performance as communicators. This is not a deliberate attempt to confuse; it is not a joke; it is simply a recognition that we can't easily separate the idea of communication from the idea of a relationship. They feed each other.

From now on, Bill's communication with the Croydon Bridge branch will improve because he has begun to develop a personal relationship with David. The more they communicate, the better that relationship will become, and the easier it will be to communicate.

Remember that we don't come to a communication encounter with an open mind: we are not blank slates waiting to have messages written upon us. We come to the encounter with all the power of the cage working for us, looking for messages which will give us the reinforcement we so much enjoy getting. This means that, for us to be open to the idea of communication with another person, we must feel as though our cages are safe; as though we can trust the other person to respect the integrity of our point of view; as though we could be as secure in the encounter as we are in the cage.

Indeed, 'security' is almost as important a word as 'reinforcement'. If a person feels secure in a relationship with someone else, even messages which might otherwise be unwelcome may be 'taken on board', because the security of the relationship lends its own protection to the cage.

Insecurity is the great enemy of communication. When men and women feel insecure in their relationships with each other (as many currently do, because of the impact of the gender role revolution) the quality of their communication with each other will inevitably suffer. In my book about the impact of social change, *Reinventing Australia*, I wrote:

> When women are themselves feeling insecure about their own pioneering attempts to redefine their roles, they are less able to communicate calmly and confidently about their goals and their needs. And when men are feeling insecure as a result of not fully comprehending what is going on (and, it must be added, as a direct result of being so relentlessly attacked by women who find male attitudes and behaviour unsatisfactory), they are much less likely to be receptive to open communication.

Trust and security do not come easily. They are earned and learned. Anyone who is serious about being an effective communicator, therefore, must think about the need to build up the sense of security in any relationships which are important. One useful strategy for achieving this is to make your *general* communication aim to keep the relationship alive; to regard every encounter as being a stepping stone to the next; to ensure that whatever specific bits of communication might or might not be achieved in this particular conversation, at least we will have made it easier to communicate again when next we meet.

In other words, we can try to say things to each other in such a way that we not only achieve our immediate goal (of sharing meaning about a specific subject) but also the more general goal of making the channel of communication between us more open, more comfortable and more secure.

Try not to think of a communication encounter as an

end in itself. Try to see it as a step in a journey, or a stage in a process. Then try to see how your handling of *this* encounter might make the next encounter easier for both of you. Argument, intimidation, insensitivity or indifference are likely to erode the other person's confidence and reduce the sense of security in the relationship, making it even harder to communicate next time. Keep the door open. Keep the flame burning. Keep in touch.

The importance of this deeper purpose is captured in the Fifth Law of Human Communication:

> *People who feel insecure in a relationship are unlikely to be good listeners*.

Think again about the conversation between Margaret and Kelly near the beginning of this chapter, on the subject of Damien. That situation was difficult for both of them partly because neither of them felt really secure with the other. This was a subject which Kelly didn't even want to discuss with Margaret. For her part, Margaret's compelling need to say what she wanted to say was not based on any prior experience which might have suggested that she was likely to be successful in communicating with Kelly about such a touchy subject.

Margaret may have felt that it was her duty as Kelly's stepmother to raise some questions about the relationship between Kelly and Damien but, more importantly, she probably needed to express some feelings which she was experiencing very strongly. (There's nothing wrong with that, of course, and we explore the legitimate need for self-expression in Chapter 8.) But saying what you want to say, regardless of the other person's frame of mind and regardless of the state of your relationship with the other person, is not the most solid basis for successful communication, and it is most unlikely to build up a sense of security in the relationship.

If Margaret's goal had been communication (rather than mere self-expression), then she may have achieved more by recognising that this conversation could be just one small step in the direction of developing greater mutual understanding between her and Kelly.

Because Kelly felt that Margaret was generally unsympathetic towards Damien, it might have been more constructive if Margaret had been able to admit to Kelly that she felt she didn't know Damien very well, and that she would like Kelly to tell her a bit more about him. Kelly would no doubt have been delighted to do so and, in a conversation which was not threatening to Kelly, it would have been possible for Kelly and Margaret to share the intimacy of discussing Damien. At that preliminary stage, there was really no need for Margaret even to react to what Kelly told her: her primary goal could have been to lay a foundation for a better relationship with Kelly; to build a bridge to future conversations, rather than trying to achieve too much at once.

Instead, Margaret was making the mistake which most of us make: the mistake of going for our ultimate goal on the first attempt. In almost every situation, big communication goals will only be achieved after a great deal of preliminary work on the relationship with the other person. This is why political and other lobbyists work as hard as they do at creating the channels of personal relationships with people, so that when they need to communicate about something in the future, the relationship channels are already working.

Unless people feel secure in their relationships with

each other, there is little chance that they will respond with openness to any but the most straightforward and agreeable messages. After all, why should I take seriously what someone says to me if I have no reason to trust that person, no history of personal contact, and no sense of the confidence which comes with having an established relationship?

Communication is good for you

Quite apart from the intellectual and emotional satisfaction of knowing that you have successfully shared your thoughts or feelings with another person, the long-term effect of being involved in communication relationships with other people is intensely therapeutic.

It works in two ways. First, the more we communicate with other people, the clearer we become about our own sense of identity. Most of us spend a lifetime inching towards an answer to the question, 'Who am I?' The answer is most likely to emerge from our relationships with other people. Being understood and accepted by others is one of the most reassuring and comforting of human experiences, and it is an experience which flows directly from communication with them.

When you seem to understand me, I feel more confident about what I have said, and a little clearer about who I am. Even if you disagree with me, your acceptance of the legitimacy of my point of view will be therapeutic for me.

The urge to communicate is probably, at the deepest level, the urge to clarify my own thoughts and feelings. They are never clearer than when I try to share them with someone else.

The second therapeutic benefit of communication is that through my relationships with other people, I get a clearer sense of my tribal identity; of where I fit in to the community; of my social character as well as my personal character.

In other words, the urge to communicate is partly a response to our herd instinct. In the same way as my communication with others helps me to see myself in the mirror of those relationships, it also helps me to make the social connections which reassure me that I am not alone; that I can be taken seriously by other people; that I belong somewhere.

Of course, the converse is true. When I fail to do the hard work required to establish and maintain communication relationships, I will be less certain of my own identity and I will lose the reassurance of feeling that I belong.

It is easy to see why we want people to listen to us, and why they want us to listen to them. What we want— and what they want—is therapy. When we share meaning with another person in a communication relationship, it is ultimately much more than meaning which is being shared: we are sharing the responsibility for each other's mental health.

Conversely, the deliberate and determined refusal to communicate can destroy another human being by withholding that therapeutic benefit. Even the petty refusals of everyday life take their toll.

A person who receives the full therapeutic benefit of communication in the context of a secure personal relationship is the person who is able to say, 'I am understood', 'I am accepted', 'I belong here' or even, 'I am loved'. Many committed communicators find that the intimacy of communication is at least as therapeutic as the intimacy of sex.

If we want to receive that therapeutic benefit, we shall have to be prepared to give it as well. In Chapter 5, we begin to explore how that might be done.

The Art of Listening

*A*t first light, Margaret is lying in bed, fully alert. She feels as if she has been awake all night, drifting briefly into exhausted dozing only to snap back into painful re-collection of last night's screaming match with Kelly. How could she have done it? After all those months and months of trying so hard to be tolerant and understand-ing—and not get in the way of Bill's own difficulties with his daughter—how could she have failed so miserably?

Calling Kelly a slut. Actually wanting to hit her. Shout-ing like that. Kelly telling lies about where she'd been. Not coming home until two in the morning. A sixteen-year-old. Not telling them she'd be late. No answer from the home of the girlfriend where she was supposed to be. What were Margaret and Bill supposed to think? And what if something had happened to Kelly? No one seemed to know where she was—least of all her family. Then just mooching in like that. Shrugging. That infuriating little ghost of a smile . . .

But 'slut' was going too far. Margaret knows that. It is like throwing up a huge wall between her and Kelly which will now have to be demolished, brick by painful brick. But how? Why are her attempts to get closer to Kelly so consistently unsuccessful? Why does trying so hard only seem to make it worse? Not that Bill is doing any better with his 'she'll be right' approach. Maybe she should be shipped off to her mother in the States . . .

What is it that funny little market research man at work is always saying? You can't get a response out of a consumer when it isn't there to get. Something like that. In amongst all his irritating flip charts and overhead projector slides, he makes a lot of sense. He says the most successful advertising campaigns don't try to **change** people: they try to reflect how people are already feeling. They won't respond to your ad unless your ad is a response to them.

He has a point. It certainly works in the advertising business. The agency and its clients invest a fortune in market research—trying to understand the feelings and attitudes of consumers before any advertisements are written. 'You work within the consumer's frame of reference or you don't get to first base.' His constant theme is that you have to concentrate on evoking a response, not shovelling information into their heads. You can't evoke a response that isn't there to be evoked, and you have to find out in advance whether it's there or not.

Recalling those presentations, Margaret begins to see it all in a very personal light. It is true that she is constantly trying to get Kelly to see things her way: Kelly is right when she complains that Margaret doesn't really listen, because she is sure she wouldn't like what she heard.

Margaret suddenly feels that she is on to something. She has always separated her work at the agency from her life at home—partly because Bill rubbishes advertising people so mercilessly, and he's so scathing about TV commercials. But now she sees that it is all connected. Here are all these multimillion-dollar clients, desperately trying to create effective advertising messages. They **have** to get it right. It's their business. So what do **they** do? They go out and listen to their consumers, so they can understand their point of view first, and then respond to it.

Why can't she do the same thing with Kelly? And with Bill, come to think of it. She is always pushing. Always trying too hard. Always trying to persuade and manipulate. And they are always complaining that she nags them.

Isn't it funny? Here she is, working in the very industry which people think of as being all about manipulation and persuasion, and yet this is where she is beginning to learn about the real art of communication. Work with your audience, not against them.

She digs Bill in the ribs and he struggles to the surface of his troubled sleep. Then he recalls the night's events, groans and rolls over.

'No, Bill, listen. This is important. I've just realised something and I'm sure it can help us with Kelly. Or me, anyway.'

Bill groans again, but turns to face Margaret. He is always enchanted by her enthusiasm. He can remember all the reasons why he loved her in the first place.

When she has finished, Margaret sinks back on to her pillow and sighs. 'It all seems so clear. Even that business with Michael and poor old Mr Jansen. I could have heard Michael out and shown him I understood how he felt. If he thought I was capable of seeing his point of view, he might have been more open to what I was saying, don't you think? That's the thing this chap at work is always saying: we have to respond first, and then they will respond to us. Don't you think that's right? Why should people listen to us if we don't listen to them?'

Bill cradles her head in the crook of his arm and gazes at the ceiling. 'The HR bloke at work is always saying the same thing. See it their way. Put yourself in their shoes. Good stuff. There's only one thing, though.'

'What? And what's HR mean?'

'Human resources.'

'Ugh. How horrible. Does that mean "people"? And you reckon marketing people treat consumers like numbers. Anyway, what's your problem?'

'Well, if advertising people go to all that trouble and expense to find out about consumers' motives and attitudes and everything, how come so much advertising is still so stupid? If you ask me, they still get it wrong most of the time.'

'Mmm. **We** don't. And anyway, just think how much worse it would be if they didn't do any research. There's no magic formula, you know. I just think I've been approaching Kelly the wrong way round. I'm really going to try from now on, but I'm not going to push. And I don't care what you think.'

'Thanks. That doesn't sound like a terribly sensitive beginning, if I may say so.'

Margaret smiles. 'Only kidding. But I'll tell you what it feels like. It feels as if we are all inside our own little worlds, too scared to step outside and not prepared to venture into each other's. I'm sure I could do a better job of seeing things from Kelly's point of view. She has had a rotten time, and I haven't made nearly enough allowance for that. I thought I had, but not really. I'm going to try to visit her in her world, and see what it feels like. Do you know what I mean? I want to try to get into her shoes, like your HR man says. I just have to get to know her better. I suppose that's all I'm saying.'

Being sensitive and responsive to the cages of other people does not mean that we have to *agree* with their attitudes, values or points of view. Understanding is not the same thing as agreement. While we may not be able to accept their views, one of the disciplines of communication is learning to accept that those *are* their views, and they are entitled to them.

They are not going to operate from our point of view. Why should they? We want to communicate; we want to be listened to; it is therefore *we* who must make the accommodation. Their cage is the framework within which we must operate if we are serious about communication.

There is no law which says we *must* communicate with anyone, or even that we must *want* to communicate. (The life of a hermit has its attractions, after all.) But if we do want to communicate because of our affection for someone, or simply because of our responsibilities, then we will have to learn the discipline of working with the cage of the other person.

WHAT MAKES A GOOD LISTENER?

'Bill, Kelly hasn't used any tampons for six weeks or more. I'm sure I'm right.'

'Don't get agitated. She's only sixteen. Her cycle prob- ably hasn't settled down yet.'

'Come on, you know as well as I do that she's as regular as clockwork. No, you probably don't know, but take my word for it: she is. Ever since she moved in with us, she's shared my tampons and I've always kept an eye on it. There's never even been a hiccup before.

I'm afraid I fear the worst, Bill. If that little creep Damien has got her . . . '

'*Hang on. Aren't you a bit ahead of yourself? She might be buying her own. She might be a bit off-colour. She might have gone on the pill. God, what am I saying? But don't rush in. There's got to be a reasonable explanation.'*

'*I'm sure there's a reasonable explanation. That's exactly what I'm afraid of.'*

Bill takes Margaret by the shoulders and holds her at arm's length. He looks into her worried face. 'Marg, remember what you were saying just a couple of days ago? About getting inside Kelly's world? About how you really hadn't made enough allowances . . . putting yourself in Kelly's shoes? All that? If Kelly's got something to tell us, we've got to make it easy for her to tell us. The only thing worse than her being pregnant would be her not being able to tell us that she was pregnant. But I'm not convinced anyway. Could she be buying her own?'

'*I suppose she could. But why would she, all of a sudden? And why would she hide them away from me? There aren't any in the main bathroom cupboard, and I don't think there are any in her room.'*

'*This all sounds a bit snoopy to me. Kelly would hate to think you were hunting in her room for tampons or anything else.'*

'*Bill, I'm worried. I'm her stepmother, for God's sake. I care about her. You know that. She knows that . . . well, she did, before the other night. We still haven't really cleared that up, I'm afraid. We've all been on the usual treadmill and there's been no time to talk. I've been waiting for the weekend. But now . . . well, don't you think I should say something?'*

'I most certainly do not. Imagine the effect of raising a subject like this if there's nothing in it. What are you going to say? Are you pregnant, Kelly? You haven't been raiding my tampons like you usually do? Fair go. Do us all a favour, Marg. Don't say a word about it. Keep a bit of an eye on her, of course. If what you think is true, we'll know soon enough. She can't hide it forever. Bloody hell. What next? Anyway, if it isn't—which I'm sure it isn't ... well, no harm done.'

Margaret is quelled, but unconvinced. She sees the wisdom in what Bill is saying, but she is amazed by his calm response. She finds the urge to confront Kelly almost irresistible. What if Kelly is pregnant? Wouldn't it be better to know early, in case they decide that she shouldn't keep the baby. No. What a thought. And if she isn't pregnant, then there is something wrong with her cycle, and that should be looked at. On the other hand, she might be only a few weeks overdue and that wouldn't be the end of the world. But Bill is right. This is a classic case where listening is going to be better than talking. If only that row hadn't happened the other night ... if only we were a bit closer ... if only we were already at the stage where Kelly felt that she could trust me. **Can** she trust me? Suddenly I feel as if I'm living in the middle of a soap opera.

If Margaret is not going to talk to Kelly, she is certainly going to talk to Kate. When no one else quite understands, Kate always seems to. Ever since they were at school together, they've maintained contact with each other. As teenagers, they were always there to commiserate over failed romances or other disappointments; as young women, they stiffened each other's resolve—about everything from men to careers—when the going got tough;

as second wives and stepmothers, they seem to have more in common now than ever. With Kate, Margaret always feels she can literally say what she thinks. There will be no judgment, no argument, not even any advice, usually: just solid, careful listening and the reassurance of being understood and accepted.

With the sense of pleasant anticipation she always feels when she calls Kate, Margaret picks up the phone.

If Margaret is going to stick to her first-light resolution and start to explore the shape and structure of Kelly's cage, then the first step will be to commit herself to serious, sustained listening.

But what is listening?

For a start, there's a very big difference between listening and merely hearing. Hearing is a physical process which is passive. When we hear something, that just means that our ears are working. But when we listen, we are active; alert; focused.

Most of us find it irritating when someone says to us, 'I hear what you're saying', because that sounds as if the listener is not wholehearted about listening. 'I hear what you're saying' seems to imply that 'I'll hear you out, but I'm not really entertaining what you're saying; I'm not in the market for your ideas'. Almost every time it is said, 'I hear what you're saying . . . ' is followed by the word 'but', suggesting that the listener is keeping our message at bay.

It's tempting to reply as Margaret has to Bill on more than one occasion when he has cautiously, but unwisely, said that he hears what she is saying: 'I don't want to know whether your *ears* are working; I want to know whether your *brain* is working. Don't hear me; *listen!*'

The difference between hearing and listening is crucial

in communication. When I hear, I simply receive a message which I may or may not think about. When I listen, I am involved in the transaction: I am not just hearing what you say, but I am attending, understanding and interpreting. There's an old Anglo-Saxon word, *hlosnian*, which was used to express the idea of 'waiting in suspense'. Our word 'listening' derives partly from that word because part of the listening process *is* waiting in suspense; being committed to the encounter; seeing where this may take us.

Because listening is an act of commitment, it should look as if it is. Eye contact, an alert expression and an attentive posture will send reassuring non-verbal messages to the speaker that we are listening; that we are, indeed, in that state of suspenseful anticipation which listening entails.

(At least, that's how we *should* be when we are really listening but because listening is such hard work for us, we often engage in a very convincing performance of something called 'mock listening'—nodding, smiling, making little noises of assent or encouragement—while we are actually working on the much more interesting task of deciding what we are going to say next, or even pursuing some engrossing thought of our own.)

The courage to listen

Our reluctance to listen is legendary, and there are many physical and psychological reasons why that is so. The first and most important reason why we so often fail to listen is that we don't have the courage to do it.

Courage? Why does listening require courage?

In fact, listening is one of the most psychologically courageous things we ever do in our normal personal relationships simply because listening—*real* listening—involves seriously entertaining the ideas of the other person. That entails the risk of having to change our minds in response to what we hear. If we listen properly, if we listen attentively, if we listen as if we are truly entertaining—trying out—the ideas of the other person, we may find that we will have to take what is said into account, and that may well involve some cage-work on our part.

Listening is an act of great courage, because when we listen, we make ourselves vulnerable. When we listen, we run the risk of finding that we were wrong. When we listen, we move outside the comfort and security of our own cage, in order to see for ourselves how things look from inside the cage of the other person.

In his book, *On Becoming a Person*, the American psychotherapist Carl Rogers put it like this:

If you really understand another person ... if you are willing to enter his private world and see the way life appears to him, without any attempt to make evaluative judgments, you run the risk of being changed yourself. You might see it his way, you might find yourself influenced in your attitudes ... This risk of being changed is one of the most frightening prospects most of us can face.

Why frightening? The answer lies in the cage: to change our minds about something is to demolish and rebuild part of the cage; to admit that we got it wrong; to accept that an alternative view is better than the one we had learned from our own experience, or constructed out of our own prejudices. The cage is there to protect us, but it becomes counter-productive if we let it lead to unnecessary and unreasonable defensiveness.

Carl Rogers spoke of the courage required to listen openly and non-judgmentally in the context of counselling and psychotherapy. But what is the difference between the professional listener and the person who is genuinely trying to listen to another person in the context of family life, work, education, or any other personal relationship? As we have already seen in Chapter 4, communication works as a kind of therapy for all of us. We are each other's 'therapists'; we are each other's 'clients'. Listening is fundamental to that therapeutic effect: to be truly listened to is to receive a precious gift from someone who is saying, in effect, 'I am prepared to put my own interests and concerns on hold; I am putting you first; I am going to entertain *your* ideas'.

That's listening. Anything less than that is mere hearing.

If you're not feeling the suspense, not taking the risk, then perhaps you are not committing yourself properly to the listening task. If you're not sensing the strain involved in stepping outside the cage to listen, then you are probably not listening fully, openly, non-judgmentally.

Suppose you say to me, 'Try on that coat over there on the peg'. I reply, 'Oh, that wouldn't suit me ... it wouldn't fit, for a start'. Wouldn't you feel entitled to say, 'How would you know? You haven't even tried it on.'

Listening is like that. We have to walk over to the peg,

take down the coat, and try it on. Then, and only then, will we know if it fits. Then, and only then, will we know if we agree or disagree with what is being said; whether we can accept or reject it; whether we can incorporate it into our own set of opinions or our own body of knowledge, or not.

Courage. Risk. These are key words in listening. But there's another ... Generosity.

The generosity to listen

When we listen, we are being remarkably generous: we are offering the other person the gift of understanding; the gift of acceptance (even if not agreement); the gift of taking that other person seriously.

But the generosity of listening runs even deeper than that. To listen to someone with a genuine willingness to entertain their ideas means that you *join with the other person* in the task of concentrating on (and perhaps clarifying) *their* point of view, *their* opinions, *their* attitudes. Listening is a gift of much more than time; it is also a gift of mental energy and a willingness to undertake a cooperative exploration of the other person's cage.

After all, when someone wants to talk to us (or write to us) they are giving us a glimpse of the view from their own cage. When we fully attend, we are saying, 'I am prepared to look at the view from inside your cage ... even if it pains me to do so. I can think about myself and my views any time I like: just for now, I am going to think about you and your views.'

Nothing is more reassuring than to be listened to in an attentive way. Quite apart from the fact that when you listen to me, I know that my views are being entertained, your listening also reassures me that I am being taken seriously *as a person*. To be listened to is to be valued. To be listened to is to be fully acknowledged. To be listened to is to be recognised as an individual with thoughts worth expressing.

Children intuitively sense all this when they feel hurt by the failure of adults—parents or teachers, in particular—to listen to them with non-judgmental understanding, and with patience. When the child is fobbed off, it is more than the message which is being rejected; the child also feels rejected as a person.

And so do we all. The manager who is a poor listener is saying to his or her subordinates, in effect, 'I don't regard you seriously enough to attend closely to what you are saying'.

If you want to appreciate just how generous listening really is, think of what it means *not* to listen to someone. The act of 'mock listening' is a cruel deception, because it carries the promise of attention which is not delivered. But the wall of silence erected by those who don't even pretend to listen is an act of aggressive denial and rejection. When you don't listen to someone who needs you to listen, it will feel to them as if you are being mean with your spirit.

None of this implies that we have an obligation to listen to everyone who wants our attention, on every occasion. That would be unrealistic and far too demanding of our capacity to listen. But there are many occasions when we have the time and the opportunity to listen to people who *need* to be listened to, yet we lack the generosity to attend fully to what they are saying.

Listening is hard work, but it is never wasted work.

Like any other gift we give, our listening is a reward to those who receive it. Our listening to others is our contribution to their mental health—no less than that.

The deep satisfaction of being listened to was described by the nineteenth-century poet Stephen Crane in his rather melancholy poem, *There Was a Man*:

> There was a man with tongue of wood
> Who essayed to sing,
> And in truth it was lamentable.
> But there was one who heard
> The clip-clapper of this tongue of wood
> And knew what the man
> Wished to sing,
> And with that the singer was content.

People who rarely receive the gift of being listened to tend to become naggers. Garrulous and indiscriminate talkers are often exhibiting the symptoms of their own insecurity and low self-esteem. They tend to be people who have lacked the therapeutic reassurance of being listened to with generosity: because they have not been reassured by the attention of others, they try to reassure themselves—sometimes by endless repetition of the same messages or by talking about anything to anyone. Such people then set up a vicious circle which is difficult to break. Because they are not carefully and responsively listened to, they talk too much; then, because they talk too much, people tend not to give close attention to what they say.

Difficult though it may be to put into practice, the best strategy for stemming the flow of garrulous talk is to listen carefully to it and then to provide constructive feedback upon it (see 'From Playback to Feedback').

Obviously, you would have to be well motivated to decide to break into the cycle of the nagger or the bore. But the motivation is the same as the motivation for *any* serious, therapeutic listening: we do it out of love, or care, or we do it out of duty.

That is the essence of the generosity of listening: it is something we do *for the other person*. We certainly don't do it for our own satisfaction (except that, in the longer term, people who listen tend to be listened to ... so there is a pay-off).

There are occasions when we listen for our own pleasure because the speaker is fascinating, entertaining or informative. But in the ebb and flow of most personal relationships, we have to commit ourselves, often against our natural inclinations, to listen to what other people are saying, especially if it looks as if the message will be unattractive, uninspiring or not even particularly interesting. What will motivate us, then, to bother to listen with our full attention? The answer, again, is love, care, or duty: we either do it because of our affection for or commitment to the person, or we do it because our position— in the family, in the organisation, or in the community— requires that of us.

The patience to listen

Notice how often you find people answering questions before they have been fully asked; responding to comments before they have been fully made; leaping into the conversation to make a fresh point without having first acknowledged the point being made by someone else.

If words were actions, we would never tolerate the interpersonal violence which we inflict on each other in the name of conversation (or, worse, in the name of communication). The failure to listen is a violent act, because it represents a violation of the integrity of the person who is trying to capture our attention.

One of the difficulties is that it is often easier to talk than to listen. I am naturally more interested in telling you about the view from my cage than in listening to you talking about the view from yours. So some impatience in the listener is very easy to understand.

Nevertheless, impatience is one of the great barriers to listening. If we are going to listen to other people, then we are going to have to develop reserves of patience which will allow us to hear them out, and even to discuss with them what they have said, rather than rushing in with statements of our own.

We have to acquire the patience as well as the courage and generosity to listen in a non-judgmental way: that is, accepting and understanding the other person's message *before* we make any judgments about it.

This might be one of the most difficult of all our communication challenges. Our natural inclination is to rush into making our own judgments upon everything that is said. We agree, we disagree, we object, we support ... judgments come all too easily. What doesn't come easily is our ability to entertain the ideas of the other person— to operate within the other person's frame of reference— at least for the time being.

Yet how are we going to claim that we have listened if we haven't fully absorbed the other person's point of view? What is generous about listening only long enough to form our own reaction to what has been said? Where is the risk involved in listening only as a prelude to making a reply?

When it comes to listening, patience is the cardinal virtue. I am going to concentrate on what you are saying until I am sure that I have grasped it and 'tried it out'. I am going to keep listening until I am confident that I know what it feels like to be you. I am going to keep listening until I feel confident that I have appreciated the view from your cage.

Then—and only then—am I in a position to respond.

From an early age, we learn to be impatient as listeners; we learn to make instant judgments. 'Did you like that book?' we ask a child, rather than, 'Tell me what the book was about'.

'How did you like the movie, or the play, or the lecture?' is our natural line of inquiry when we are asking people to respond to something they have seen or heard, as though the only important responses are judgments. Those habits are readily adapted to the world of inter-personal communication.

How much better our performance as communicators would be if we practised the withholding of judgments, at least until we were sure we had fully received the messages we were being sent.

'Oh, we tried that ten years ago and it didn't work,' says a manager, cutting across the message of a subordinate who is proposing a change in some work practice. But the subordinate had not finished outlining his plan: he had used a couple of key words and phrases which triggered a recollection in the manager of something which had, indeed, been tried previously. The manager was making a mistake in assuming that because the new proposal had some similarities with the old, he could respond to it as if it were the same thing.

'Trigger words' always test our patience as listeners: they are the words which evoke such a strong emotional eruption within us that we are likely to lose the thread of what is being said and retreat into the private world of our own thoughts. Everyone has his or her own set of 'trigger words' which change, from time to time, according to our preoccupations, fears, fantasies and focus. See how you feel about words like these:

paedophile	gay
computerisation	de facto
multiculturalism	mother-in-law
the 1960s	Jesus
republic	authority
head office	information superhighway
rainforests	baby boomers
log fires	Middle East
retrenchment	virus

As you read some of those words, you may have experienced an emotional 'trigger' which set off a kind of chain reaction in your mind. It is that 'chain reaction' which tries your patience as a listener: if the person who is speaking to you happens to use a trigger word (probably without even realising that it happens to be a trigger for you), you have to fight the natural urge to release in yourself the rush of responses to that word which may have nothing to do with the speaker's message. (See 'Seven Tricks of the Trade'.)

Our patience is also sorely tested by the fact that we have the mental capacity to think much more quickly than the rate at which most people will speak to us (or even the rate at which most of us will read the printed word). Researchers who have tried to quantify this gap between 'thought-speed' and the rate of speech estimate that most of us talk at about 125 words per minute, whereas, when we think in words, we may think as quickly as 500 words per minute, or more.

Obviously, that gap between the rate at which people speak to us and the rate at which we can think poses a hazard for our listening. We are perfectly able to think about three or four things at once and that creates the ever-present risk that one of those concurrent thoughts might expand to occupy our complete attention and distract us from what is being said.

(In 'Seven Tricks of the Trade', we explore some of the techniques for making positive use of our thought-speed to enhance our skill as listeners.)

So we have to be patient in our listening if for no other reason than that messages come to us more slowly than we can think about them. People who are trying to communicate with very young children are often frustrated by the slowness of the children's messages. People who are struggling to express their thoughts in a foreign language notice how native speakers of the language become impatient with their efforts. The same is true, to a lesser extent, with all our communication encounters: from moment to moment, the listener has the capacity to deal with more information than is being sent through normal speech or writing, so something has to 'fill the space'.

This is why we sometimes find that we have read a complete page of a book and yet felt that we have not really absorbed what it said: while reading, we have probably been thinking about several other things. What's for dinner? ... Will the car be ready when I go to collect it? ... I wonder how the children got on with their exams ... Parliament is such a shambles ... I hope that pain in my shoulder isn't anything serious ... One of those unbidden thoughts may well have distracted us from concentrating on the written word. Speed readers report improved rates of comprehension partly because they are harnessing their thought-speed to the task of reading so quickly that there is no 'mental space' for thoughts which might distract them.

Listening is an experiment: I'm trying out your ideas

Hearing is a perfectly natural human function but active, committed, focused, non-judgmental listening is not: it requires effort, training and skill. It calls on our reserves of self-discipline, patience and generosity.

Even when we are motivated by genuine interest and concern for the other person, listening is often hard to do. Why should we entertain the ideas of another person (especially if we are reasonably sure we are not going to agree with them)? Why should we hear someone out when we are already committed to the response we are going to make? Why should we let someone ramble on when we feel sure that what they are saying is either wrong or simply stupid?

The answer to all those questions is that listening is an important part of the contract we make with other people in any personal relationship. After all, why should anyone listen to us if we haven't first listened to them?

When the going gets tough, it is sometimes helpful to make listening into a kind of 'let's pretend'. Even if we don't want to entertain the ideas of another person, or even if we feel that our chance of being able to accept what is being said (let alone agree with it) is remote, we can still focus on the listening task by reminding ourselves that listening is an *experimental* process: we are 'going along' with the message to see where it takes us. We are trying out another person's ideas. That's what listening *is*.

In fact, serious listening often involves some element of 'let's pretend', simply because the whole idea of entertaining the point of view of another person is an experiment, and that requires an unusual mental discipline. It is not natural for us to be so accommodating, so patient and so accepting. The discipline finally develops through practice but, in the meantime, 'let's pretend that I am taking you seriously' is an effective stepping stone on the way to ensuring that I will take you seriously.

Parents who are sensitive to the needs of their children (particularly their need for self-esteem) play 'let's pretend' all the time: they take seriously propositions advanced by their children which they know to be outrageous or impractical. But they hear them out, and respond kindly because they know that the relationship will be enhanced by their doing so, and that the child's sense of worth and identity will be promoted.

If you refuse to listen to another person—that is, if you refuse to entertain their point of view—you will threaten the security of your relationship with that person. Once insecurity creeps into the relationship, the possibility of communication is seriously threatened. (Remember the Fifth Law: People who feel insecure in a relationship are unlikely to be good listeners.)

The moral dimension

In his book *The Moral Sense*, James Wilson reminds us that 'human existence requires co-operation; co-operation requires reciprocity'. That is certainly true of communication. To communicate we must cooperate with each other—we must work together—and the basis of our cooperation lies in the reciprocity of listening. If we are going to communicate with each other then, sooner or later, *we are going to have to listen to each other.* That's the contract. If I don't listen to you, what right do I have to expect you to listen to me?

Why don't people listen? One of the most simple and obvious answers is that they don't listen to us because they know we don't listen to them.

'Why don't my kids listen to me?' asks the angry and frustrated father. The answer won't be welcome, but the truth is that he probably doesn't listen to them, either. By not listening to our children, we actually teach them by our example not to listen to us. However much we might want them to do as we say, they will usually end up doing as we do.

The manager who doesn't listen to her or his subordinates is not only denying their significance as people with a right to be heard; there is another message as well: 'Around here, you get to become a manager by not listening'. (Is that a message a manager would ever want to make explicit?)

If we are going to be serious about communication, we may as well acknowledge that there is a moral dimension to it; that it does involve a kind of social contract; that 'tit for tat' is pretty much what you are going to get when it comes to listening.

The moral sense is a social sense: we learn about good and bad, right and wrong, from the experience of living in community with others. It is in the context of our personal relationships that we acquire some

understanding of the value of mutual obligation, cooperation and reciprocity. Communication is therefore
fundamental to our moral awakening, and listening is
the key to it.

All of us struggle between our desire to please ourselves
and our recognition that cooperation with others is essential for our long-term happiness and welfare. Nowhere is
this struggle more apparent than in our approach to listening. We *want* to talk; to express ourselves; to be heard
and understood. But we *have* to listen, if only because we
will not otherwise be listened to when it is our turn to
speak.

Out of the realisation that listening is a reciprocal
process comes the Sixth Law of Human Communication:

> **People are more likely to listen to us if we also listen
> to them.**

'Kelly, may I come in for a moment?'

*'Sure, help yourself. There's nowhere to sit. Sorry about
the mess.'*

'I'm not worried about the mess. But I **am** *worried.
About us, I mean. You and me, and your Dad. Life just
seems to be such a rush at the moment and we never
really have time to talk about anything much. And there
was that awful business the other night . . . '*

'Forget it.'

*'Well, I can't forget it so easily. I behaved very badly
and I'm not proud of myself. I was angry and I was
worried about you. We both were. But I shouldn't have
said what I said, and . . . well, I'm sorry. I know it must
have hurt you and I really wish I could do something to
make amends.'*

Tense, Kelly shakes her head quickly and keeps looking down.

'Do you feel like talking about how things are going? Is everything all right at school? We haven't seen Damien for a while.'

'Oh, Damien.' Kelly gives a non-committal shrug but doesn't look up. Margaret is suddenly desperate for something to say. She came to listen, but Kelly is obviously not in the mood to talk and this doesn't feel like the moment to drop the subject of tampons into the conversation. Kelly is a bundle of misery. Margaret's resolve to try and get closer to her is already wavering. Suddenly, she has an idea.

'I'm going to go shopping for some clothes on Saturday. Would you like to come? We can leave Bill and Michael to themselves for a while and take our time. You need some new things, too. What about it?'

Kelly's face betrays a flicker of interest. 'OK. Yeah.'

Margaret has been standing rather awkwardly in the middle of the room. Kelly is perched on the end of her unmade bed. The only chair is covered with a jumble of school books and dirty clothes. Now Margaret sits tentatively on the bed beside Kelly, saying nothing. One of the thoughts skating on the surface of her mind is that Kelly is really a very badly brought-up girl and that Michael would not get away with any of this surliness. She represses the thought and recalls her declaration to Bill that she is really going to try to see things from Kelly's point of view. So what is Kelly's point of view at this moment? she wonders. All the signs suggest that Kelly is desperately unhappy, disinclined to talk and wishes Margaret would go away. On the other hand, Kelly has sent those signals a thousand times before, so that's not much help.

Hold up a mirror to your audience, says the market researcher. Respond to them if you ever want them to respond to you.

Yes, but how? Margaret feels a curious combination of inadequacy and fury. What am I doing, sitting here like some social worker? This kid is just putting up with me. What am I trying to prove? Put yourself in their shoes, says Bill's HR person. HR! Margaret catches sight of a textbook peeking out from under a pile of socks and underpants on Kelly's chair. **Human Geography**. God. That's what I need—a map.

'What's human geography?'

'What? What are you talking about?'

'That book on your chair. **Human Geography**. What is it?'

'Oh, that's Mr Martin. He's great. It's all about studying the environment from the point of view of people living in it. Cities, the use of resources . . . stuff like that. But he's really nice. He listens to you, and he makes it interesting. We're doing a project on patterns of development around here. It makes you look at things in a different way.'

Margaret is thrown off-balance by this sudden declaration of interest and burst of genuine enthusiasm. She feels immediately old, and out of her depth. 'Can I see what you're doing some time?'

'Of course. It's all at school. But I'll show you next time I bring it home if you like. You can borrow the book if you want to.'

Margaret leans over and picks up the book. She holds it in her lap and doesn't look at it.

'You're not really interested, are you?' Kelly asks with a smile.

'Yes, I am. Really. Well, sort of. I really do want to know more about what you're doing at school. Like I said before, I don't want to feel so out of touch.'

'You know what Mr Martin would say. Hang in there.' Kelly smiles again.

Unsure of whether she is being mocked, advised or encouraged, Margaret puts her hand on Kelly's hand, with the gentlest of squeezes. She is amazed by how hard she finds it to do. But she leaves her hand there. Kelly doesn't pull away.

'I'll surprise you,' says Margaret. 'I'll read this book. Not all of it ... I won't promise that.'

But Kelly has retreated and she doesn't smile. The interview, it seems to Margaret, is just about over. Can she venture another question, to try and encourage Kelly to talk about how she is feeling? Probably not.

Margaret is learning one of the important lessons about early forays into cage exploration: when we are first trying to establish trust and a mutual willingness to communicate, it is generally easier to talk about 'out there' topics rather than personal feelings and attitudes. We are on safer ground in the early stages of a relationship when we talk about the weather, books, movies ... and when we stick to factual material (such as scraps of personal history or current affairs) or to practical things like making arrangements.

Only when a pattern of easy conversation about easy topics has been established can we begin to feel confident about revealing our more private thoughts or deeper feelings to each other. Communication is a gradual process, and trying to rush it may have the effect of leaving the process permanently stranded at a superficial level.

One of the functions of games and other pastimes (cards, Monopoly, Trivial Pursuit, dancing, bushwalking, sport) is that they give us things to talk about—as well as shared experiences—which facilitate the process of communication.

So, as Margaret is discovering painfully, you can't just wade in and say, 'I'm going to get to know this person better by listening to her'. A foundation has to be created; shared experiences (like the shopping expedition) have to evolve; a sense of security in the relationship has to develop. Gradually, as you talk to each other about more and more things, glimpses of each other's cages begin to emerge and communication becomes more involving, more satisfying and more complete.

But it has to start safely. Although our goal may be to get to know the other person, that goal must be approached very carefully. We must be prepared to give before we can hope to receive, and we must make sure that there is plenty to talk *about*. We rarely get inside the cage by trying to force entry.

This is why Chapter 1 laid so much emphasis on the idea that communication is about releasing, rather than injecting, meaning. Communication is a process of trying to find common ground (shared meaning), and the starting point for that exploratory journey must be discovering what the other person *already* has in mind.

Listening is how we do that.

By Thursday morning, Margaret has found herself wishing that she had never proposed a shopping expedition with Kelly. For two days, Kelly has been colder than usual and, although Bill maintains that we've all been through this on several previous occasions, Margaret can't help feeling that she is being punished for her overture. That feeling, in turn, fuels a sense of anger at having her life—and her marriage—dominated by the moods of a teenage girl. She is on the point of calling off the shopping trip, but Bill encourages her to stick to the plan.

'You said you wanted to get to know her better. You didn't say you only wanted to get to know her better if you liked what you found. From what you said about your session in her bedroom, you've actually made a bit of progress already. If all else fails, you can always fall back on Mr Martin and **Human Geography**. *Have you looked at the book, by the way?'*

'Come off it. When have I had time to look at the book? But I will.'

'I just think it might be a good idea if you ... '

'Yes, I know. I'll try to look at it before the weekend, if I can. But I'm not Superman, OK?'

On Saturday morning, Kelly is still in bed when the appointed hour of departure arrives.

'Now what?' says Margaret to a nervous Bill.

'Leave her to me.'

Bill goes into Kelly's room and, after a long time, emerges with his arm around Kelly's shoulder. Kelly sits glumly at the breakfast table and tackles a bowl of cereal. Margaret goes out to the car and waits. After a few minutes, Bill follows.

'She was already dressed and ready, but she'd gone back to bed in her clothes. Don't ask me why. She's mixed up, all right.'

'It was probably morning sickness,' says Margaret icily.

'Hey! Fair go. This is your idea of getting into her world? I'm sure ... Here she comes.'

Margaret and Kelly drive to the shops in total silence but, as they begin to walk around the mall, Kelly responds with growing animation to some of the clothes. She even shows an interest in Margaret's existing wardrobe which surprises Margaret.

They both try on a number of outfits. Margaret finds herself looking for any sign of thickening at Kelly's waist, but can't see any. The mood is becoming lighter and mutually supportive. After an hour of meandering, with nothing bought, Margaret suggests coffee.

'I have actually started reading that book you lent me. Interesting.'

Kelly's mood darkens and she stirs her coffee noisily. 'Do you mind if we don't get heavy? I thought we were here to look for clothes.'

Margaret is crushed and, for a moment, wants to lash out at Kelly. Who does she think she is? Why is everything so dependent on her? Don't my feelings count in all this? Hang on, though ... I'm the adult. I'm the one who wants to get closer. As far as I know, she couldn't care less. She doesn't want to get inside my world. I want to get inside hers. I think. Well, do I really? Right now, I feel as though I would be more true to myself if I just told her how she makes me feel. But that wouldn't help matters. That's the mistake I made the other night. I told her exactly how I was feeling, and look where it got me. But there has to be some give and take, surely. Well, perhaps I'd better just give, and see what happens. I've said it before, who'd be a stepmother?

'Sorry. I want to go back and look at that yellow suit. What about you?'

For a long time, it seems as if Kelly isn't going to answer. Then, after a theatrical sigh, she says, 'I think you can do better than that. It makes your bottom stick out. What was wrong with the navy?'

'Thanks for the compliment. I always end up with navy . . . what about you? Have you seen anything you want to buy yet?'

'I want . . . I want, well, something a bit startling. I don't want to buy the same old thing. I want to be . . . a new me.'

Later, driving home with an impressive stack of parcels on the back seat, Margaret is feeling optimistic. Kelly has smiled more than she has for months. There have been some animated—if brutally frank—exchanges about the suitability of various items of clothing. Margaret has been able to be more like herself. Even her passing remarks about Bill have not produced the usual stiffening in Kelly.

After a moment of silence, Kelly announces, 'I'm not pregnant, you know'.

Margaret pulls over to the kerb, turns off the engine, and faces Kelly. 'What did you say?'

'You heard me. I'm not pregnant. Dad said you thought I might be.'

Margaret's eyes flick away, then back onto Kelly. 'When did he say that?'

'It doesn't matter. He just said you were worried about my period not coming because I hadn't used any of your tampons lately. That's what you've been trying to find out, isn't it? Anyway, I'm not, so you can relax. I'm just a bit irregular, that's all.'

Margaret restarts the engine and pulls away from the kerb. A taxi almost swipes the side of the car and the driver curses her loudly. She stops again, confused, hurt, angry, relieved. She reaches out for Kelly's hand and they sit there, both suddenly in tears, not game to look at each other.

When they arrive home and unpack, Margaret corners Bill in their bedroom.

'Bill, you're a thorough-going bastard. Why did you mention the tampon business to Kelly? And why didn't you tell me? You've made me look a total fool and a hypocrite. Luckily for you, Kelly and I had a chance to talk about it in private. But why did you do it?'

'It wasn't a deliberate thing. Don't get so worked up. I didn't even mention the word pregnant.'

'Kelly said you did.'

'Well I didn't. The poor kid was lying there in bed looking wretched and I just asked her if she was all right. She didn't answer so I asked her if everything was all right in the period department.'

'Is that what you said? The period department? Go on.'

'Well, she looked a bit defensive, so I thought it was better to come straight out and say it. I just said we'd noticed that she hadn't been using any tampons for a while and we thought something might be amiss.'

'Something might be amiss. You said that? We noticed, and we thought something might be amiss? Great.'

'Marg, it was a spur-of-the-moment thing. This morning. I didn't have a chance to tell you. You were already out in the car. I was going to mention it when we had time to talk properly. Anyway, hasn't it all worked out for the best? We've said our piece, and she isn't pregnant.'

'What did she say?'

'Just that she must be a bit irregular at the moment. I didn't particularly want to pursue it.'

'I bet you didn't. Well, maybe it is for the best. But I must say she's cool as a cuke. She didn't say a word to me until we were nearly home.'

'That proves it, then. It's no big deal to her, so it shouldn't be for us. End of story.'

'Except that, for the first time, Kelly's cycle has become irregular. She'll have to see a doctor.' Margaret gives an enormous sigh and puts her arms around Bill. *'Haven't we all got a lot to learn? Here I am trying to be so careful. I thought you had mucked everything up. But maybe you haven't. And I think I am making some progress with Kelly. I hope I am. She's a very hard kid to read.'*

'You're a pretty hard kid to read yourself.'

'That sounds like a compliment when you say it about me. Why didn't I mean it as one when I said it about her?'

Courage, generosity, patience: Margaret is learning them all in a rush. Once we decide to commit ourselves to listening, our whole approach to personal relationships changes. If we are serious about listening, we soon discover that there's no point in nagging, coercing or trying to persuade: through listening, we gain access to others' cages and, once inside, we find it easier to understand them, easier to accept them as they are, and easier to see how they might respond to us.

Our reward for listening is that, over time, we find that when we speak, others listen—not merely because they owe it to us, but because messages created out of an understanding of another person's cage are bound to be more sensitive to that person and will therefore be hard for that person to ignore.

Now that Margaret has begun to listen, she'll be surprised by what she will learn, but even more surprised by how attentively her family will begin listening to what she says, as she gets better at designing her messages *for them*.

SEVEN TRICKS OF THE TRADE

Listening is an art. We can't afford to be too rigid about the techniques for becoming better listeners because, as in all aspects of communication, our performance grows out of our experience of personal relationships and each of those relationships has its own dynamics, its own style, its own degree of intensity and its own importance to us.

But when you reflect on the main themes in the section you've just read—courage, patience, generosity, and a willingness to experiment—it is clear that there are a number of things we can do to improve our performance as listeners. Indeed, when you look at the habits of people who are good listeners, you notice a number of 'tricks of the trade'. These are not 'tricks' in the sense of being manipulative or devious: they are simply the disciplines which good listeners impose on themselves in order to ensure that, as Margaret put it, their brains—as well as their ears—are working.

So what are some of the things that good listeners do?

1 They receive the message before they react to it

Good listeners try to postpone judgments about the speaker (or the writer) and the message until they are sure they have understood what is being said. They hold their fire. They withhold their evaluation. They know that comprehension and acceptance must come first.

This is a difficult principle to put into practice because, as we have seen, it involves running the risk of having to change our minds. We may be influenced by what we hear, and that is the risk we must take. By listening to another person, we have agreed to enter into the world of that other person; to entertain their ideas; to see what it must feel like to be them. None of that can be accomplished if we let our own judgments, evaluations and reactions overwhelm the process of receiving and understanding the message *before* we try to interpret it for ourselves.

2 They resist the distraction offered by 'trigger' words

'Trigger' words unleash the tendency in us to stick with the comfortable, the familiar and the self-indulgent: they set off a mental 'chain reaction'.

We are always ready to treat messages *as if* they fit the shape of our existing cages, because we are always hoping for some reinforcement. So it is natural for us to seize on words which seem to relate to what we already think and feel, or which activate some of our favourite memories, ideas or convictions.

When that happens, we are likely to suffer a kind of 'emotional deafness' to what is really being said to us, because we have allowed the message to be swamped by the private thoughts which it triggered.

If we allow that to happen, we are in danger of completely losing the thread of the speaker's message. Once triggered, our private ruminations can lead us back into the safe territory of our own beliefs and prejudices, and that may be a very long way from where the speaker was hoping to take us.

Listening is all about stepping outside the comfort and security of our own cages. Good listeners actively resist the tendency to scurry back to the protection of the cage, particularly in response to trigger words which might affront them (causing them to block out the rest of what is being said) or stimulate them to leap aboard their own private trains of thought.

3 They ask themselves 'What can I do about this? How can I use it?'

Remember that one of the three Rs of communication is 'relevance': when we are trying to communicate with someone, we need to ensure that our message is relevant to their needs, interests and concerns.

Good listeners apply the same principle in reverse: they keep looking for ways in which they might *make* the message relevant to their own situation.

If we keep asking, 'What can I do about this?', even messages which seem uninteresting may become interesting because we will be searching for something of relevance in what is being said. That quest itself creates interest: are there any worthwhile ideas here that I can use somewhere else? Can I benefit from this in some way? (In any case, remember what G. K. Chesterton said: 'There is no such thing as an uninteresting subject; there are only uninterested people.')

If all else fails, we can imagine that we will have to give a report of this conversation to someone else. We can focus on that task as the action which we are going to take in response to what we are hearing.

But let's not overemphasise the negative: after all, most conversations are neither boring nor irrelevant and it is a very useful discipline to keep looking for the action which the speaker might want us to take in response to what is being said: that is probably the speaker's focus, so we should make it ours as well.

4 They work hard at listening

Because listening involves physical effort, we can be easily distracted from it. For most of us, it is harder work than speaking.

For that reason, we may try to simplify the job of listening by simplifying the message we are hearing. There is a natural tendency to interpret the message in ways which will make it more palatable to us, more sensible to us, and more painless for us to absorb.

We need to remember that what is being said to us may not be simple, sensible or painless!

It is often a mistake to be too comfortable when we are listening: we need to be on the alert, and a bit of discomfort may actually help that. We listen better in a room that is too cool rather than too warm. We listen better sitting up than lying down. We listen better when we are learning forward rather than leaning back.

Because listening is hard work—both physically and psychologically—we need to ration the time we devote to it. There is simply no point in assuming that we can listen properly for indefinite periods. Ten minutes of concentrated listening seems to be about as much as most of us can handle in one go. That is why astute playwrights and movie directors ensure that we are regularly given 'time off' from the main plot by some refreshing subplot or visual distraction. It is also why accomplished public speakers generally try to give the audience the relaxation of laughter from time to time, or to contrast weighty material with lighter illustrations and examples.

If someone is 'talking you into the ground', you might as well point out that your capacity for listening is being pushed beyond its limit, and you need to take a break. (The use of feedback in a conversation is also a useful way of breaking the tension of listening: see 'From Playback to Feedback'.)

The more you can listen in small chunks rather than large slabs, the more likely it is that you will have correctly absorbed the message and been able to respond to what has actually been said, instead of your own simplified, comfortable or distorted version.

5 They harness their thought-speed

Because it is obvious that we can think much more quickly than most people speak (or even than most of us read), good listeners use up as much mental capacity as possible in the listening act, simply to minimise the possibility that they will be distracted by other thoughts crowding into their minds.

Good listeners usually make the listening task more complex: they concentrate actively on trying to summarise what has been said and, perhaps, on trying to anticipate where the speaker might be leading (although this can be dangerous because the anticipated direction might seem more interesting than the one which is actually being followed). They question the speaker's motives; they consciously   observe   all   the   messages—spoken   and unspoken—which they are receiving from the speaker's tone of voice, rate of speech, facial expression, posture, gestures, etc. (See Chapter 7: 'Other messages'.)

In fact, if we give our full attention to the *totality* of the presentation, we will find that this keeps most distractions at bay. The important thing is to fill our minds with the listening task.

One useful way of harnessing our thought-speed is to focus on the speaker's intention rather than being exclusively concerned with the way the message is being expressed. Messages are always a translation of ideas which exist in the mind of the speaker: an important part of the listener's responsibility is to 'decode' the message and to identify the meanings—the ideas and the feelings—which lie behind it.

6 They try to empathise with the speaker

Good listeners have always sensed the need to work together with the speaker in the task of communicating. They realise that a big part of the job of understanding what the speaker is driving at involves trying to feel what the speaker feels. Empathy is therefore an important part of good listening.

The psychotherapist Carl Rogers describes it as sensing 'how it feels [to the other person], to achieve his frame of reference in regard to the thing he is talking about'. Some analysts and counsellors have tried to achieve empathy by actually imitating a client's posture, in order to obtain a better appreciation of how the client is feeling.

The Australian communication trainer Maree Mac-Callum speaks of the need to match the 'energy level' of the other person, so that the possibility of empathy is increased. If a speaker is intense and serious, we need to respond to that mood if we are going to fully appreciate the message in the words. If a speaker is distraught, amused, solemn, fatigued or furious, our understanding of the message will partly depend on our ability to discern and respond to that mood. Since our job as a listener is to catch a glimpse of the view from the speaker's cage, we need to get as close as we can to finding an answer to the question, 'What does it feel like to be her/him?' We don't ourselves have to feel precisely as the speaker feels (how could we?), but the style and intensity of our response should be appropriate to and compatible with the speaker's style and intensity.

Good listeners enter into the spirit of the encounter. If we are going to allow the speaker to take us somewhere, we need to be prepared to give ourselves up to the journey.

In the case of an excited child with an urgent message, for example, nothing is more deflating and counter-productive to communication than a flat and dull response from an adult. The spark in the child demands some equivalent spark in the adult or the child will feel that none of the richness of meaning which lies behind the message has been communicated. Anyone who is enthusiastic about a particular message will be inhibited in communicating it if listeners show no sign of being prepared to rise to the occasion with a bit of enthusiasm of their own. And the contrary is equally true: when the listener is more intense or enthusiastic than the speaker expects, this mismatch can lead to a breakdown in communication between them.

If a speaker is being angry and irrational, a calm and rational tone in the listener's response is likely to make things worse, not better.

If good listeners have one quality which speakers prize most, it is their empathy—their ability to catch the speaker's mood and respond appropriately to it.

Why don't people listen? Sometimes, it's simply because their own energy level at the time can't match the intensity of the speaker. People are sometimes too 'high' or too 'low' to respond to us.

7 They reflect what they have heard

Merely listening to other people and understanding what they are saying is not enough. Good listeners develop the habit of giving the speaker a summary of their understanding of what has been said before they express any reactions to it (especially when they know those reactions might involve some disagreement or the expression of a different point of view).

In other words, the good listener *proves* that listening has taken place by reflecting or paraphrasing the main themes in what has been said. Good listeners develop the habit of saying things like, 'Let me see if I got that straight. Are you saying ... ?' Or, 'If I have heard you correctly, you are saying that ... ' Or, 'So you think ... '

Few things are more reassuring to us than to hear somebody else correctly present our own point of view—not like a parrot, but with understanding. Not only does it prove to us that we have been understood, but it also indicates the extent to which we have been taken seriously and acknowledged as a person with the right to an opinion.

(Several of these 'tricks' incorporate material which first appeared in an article by Ralph Nicholls, 'Do we know how to listen?'.)

FROM PLAYBACK TO FEEDBACK

'I told you a sort of lie.'

Kelly is curled up on the sofa, cradling a mug of coffee. Margaret is sitting in her favourite chair, half-reading, half-dozing. 'Mmm?'

'I told you a sort of lie.'

Not dozing any longer, Margaret sits up in her chair, then tries to relax herself, aware that this is not a moment to frighten Kelly off with a show of too-intense interest. 'Do you want to tell me about it?'

'I said I wasn't pregnant, and that was true, but it wasn't the whole story. Will you tell Dad?'

'Tell him what?'

'I mean, if I tell you what happened, will you tell him?'

'Are you saying that you wouldn't want me to? Or that you would want me to? I'm not sure . . . '

'I don't want him to tell Mum.'

This is the first time Margaret has heard her refer to Judith as Mum since Kelly moved in with her and Bill. She always says 'my mother' or even, in moments of extremis, 'Dad's **first** *wife'. Margaret knows she must tread carefully but feels unsure of herself. 'If we ask him not to, I'm sure he won't.'*

'I'm not so sure. I got a horrible letter from her. Have a look . . . ' Kelly spins an envelope through the air and Margaret catches it. She doesn't open it. She doesn't say anything.

'If I tell you what happened . . . ' Kelly is weeping, her words almost inaudible.

Margaret moves to the sofa, sits beside Kelly and puts her arm around her shoulders. 'If you want to tell me about it, I can't promise that I won't tell your dad, but

I won't say anything until we've worked it out between us. That's a promise.'

'The night I was late, I think I had a miscarriage. I was at Colin's place and I felt really bad. Cramps and everything. Then I started bleeding. Colin's mother fixed me up but I made her promise she wouldn't say anything.'
Long pause.

'And she hasn't. You must have felt awful ... Want to tell me the rest?'

'That's it, basically. I was stupid, I know. You don't have to tell me.'

Margaret tightens her hold on Kelly's shoulders, saying nothing. Her head is full of appalling questions. She's never heard of Colin, for a start.

'Does Damien know what happened?'

'Oh, Damien.' *That shrug again.* 'I think one of the girls has told him. I'm not really seeing Damien at the moment.'

'So you feel pretty sure it was a miscarriage.'

'I think it was. Colin's mother said it might have been.'

'And she felt that you were OK? She didn't think you needed any treatment?'

'Oh, she said I should see the doctor if I was worried. But everything was ... well, it wasn't a big deal, in a way. She's a chemist. She's nice. You'd like her.'

'Kelly, I don't think I know Colin, do I?'

'He's nice, too. You'd probably like him better than Damien.'

'But he was ... I mean, was he the boy you were involved with?

'Colin? God, no. He's Julie's brother.'

'Oh. So ... Damien?'

'Are you out of your mind? It was just one of those

things, Margaret. We were at a party and I had too much to drink and ... it was just one of the boys there. I didn't really know him that well. Damien was furious because I went home with this other boy.'

'So have you seen this other boy since? Do I know him?'

'Is this the Spanish Inquisition?'

'Kelly, I'm concerned. You're not surprised, are you? Even if it wasn't a miscarriage—and it might not have been—it still sounds as though you might have done something you wish you hadn't done.'

'I feel like such an idiot.'

'I guess you wish you hadn't got involved in anything like this. Not yet. You remember that chat we had about Damien?'

'But it's happened. And it wasn't Damien.'

'Yes. It's happened. We can't undo it, but ... well, we can learn from it.'

Kelly blows her nose noisily. 'So what do you think?'

'What do **I** think?' Margaret is lost for words. She is trying to piece together the story without asking Kelly too many questions. She is trying to listen, trying to see how it is—and was—for Kelly. She now suspects that Kelly has dramatised a late period into a miscarriage, but she can see that Kelly needed to find a way to tell her what she'd done. 'Well, I'd be lying if I didn't say I was upset. But so are you. I guess I mainly feel ... sad.'

'Disappointed in me?'

There is a long silence. Margaret struggles with her answer. 'Disappointed? Disappointed in both of us, really. We haven't spent as much time together as we should, but we're getting better at it, aren't we?'

Kelly doesn't reply, but she leans against Margaret. She feels tiny.

'I think I'd like to meet Colin's mother. Just to thank her. What do you think?'

'Can it wait a while? What are you going to tell Dad? The whole story?'

The last of the seven 'tricks of the trade' introduced the idea of reflective listening: playing back our understanding of what someone has said to us. Reflective listening is a useful tool in communication partly because it allows us to check whether we have got the message straight, and partly because it reassures the speaker that his/her point of view is being taken seriously. Reflective listening is the symptom of our desire to empathise with the speaker.

For the person who uses it, reflective listening is the restraint which ensures that we will receive a message before we react to it: if our 'playback' is inaccurate—either in content or tone—this gives the speaker an opportunity to correct our understanding of what has been said before we allow ourselves to 'get the wrong end of the stick'.

Many teachers of communication would argue that reflective listening is the most important communication skill of all. They point out that, when we accurately play back what another person has been trying to express to us, the effect is often dramatic. People who are listened to in this way find communication to be a highly therapeutic personal experience (quite apart from the effectiveness of the actual communication itself).

But reflective listening can be a minefield unless we remember the sixth of the seven 'tricks of the trade': the need to empathise with the speaker. To demonstrate our understanding of what someone has *said*, without showing that we also understand how they *feel*, is the equivalent of throwing cold water in the person's face. Playback should never be mechanical: it needs to take account of the whole message-pack.

Mechanical, 'textbook' reflective listening can easily backfire.

Bill comes through the back door, whistling cheerfully. Margaret is beside herself with frustration.

'Michael refuses to get into the bath. Kelly has been on the phone for almost an hour. The potatoes have just boiled dry. And you're whistling . . . flat, as usual.'

Bill, fresh from a management course on active listening, seizes another opportunity to put the theory into practice. He speaks calmly: 'My whistling is annoying you.'

Margaret looks at him in disbelief. 'What did you say? **What** *did you say? This place is totally out of control and you're going to patronise me with some of your active listening twaddle. I'll tell you something. Your whistling is* **bloody** *irritating and that's* **nothing** *compared with this patronising listening business you've been going on with since that wretched course. I think I preferred you when you just grunted.'*

Undeterred, Bill tries again, only half-serious.

'My method of listening is even more annoying than my whistling.'

'Get out of this kitchen. I think I'll buy a parrot in a cage. Yes, Bill, your method of listening is even more annoying than your whistling.'

But reflective listening *with empathy* would take account of the need to respond to the mood of the moment. The last thing Margaret needed was the voice of reason: what she needed was support ... someone to tune into her emotional wavelength and match the intensity of her feelings. Bill *might* have said, 'What a cow of a time you're having. I'll get Michael into the bath.'

Some response to the urgency, the drama, was called for. Yes, Margaret would appreciate reflective listening to her recital of his misadventures but what she most wanted was recognition of her *state*; recognition of the *intensity* of her message. Almost regardless of what Bill said, he needed to say it with appropriate passion and the right note of concern. Then Margaret would feel that, at least, she had made her point.

Reflective listening acts as a discipline on both speaker and listener: it encourages the listener to concentrate fully on grasping what is being said (because the message will have to be replayed with understanding) and it provides the speaker with some immediate 'quality control' on the way the message has been expressed. Reflective listening allows the speaker to answer the question, 'Have I made myself clear?' and it allows the listener to answer the question, 'Have I really grasped the point of this message?'

The essence of reflective listening is that it is non-judgmental. When we are simply trying to prove that we have listened closely to what someone has said, *our first responsibility is to play back our understanding of the message itself, not to comment on it.*

Yet, for all its value as a quality-control mechanism, and for all its great benefit to the effectiveness of the communication process, reflective listening is not, in the end, a *response* to what has been said. It is not a reaction. It gives the speaker no hint of what is going on inside the cage of the listener. It simply reassures the speaker that, yes, this person understands my point of view and is taking my contribution to the conversation seriously.

Ultimately, though, the speaker wants more than mere playback. After all, the First Law of Human Communication says that 'It's not what our message does to the listener, but what the listener does with our message that determines our success as communicators'. Once the speaker has been reassured, through reflective listening, that the message is understood, the far meatier question arises: What did the listener *do* (in a psychological sense) with the message? Now I know you have comprehended what I have said, I want to know how you have *interpreted* it.

So the focus shifts away from the message itself to the listener's response to the message. In other words, the speaker wants the listener to move on from mere playback and to offer some substantial *feedback*.

To be met by nothing more than reflective listening can be intensely frustrating—and even unnerving—for a person who wants to communicate. In fact, endless reflective listening (which might have a legitimate role to play in a professional counsellor's repertoire of techniques) can seem, in normal personal relationships, defensive and lacking in reciprocity. If, as listeners, we stop at reflective listening and fail to move on to make the offer of feedback, it can easily seem to the speaker as if we are *hiding ourselves* inside the listening process by focusing such exclusive attention on the speaker that we are refusing to reveal ourselves and our own reactions.

'For goodness' sake, *react!*' is the desperate cry of a person who may not be feeling misunderstood, but who needs more than playback. It is the cry of a person who is hungry for access to the other person's cage. 'Don't just listen ... *say something*' is a legitimate complaint, even against someone who has been engaging in the most committed, focused reflective listening. In the end, most speakers want more than playback: feedback is going to be the sign that we are fully participating in this relationship. Feedback is a message sent by a listener which is designed to tell a speaker what is going on in the listener's cage in response to the speaker's message. The switch from playback to feedback is the shift from saying, 'We have been concentrating on what's going on inside *your* cage' to saying, 'Now I am going to tell you what's going on inside *my* cage as a result of what you have said to me'.

Feedback is still part of the listening contract, because our feedback is designed to give the speaker as much information as possible about our response to the message. So, although the focus shifts from the speaker's cage to the listener's cage, the whole point of feedback is that it enriches the gift of listening by adding some *new* information to the encounter.

Feedback is therefore a distinct step forward in communication, whereas playback is simply an acknowledgment—or clarification—of a step already taken. (But note, once again, the important proviso: we don't earn the right to react through feedback until we have reassured the speaker through playback that we have really listened to the message and entertained the ideas which lie behind it.)

The art of giving feedback: Describe yourself

As with listening, there are some 'tricks of the trade' in giving the kind of feedback which is going to enrich a communication encounter.

The hardest thing of all is to restrain ourselves from

making evaluative comments about the speaker and the message. The cardinal rule of feedback is that it should be *self-descriptive*. As long as we express our reactions to what a speaker has said by describing only those reactions (rather than criticising the speaker or the message), then we have achieved the object of feedback, which is to *add something* to the speaker's understanding of our response to the message.

It is endlessly tempting to offer judgmental and evaluative feedback, especially when our response is negative or when we are confused by what we hear. We are inclined to jump in with reactions like these:

'You didn't explain that very well.'
'I don't think you are making yourself clear.'
'You don't know what you are talking about.'
'You're wrong, you know.'

Another temptation is to express feedback in terms of our diagnosis of the speaker's motives, or our assessment of the speaker's feelings:

'You seem to be a bit obsessive about this.'
'I think you are letting your feelings get in the way of your judgment.'

There are two obvious problems with feedback which offers judgments about the speaker or the message, rather than simply offering self-descriptive statements about the listener. The first problem is that the speaker is bound to be defensive if our feedback feels like an attack on what we have heard. (The speaker's cage works just like everyone else's.)

The second problem is that it is always dangerous—and rarely justifiable—to offer someone else a hypothetical description of what we think might be going on inside their cage. We only have access to our own cage and, although skilful listening gives us some clues about the view from inside the speaker's cage, we are still on dangerous ground when we try to second-guess what someone else might be thinking, or feeling.

Even if we are correct in our assessment of what is going on inside the speaker's head (she may well be feeling confused or unsure of herself), the speaker already knows that: we are not *adding* anything to her understanding of our reaction by telling her how *she* is feeling!

The only fully legitimate feedback we can give a speaker is information about the state of our own cage. We can say how we feel—or what we are thinking—in response to the speaker's message and that information will be valuable to the speaker because it adds to the information we are sharing with each other.

When we confine our feedback to self-descriptions, we are *developing* communication by giving the speaker access to information which is otherwise hidden inside our minds.

This is the essence of feedback: self-disclosure; self-description.

If we are going to play by the rules, and make our feedback constructive, we would not accuse someone of 'not explaining that very well'; rather, we would offer a self-description: 'I don't think I quite understand what you are saying.'

Similarly, we wouldn't accuse someone of 'not making

yourself clear'; rather, we would admit to feeling a bit confused about the message.

If a message has made us angry, we can express that anger in a self-descriptive statement: 'I can feel myself getting angry in response to what you have been saying.' That will work much better, as feedback, than an angry outburst against the speaker. The speaker needs to know that we are angry, but being told about our anger is much easier to handle than an angry outburst.

The great value of self-descriptive feedback is that it doesn't put pressure on the speaker—by criticism or judgment—even when the feedback is negative. It is quite possible for us to disagree vehemently with each other without mounting attacks on each other (which, because of the operation of the cage, are likely to result in defensive reactions and closed minds).

When we tell the speaker something about us and our response to the message, this is information which the speaker can take on board. But if we turn it around and express it as a comment about the speaker, it is much harder for the speaker to accommodate it without feeling defensive.

Imagine that I am speaking to you and, while I'm speaking, you are sending me (whether consciously or unconsciously) messages via body language which suggest that you are not very interested in what I am saying. If I say (as feedback on your body language), 'You're not paying attention', this is likely to produce a defensive reaction. If I say, 'I feel as if I'm not really getting through to you', you will still get the same general message but, because I have couched it in self-descriptive terms, it will be much easier for you to handle and to respond to.

Feedback builds the security of a relationship

Provided feedback always *follows* playback, it has the potential to deepen the sense of trust which we feel towards each other and the sense of security in our relationship.

When we play by the rules, feedback is the mark of a healthy and developing communication relationship. Playback proves that we have been listening attentively; that we accept the speaker's right to speak; that we have a genuine desire to understand the message. But feedback says much more: it says that we are going to match the speaker's willingness to be frank and open.

From the speaker's point of view, there is a certain vulnerability in receiving nothing more than playback. 'I've gone out on a limb to tell you what I think . . . when are you going to tell me what you think about what I have said?' Feedback closes the communication loop. It is the sign that the listener is prepared to do more than listen. It is only when the listener offers feedback that speaker and listener can begin to peg out the common ground between them.

Feedback may be a less generous gift than the giving of true listening (simply because it is actually easier for us to describe our own responses than to discipline ourselves to concentrate exclusively on the speaker's message), but it is a gift nevertheless. It is a gift of a cooperative spirit; a gift of willingness to go deeper into the communication process than merely listening to what the speaker has said. Feedback is a sign that we are prepared to make our *own* contribution to the process.

When I speak to you, I greatly value your listening and your playback. But when you open your cage to me and tell me about your reactions to what I have said, I know that this is a relationship.

By contrast, if you persistently withhold feedback (even if you are willing to offer reflective listening), I will feel inhibited: knowing that I will receive nothing in return for my message than a repackaged version of the same message, I am bound to feel a bit insecure, a bit vulnerable, and a bit wary.

Once we recognise that feedback has the capacity to build the security of a relationship, this should encourage us to be careful in the way we express our feedback. It is helpful to remind ourselves that feedback—like listening—is still a gift to the speaker, because it is a response to what the speaker has said (rather than an entirely fresh communication initiative).

Although feedback is based on my response to what you have said, this does not give me carte blanche to express myself without appropriate respect for the fact that I am responding to another person's initiative. For the time being, the other person still owns the game.

Apart from the need to be rigorous in our commitment to self-descriptive feedback, there are a couple of other 'tricks of the trade' which will help to make our feedback more effective (in the sense of making it acceptable to the speaker):

Avoid generalisations
When feedback is expressed in generalisations, it is harder for people to absorb than when it focuses on specific statements or a specific incident. The wife who complains to her husband that 'You never put out the garbage' is giving feedback on his behaviour which is too general to be accepted. She will register the same point in a more acceptable way if her feedback is more focused and specific: 'I was disappointed that you didn't put the garbage out last night, after I had asked you to.'

Similarly, 'You always try to dominate the conversation' will be much harder for the speaker to handle than more specific feedback such as 'Right now, I feel as if my point of view doesn't count.'

'I can never understand what you say' is going to be much harder for the speaker to handle than, 'When we were discussing your ideas for the new system, I felt that I was a bit out of my depth.'

(A good practical rule, by the way, is to keep 'never' and 'always' out of our feedback statements.)

Be tentative rather than dogmatic

Remember that feedback—like listening itself—is something we are doing for the good of our relationship: it is something we are offering to the other person. Once we realise the contribution which feedback can make to building up trust and security in a relationship, we also come to realise that people will respond more easily to feedback which leaves them with some room to move. Feedback which is expressed in tentative and exploratory terms will generally be less threatening to the security of the relationship than black-and-white, dogmatic or aggressive statements. Feedback represents a distinct step forward from mere playback, but it is still a *response* to what someone else has said, and it is still part of the process of negotiating shared meanings.

Statements like 'I may be off the track here, but I feel that ... ' or 'My present feeling about this is not very enthusiastic, but I need more time to do justice to it' keep our options open and do not have the effect of slamming the door in the speaker's face.

Feedback is a flow-on from listening and, like listening,

it is something we are doing for the other person. It is a gift, not a bludgeon.

RESOLVING CONFLICT THROUGH LISTENING

All of us find ourselves in a state of conflict, from time to time. Most of us hate it and try to avoid it, and the stresses and tensions it produces are the very reasons why we generally find conflicts hard to resolve.

Resolution demands some rationality, but conflict is often irrational. Resolution requires a steady focus on an outcome but, when we're in conflict, steadiness doesn't come easily. Resolution almost always requires some compromise but the mood of conflict is rarely open or generous enough to accommodate the idea of give and take.

But if we have children, or parents, or partners, or neighbours, or colleagues ... if we have any relationships at all, we are bound to run into conflict, so we might as well prepare ourselves for it and equip ourselves to cope with it when it happens.

Conflict isn't always bad, of course. Almost every loving relationship is enhanced by the occasional conflict which helps to clarify differences of opinion and to put little difficulties into a larger perspective. Most people have experienced the sort of conflict that 'clears the air' and creates a positive outcome.

The sociologist Gibson Winter says that 'we cannot find personal intimacy without conflict' which is why, presumably, Shakespeare assured us that 'the course of true love never did run smooth'.

Robert Bolton, in *People Skills*, quotes research which

suggests that high self-esteem in children is more likely to be found in families where there is open dissent and disagreement. Business organisations, also, find that *some* conflict stimulates creativity and energy.

Of course, when conflicts arise, we all tend to defend our existing points of view. Even if we can't use the structure of our cages to filter (or distort) messages which are in conflict with our own point of view, we can always simply restate our position and obtain welcome reinforcement from that.

(Remember the Third Law of Communication: when people's attitudes are attacked head-on, they are likely to defend those attitudes and, in the process, to reinforce them.)

The fact that argument generally results in people clinging to their original points of view does not mean that arguments are useless: they are often healthy and therapeutic; they are sometimes essential for the clarification of our own points of view; they can help to expose and define differences between us (and an understanding of those differences is important in any realistic personal relationship).

Some conflicts do not need to be resolved at all. It may be possible for us to accept each other's different points of view without necessarily having to agree: mutual acceptance might be sufficient in a relationship where there is plenty of other common ground. When people say that they have 'agreed to disagree', they generally mean that, in their relationship, a particular difference of opinion is not significant enough to provoke continuing conflict.

Sometimes, however, unresolved differences do lead to simmering conflict which puts pressure on a relationship, and that pressure must eventually be relieved. Of course, it is not always relieved by the resolution of the conflict: there are many other ways of relieving pressure in a relationship. We may simply walk away from each other; we may continue to distort each other's messages so that we both obtain the comfort of (unjustified) reinforcement; we may make negative private judgments about each other without admitting to explicit conflict.

But if we want to maintain a healthy, long-term relationship with another person, short-term relief of that kind will generally not be enough: it will often have the effect of reinforcing the prejudices which created the pressure and, inexorably, increasing the pressure.

It is this building up of pressure through unresolved conflict which often leads people to erupt in violent argument over matters which themselves seem quite trivial: where there are underlying tensions, little disagreements can be 'the last straw' or 'the spark that ignites the fire'.

It is a curious fact about human beings that, when conflicts do arise, our natural tendency is to prefer one of the least efficient ways of trying to resolve them: namely, out-and-out struggle or head-on argument. Since everything we know about the cage suggests that this kind of approach is very unlikely to succeed and may actually be counter-productive (in the sense that it may reinforce the very attitudes we are trying to modify), why do we do it, when it seems so obvious that careful negotiation would be more likely to resolve conflict to everyone's satisfaction?

Writing in the *Annual Review of Psychology*, Peter Carnevale and Dean Pruitt offer these explanations:

Communication may be difficult, because the parties cannot meet or do not understand each other when they do. Trust levels may be so low that the parties dare not enter into an explicit agreement. One party may be too proud to concede or too angry to do anything that favours the other's welfare. It takes two to negotiate, but either party can decide to go the route of struggle, forcing the other to adopt the same approach.

In addition, it is common for one or both parties to believe that they can achieve more through struggle than through negotiation.

Carl Rogers and F. J. Roethlisberger mention an additional reason why we might be more likely to rush into head-on argument than to try more carefully negotiated resolutions of our conflict. In an article published in *Harvard Business Review*, they point out that 'In heated discussions, emotions are strongest, so it is especially hard to achieve the frame of reference of another person or group. Yet it is precisely then that good listening is required if communication is to be established'.

The implication of these statements is that, when we find ourselves in a state of conflict with another person, the very communication skills which we most urgently require are likely to be functioning less effectively than usual.

This is not a book about techniques for conflict resolution. (There are many such books available. See, for example, *Getting to Yes: Negotiating Agreements Without Giving In*, by Fisher and Ury.) But, since conflict resolution obviously draws on our communication skills—our listening skills in particular—how might we harness what we know about listening in the process of trying to resolve conflicts?

Before we explore one method of conflict resolution based on reflective listening, we should note that there are two conditions which will almost always need to be met before there is any hope of resolving conflict.

The first is that *both of us must want a resolution to our conflict*. There is little to be gained from pretending to negotiate with someone in order to reduce conflict: the outcome will be worse than the original conflict because, while nothing will be resolved, frustration and disenchantment will have been added to our original difficulties. There are people who appear to thrive on conflict and who do not want to resolve it because it would reduce the level of excitement or emotional arousal in their lives. Tragically, some people enjoy conflict because that is the only time when they feel as if they are being taken seriously.

Spouses have certainly been known to bait each other in the hope of stimulating conflict, simply because, as one wife put it, 'When he is shouting at me, at least I know he is aware of my existence'. So, for some people, the idea of *wanting* to resolve conflict may hold no attraction at all.

For most of us, however, serious and unresolved conflict feels like a negative and corrosive experience in our lives. When we can tell that conflict is disrupting the harmony or security of a relationship which is important to us, we will probably want to resolve it. The essential first step is to establish that each of us is committed to the resolution of our conflict.

The second condition is that *both of us must be prepared to compromise*. While we both naturally want to win, we must recognise that winning will involve giving something away. It is fashionable to speak about 'win-win' resolution of conflict and that is a laudable ideal, but we need to be realistic enough to recognise that 'win' does not mean total victory. If we are both going to 'win' (that is, if we are both going to feel as though the conflict has been resolved in a way which is satisfactory to us), then we shall have to go into the process of resolution with a clear understanding that each of us will probably have to give something away as well. (In practice, we will sometimes find that we can both be satisfied without having to give anything away, but it is our *willingness* to do so which will make the resolution of conflict possible.)

Suppose, then, that you and I are in conflict and that we both want to resolve it and we are both prepared for compromise, if necessary. How might we go about it?

The key to success in conflict resolution through negotiation is active listening—the kind of listening we explored in 'What Makes a Good Listener'—which is supported by reflective listening. That kind of listening can create the climate in which conflict resolution can be negotiated, but it requires strict discipline.

Six steps towards a negotiated settlement

1 I state my own point of view on the subject.
2 You tell me what you understand my view to be. This is playback, not feedback: you must not express your agreement or disagreement with my point of view. Your task, at this stage, is simply to prove to me that you understand what my attitude is on the subject of conflict.

3 I then tell you whether I am satisfied with your understanding of my point of view; whether you have correctly represented my position.

If I am satisfied with your reflection—or representation—of my point of view, then we have reached an important stage in the process of negotiation. Whereas, in normal no-holds-barred arguments, our views are rarely absorbed by the other person (because we are concentrating on reacting rather than receiving), this listening-based strategy ensures that each of us is going to be quite clear about what the other one thinks. Even though we are still in conflict, we have reached a point of preliminary agreement: namely, agreement about what constitutes my view of the situation.

(If, on the other hand, I do not feel that you have accurately stated my view, then I need to go back and repeat Step 1, and we then repeat Steps 2 and 3 until I am satisfied that you have reached an understanding of my point of view.)

Next, we repeat that three-step process with the roles reversed.

4 You state your point of view.
5 I tell you what I understand your point of view to be. Again, the rule is that I am not allowed to express any agreement or disagreement with what you are saying: my task is simply to establish that I understand your attitude on the subject. This is strictly playback, not feedback.
6 You now tell me whether you are satisfied with my

understanding of your point of view; whether I have correctly represented your position.

(If we find at Step 6 that I have not correctly represented your point of view, then we must repeat Steps 4, 5 and 6 until you are satisfied.)

We have now achieved the situation where I have proved to you that I understand your point of view and you have proved to me that you understand mine, and some substantial common ground has been created. We agree about the substance of each other's views—even if we agree about little else.

It would be wrong to pretend that any of this is easy when emotions are running high and when we are, after all, in conflict. Not surprisingly, the hardest part of the whole process is Steps 2 and 5: those points where each of us must submit ourselves to the discipline of reflective listening without permitting ourselves to say why we are unhappy about the point of view which we are trying to comprehend and restate. If we get caught up in judgments or even snide remarks or sarcastic tones of voice at that point, the strategy will fail. The key to success is that, because we *want* to resolve the conflict, we must use the technique of reflective listening in an absolutely strict way.

Some people find this a rather artificial process; some people find themselves breaking out in laughter at the formality of it. Sometimes, it is helpful to have an umpire or 'facilitator' who will ensure that we work through the six-step process according to the rules. But those who persist with Steps 1 to 6 are bound to find that the experience of fully understanding each other's point of view is enlightening (to say the least) and may well have defused the conflict, even before we get to the stage of proposing compromises or solutions.

Indeed, Carl Rogers claims that 'When the parties to a dispute realise that they are being understood, that someone sees how the situation seems to them, the statements grow less exaggerated and less defensive, and it is no longer necessary to maintain the attitude, "I am 100 per cent right, and you are 100 per cent wrong".'

This is not an easy strategy, for all the reasons outlined in 'What Makes a Good Listener': committing ourselves to the job of representing the point of view of the other person in a conflict is a courageous and generous thing to do. Not everyone in a conflict will be able to accept the discipline involved (in which case, some other conflict-resolution strategy will be called for, such as mediation or arbitration involving a third party). But, for people who are prepared to use their own personal communication skills to resolve their own conflicts, the reflective listening strategy is very likely to succeed.

So far, we have only talked about achieving a situation in which we have understood each other's points of view: we have not actually talked about resolving the conflict. The truth is that, when we have achieved the important breakthrough of mutual understanding, the intensity will almost certainly have gone out of the conflict, many points which we thought were in dispute will turn out not to be in dispute, and we can now agree on the areas of remaining conflict between us.

Having achieved so much common ground, we may well find that, since we now understand each other's points of view so well, we can indeed 'agree to disagree' because the scope of the conflict has been narrowed, and it no longer feels as if it is a significant threat to the harmony of our relationship.

In other cases, we will have discovered that the conflict is still significant for us and that we must define very carefully the compromises we are prepared to make in order to resolve it. By having proceeded through Steps 1 to 6 of the reflective listening strategy, we will have prepared the ground for a sensible, cooperative discussion of compromises which will appeal to both of us. If further conflict erupts over the nature of the compromises being proposed, then we simply proceed through the sequence of Six Steps until we have, once again, clarified the basis of our disagreement.

The primary challenge in conflict resolution is to maintain the highest possible quality of communication between us; to preserve the trust we have in each other; to protect the underlying security of our relationship. By agreeing, at the very least, that we are prepared to work though the discipline of listening reflectively to each other's viewpoints, we are, in effect, saying, 'this conflict will not be allowed to damage our relationship; we are not going to attack each other; we are determined to understand the nature of the differences between us'. People who reach that point are the kind of people who are capable either of resolving their conflicts or learning to live with them.

Once we have learned to *accept* each other's point of view (through mutual understanding), the question of whether we also happen to *agree* with each other usually seems less significant than it did before we learned acceptance. Some of the unhappiest moments of our lives occur when we are so preoccupied with trying to justify our own point of view that we lose the capacity to accept that there are alternative points of view which are just as legitimate for those who hold them as ours are for us. As long as we are limited in our capacity for acceptance of other people's points of view, we will tend to assume that every conflict is a dispute between right and wrong, and to feel that hostility is the appropriate response to a difference of opinion.

Somehow, sometime, we have to find room in the cage for the transcending concept of acceptance. Listening is the primary skill we need to take us to that important stage in our personal development.

CHAPTER 6

Changing People's Minds

'You knew it must come to this, sooner or later, Toad,' the Badger explained severely. 'You've disregarded all the warnings we've given you, you've gone on squandering the money your father left you, and you're getting us animals a bad name in the district by your furious driving and your smashes and your rows with the police. Independence is all very well, but we animals never allow our friends to make fools of themselves beyond a certain limit; and that limit you've reached. Now, you're a good fellow in many respects, and I don't want to be too hard on you. I'll make one more effort to bring you to reason. You will come with me into the smoking room, and there you will hear some facts about yourself; and we'll see whether you come out of that room the same Toad that you went in.'

He took Toad firmly by the arm, led him into the smoking room, and closed the door behind them.

'*That's* no good!' said the Rat contemptuously. '*Talking* to Toad'll never cure him. He'll *say* anything.'

They made themselves comfortable in armchairs and waited patiently. Through the closed door they could just hear the long continuous drone of the Badger's voice, rising and falling in waves of oratory; and presently they noticed that the sermon began to be punctuated at intervals by long-drawn sobs, evidently proceeding from the bosom of Toad, who was a soft-hearted and affectionate fellow, very easily converted—for the time being—to any point of view.

After some three-quarters of an hour the door opened, and the Badger reappeared, solemnly leading by the paw a very limp and dejected Toad. His skin hung baggily about him, his legs wobbled, and his cheeks were furrowed by the tears so plentifully called forth by the Badger's moving discourse.

'Sit down there, Toad,' said the Badger kindly, pointing to a chair. 'My friends,' he went on, 'I am pleased to inform you that Toad has at last seen the error of his ways. He is truly sorry for his misguided conduct in the past, and he has undertaken to give up motorcars entirely and forever. I have his solemn promise to that effect.'

'That is very good news,' said the Mole gravely.

'Very good news indeed,' observed the Rat dubiously, 'if only—*if* only—'

He was looking very hard at Toad as he said this, and could not help thinking he perceived something vaguely resembling a twinkle in that animal's still sorrowful eye.

'There's only one thing more to be done,' continued the gratified Badger. 'Toad, I want you solemnly to repeat, before your friends here, what you fully admitted to me in the smoking room just now. First, you are sorry for what you've done, and you see the folly of it all.'

There was a long, long pause. Toad looked desperately this way and that, while the other animals waited in grave silence. At last he spoke.

'No!' he said a little sullenly, but stoutly; 'I'm *not* sorry. And it wasn't folly at all! It was simply glorious!'

'What?' cried the Badger, greatly scandalised. 'You back-sliding animal, didn't you tell me just now, in there—'

'O, yes, yes, in *there*,' said Toad impatiently. 'I'd have said anything in *there*. You're so eloquent, dear Badger, and so moving, and so convincing, and put all your points so frightfully well—you can do what you like with me in *there*, and you know it. But I've been searching my mind since, and going over things in it, and I find that I'm not a bit sorry or repentant really, so it's no earthly good saying I am; now, is it?'

'Then you don't promise,' said the Badger, 'never to touch a motorcar again?'

'Certainly not!' replied Toad emphatically. 'On the contrary, I faithfully promise that the very first motorcar I see, poop-poop! off I go in it!'

'Told you so, didn't I?' observed the Rat to the Mole.

'Very well, then,' said the Badger firmly, rising to his feet. 'Since you won't yield to persuasion, we'll try what force can do.'

The Wind in the Willows
Kenneth Grahame

Almost all communication involves some degree of persuasion. Someone asks you the time: they are persuading you to tell them. If you do, you are persuading them to accept what you say is true. When you seem to be trying very hard not to change someone, you may still be being persuasive: 'Stay as sweet as you are' is an appeal to resist change.

What about a simple 'goodnight'? Neutral? Not quite: it doesn't have to be laden with passionate connotations to carry some persuasive implications: recognise me as a polite person; remember me kindly, perhaps. At the very least, it would express the intention to create a particular sort of impression on the listener (which would be different from saying, for example, 'Get out of my sight, you old goat').

I don't want to push this too far. I simply want to register the fact that the distinction which seems to exist between 'simple' communication and persuasion may not be so easy to define. It is tempting to say that persuasion is about trying to influence another person to think, feel or act in a certain way, whereas communication is simply about the sharing of meaning with someone else—even when no influence is intended—but that's a rather blurred distinction.

What about the filing of a routine report? Even with a simple record of information—a set of statistics—the author wants to reassure you that the report is credible and its author competent and authoritative, and the way the report is presented will no doubt incorporate some signals designed to persuade you of that.

Even a desultory conversation around the dinner table has some persuasive content. 'Have a little more beef.' 'Wasn't it a lovely day?' 'Have you done your homework?' 'I think I'll do a bit of reading' (implication: 'so leave me in peace, please').

Messages which seem to be a simple case of keeping a relationship 'ticking over' are not always quite as simple as they look. When we want to 'keep in touch', there is still a hint of persuasion in wanting to keep other people interested in us, supportive of us, or prepared to keep their side of the relationship alive.

We often think of advertising as being a persuasive

form of communication—and so it is. But the astute advertisers know that their most effective strategy is not to concentrate on changing people's minds, but to persuade through reinforcement: to strengthen the bonds of loyalty among existing consumers and to encourage others to try brand X because of how they feel now (rather than trying to get them to feel differently first). So, is 'preaching to the converted' a form of persuasion? Is further reinforcement of an existing attitude a form of 'changing people's minds'? (It is certainly a form of influence ... and that's what we normally mean by persuasion.)

One difference between communication and more obvious forms of persuasion may be that, in some circumstances, we really *want* to influence another person, whereas in other cases (such as 'Have a little more beef') we may not care one way or the other. Whatever the difference might be in marginal cases, it is obvious that there are many times when we very definitely want to *change* the attitudes or behaviour of another person: we want to modify—rather than merely reinforce—the cage. We may call it training. We may call it correction. We may call it advice. Whatever we call it, persuasion is clearly involved. One person is trying to 'change the mind' of another person.

Not all attempts to influence other people are benign: unscrupulous politicians, religious fanatics, con-artists, aggressive salespeople—anyone driven by a desire for personal power or commercial advantage—may well want to change other people's minds to serve their own ends rather than to benefit those whom they are trying to influence.

But it is often necessary to exert persuasive influence over other people *in their own interests*. Traffic authorities want to modify the behaviour of motorists in order to ensure their safety. Teachers want to influence their pupils in the interests of their own education. Parents want to socialise their children so they can take their places in adult society. Counsellors and health professionals want to help their clients to modify aspects of their attitudes or behaviour, in order to overcome problems which may be interfering with the satisfactory conduct of their lives. Conductors want to influence the behaviour of their musicians in the interests of better music making. Sporting coaches want to influence their players to improve their performance.

The desire to influence other people is most obvious in the workplace, where people must be trained to do things in a certain way; guided to become more efficient or productive; shown how to adapt to new processes. For most of us, the world of work is a world of change and that change is ultimately brought about by people influencing each other to do things differently.

Defending the cage

One of the myths about the process of personal influence is that, if you want to get someone to act differently, you must first get them to think differently. (Anyone who understands the cage knows why that is a myth).

We are most unlikely to change people's minds by asking them to change, simply because almost any direct attack on the cage is bound to be defended. Even the most sophisticated techniques of propaganda don't change people's minds in the direct way that is popularly imagined.

When the cage is attacked by people who are trying to

change our minds, we have three favourite defences. The first is the '*Yes, but . . .* ' defence which concedes the point of the attack, but smothers it in counter-arguments.

For example, the committed smoker hears all the anti-smoking arguments and says, 'Yes, but my father smoked sixty cigarettes a day and lived to the ripe old age of ninety. Anyway, I'm here for a good time, not a long time.'

The child who is being told that a particular TV program may not be viewed says, 'I know you don't like me watching that program, but all the other kids in my class watch it and, anyhow, I have done all my homework and there's nothing else to do except watch TV.'

The employee who is being told that her punctuality leaves something to be desired says, 'Yes, I am often late, but I get all my work done and I always take a short lunch break to make up for it. In any case, I think I achieve much more than some of the clock-watchers around here.'

The motorist, being warned about the hazards of drink-driving, says, 'Yes, I know what all those experiments about reaction-time are supposed to prove, but I personally find that my reflexes are actually sharpened by a couple of drinks. I feel more confident and that makes me a better driver.'

The patient who is being warned by his doctor about the dangers of a high-fat diet may say, 'I'm sure I could reduce the risk of heart disease if I cut down on fat but, on the other hand, I could be knocked over by a bus tomorrow. When your number comes up, your number comes up. In any case, it's all in your genes.'

The 'Yes, but . . . ' defence is so spectacularly successful in resisting attempts to change our minds because it saves us from being drawn into the argument. It shifts the focus away from the troublesome proposition and focuses, instead, on the unrelated proposition which seems to have equal or greater weight. By retreating into the 'Yes, but ... ' defence, we never have to respond to the attack: we mount a counter-attack of our own. The original argument is treated as if it is no longer relevant: we've moved on.

The second classic defence is the '*What would they know?*' defence. Once again, the listener chooses not to reply to the argument but tries, instead, to discredit the source of the argument.

This is a common strategy in politics where attacks on the character of a politician are thought to weaken the force of his or her arguments. Similarly, people who are in disagreement with research findings will often try to discredit the reputation of the researcher (and, by implication, the validity of the research) so that they don't have to respond to the findings.

Young people typically use the 'What would they know?' defence to protect them from the advice (or the criticism) of older people: 'What would they know? Things were so different in their day. The world has changed.'

When an academic offers some unpalatable advice to the community, the response may well be, 'What would he know? He lives in an ivory tower.'

When a child attempts to modify the attitudes or behaviour of a parent (for example, in relation to health issues, or adoption of new technology, or even in the interpretation of current affairs), the parent may well deflect the message with an attack on the immaturity of the child: 'What would you know? When you are older, you will understand these things.'

The young, enthusiastic engineer who is trying to convince factory workers of the value of new work practices may well run up against this particular defence: 'These blokes are all the same. Straight out of university. I've been doing this job for thirty years ... I think I have got a pretty fair idea of what works and what doesn't. What would he know?'

The third defence against messages designed to change our minds is that *'It couldn't happen to me'*.

This is a favourite response when someone is threatening us with dire consequences if we go ahead with something we want to do; when people warn us of the dangers of a desirable course of action; when we hear of difficulties faced by other people who have attempted what we are planning to do.

A person is fired with enthusiasm for the idea of opening a gift shop in a new suburban shopping centre. Various friends and advisers are urging caution, quoting countless examples of small business enterprises which failed because of lack of adequate capital, lack of business training and expertise and lack of proper market research. But no: the person is so excited by the prospect of owning a shop that all arguments seem to fall on deaf ears. 'I've heard all those stories you're telling me; I'm sure lots of people have made a mess of this kind of thing. But I just have a really good feeling about this—as soon as I saw the shop, I knew I could make a go of it. All those things won't happen to me. I'm keen and I'm prepared to work hard. You'll see.'

A teenage girl is being warned by her friends about a heartless Lothario who is showing some interest in her. 'He has a real reputation,' they tell her. 'He'll be all over you like a rash, then as soon as he thinks he's won you, he'll be off after someone else. Don't be fooled by him. You'll be sorry.' Undeterred, the girl continues to encourage the boy's overtures. 'Don't worry,' she tells her friends, 'this is different. I'm sure he wouldn't treat me like those other girls. He's really nice. It won't happen to me.'

This defence allows us to protect our cages by denying the relevance of other people's experience. It also protects us when we are being threatened by horrifying messages—such as road safety or health propaganda—which are designed to change our minds through fear.

'People can lose a limb from smoking? Come off it. That couldn't happen to me. I jog every morning.'

The normal response to messages based on fear of horrific or even fatal consequences is either to 'switch off' or to reject the message as being too extreme to be relevant: 'Isn't that awful ... it's too awful to happen to me ... awful things like that don't happen to me ... it couldn't happen to me.'

All three defences work as well as they do simply because our desire for reinforcement of the cage is so strong. Even when we can't deny the truth of an attack, we can divert it by relying on some other 'truth' entirely. When all else fails, we can argue that since the threatened event hasn't yet occurred, it isn't going to occur: 'After all, our own experience is the thing we should pay most attention to, isn't it?'

Resistance to attacks on the cage is part of a perfectly natural and predictable pattern of human behaviour. Knowing that, it's remarkable that we persist with the idea that such attacks are worthwhile. One reason, no doubt, is that we still find ourselves in the grip of the Injection Myth described in Chapter 1. Another reason is that, when we want to influence someone, talking strikes us as the easiest and most obvious way to go about it, so we are reluctant to face the evidence which suggests that talking might actually be counter-productive (especially if we have some inkling of the fact that the strategies which are most likely to work are trickier to design and harder to put into effect than a bit of good old nagging, or a full frontal attack on someone's existing point of view).

But the most compelling reason why most of us persist with attacks on the cage is that we tend to think of attitudes and values (the bars in the cage) as being the *cause* of behaviour. People act a certain way, we think, because of the attitudes they hold. Therefore, the argument runs, if we want them to act in a different way, we must obviously get them to think differently first.

Like so many other popular theories about communication, this one has some big holes in it. When we examine the relationship between attitudes and behaviour, we may be in for a surprise.

Attitudes and behaviour: which causes which?

We notice many examples of people who act in ways which seem to be consistent with the attitudes and values they express. People who talk about ways to 'rort the system' tend to rort the system. People whose values seem to be materialistic tend to act as if material possessions are the most important thing in their lives. People who seem, in conversation, to have a caring attitude towards others tend to be involved in acts of charity and kindness.

Such observations fuel the conviction that our attitudes

and values shape our behaviour: from there, it is a short step to the conclusion that a *change* in our attitudes and values would *change* our behaviour.

But the relationship between attitudes and behaviour is not quite as straightforward as it may first appear to be. Think again about our cages and the way we construct them. From where do we obtain the raw material for those discoveries, learnings and decisions which form the bars of our cages? Where do our attitudes, beliefs, values and prejudices come from? (Wherever it is, surely that will also be the place where attitude *change* comes from.)

The answer, of course, is that our cages are built out of our experience. Our attitudes are the fruits of that experience. We construct the cage gradually, over a lifetime, *in response* to our experience of the world. (And, as we shall see later in this chapter, we modify the cage—change our attitudes—in response to new experience.)

So it actually makes more sense to think of attitudes as being the result of experience than to think of them as being the 'cause' of behaviour. That is an oversimplification, of course, because the relationship between attitudes and behaviour runs both ways.

Perhaps it would be fairer to say that our experience shapes our attitudes and our attitudes, in turn, shape our subsequent behaviour—pending *new* experience. This is precisely how we defined the operation of the cage in Chapter 3: we build the cage out of our experience and we then view the world through the bars of the cage. The cage is the mechanism for storing and using what we learn from our experience.

So the relationship between attitudes and behaviour is a two-way street, but the heaviest traffic flows *from* behaviour *to* attitudes, rather than in the opposite direction.

Because we form attitudes, values, opinions and beliefs in response to what happens to us, it is not surprising that, over time, there emerges a pattern of broad consistency between what we think and how we act. Indeed the comfort of the cage depends upon achieving that kind of consistency.

But the consistency is by no means absolute: we often say one thing and do another. The American psychologist Leon Festinger has studied the relationship between attitudes and behaviour and, in particular, focused his attention on the emotional problem created for us when we find that our attitudes and behaviour are out of kilter. According to Festinger, when we think one way but act another, we experience what he called 'cognitive dissonance' (that is, mental disharmony).

Being in a state of dissonance is uncomfortable for us, because of the tension created by a lack of consistency between the pattern of our behaviour and the pattern of our cage. We will want to reduce that tension by closing the gap between attitude and behaviour. The interesting question is: *how will we do it?*

If we believe that attitudes are the cause of behaviour, then we would expect to see people relieving the pressure created by a gap between attitudes and behaviour by modifying their behaviour so that it lines up with their attitudes. In reality, the more common response to 'cognitive dissonance' is to modify our attitudes so that they line up more comfortably with our behaviour.

For example, a boy might regard himself as being basically honest. He has incorporated into his cage the lessons of his parents which have been broadly supported by his own experience: he believes that 'honesty is the best policy' and that stealing is wrong. The boy is rather lonely at school and seems to have trouble being accepted by the other boys. Gradually, he finds acceptance within a particular group of boys who don't happen to share his view of the morality of stealing. After school, they frequently visit the local shops and engage in shoplifting as an act of bravado.

Desperate to be accepted by his new-found friends, the boy goes along with them and, under pressure from the other members of the group, he steals something from a shop. This makes him feel guilty: he is stressed by the tension between what he believes (shoplifting is stealing, and stealing is wrong) and what he has just done.

As time goes by and his shoplifting becomes more habitual, the boy finds that his guilt recedes and the tension between his attitudes and behaviour is reduced. This has not happened because he has modified his behaviour in the light of his attitudes; on the contrary, his attitudes have become more consistent with his new pattern of behaviour. Now, he is prepared to say to himself, 'Shoplifting is not really stealing ... no one really suffers from it ... it is just harmless fun'. He is in the process of changing his mind in response to new experience.

Another example of the urge to achieve consistency between attitudes and behaviour comes from Edgar Schein's classic study of American soldiers who were taken prisoner during the Korean War. Whereas the North Koreans favoured harsh punishment of prisoners to 'change their minds' in favour of communist ideology, soldiers who found themselves in prisoner-of-war camps run by the Chinese received very different treatment— although the object was the same.

In attempting to convert Americans to the communist cause, the Chinese would typically ask their prisoners to make mildly anti-American or pro-communist statements—statements which were so mild as to seem inconsequential. For example: 'The United States is not perfect.' 'In a communist country, unemployment is not a problem.'

Once such mild statements had been made, the Chinese interrogators would then increase the pressure: having agreed that 'the United States is not perfect', a prisoner would be asked to list some of the ways in which America was not perfect ... then to identify some of the 'problems' with life in America, and so on. He would be asked to sign his name to these relatively innocuous statements on the grounds that they were, after all, his own beliefs.

Later, the soldier might find that his signed statements were being broadcast to the entire camp, to other POW camps, as well as to American forces in South Korea. Now being identified as a 'collaborator', and realising that his statements had been made without any real coercion, a prisoner might modify his attitudes still further (in the pro-communist direction) in order to line them up with his publicly exposed behaviour. Under such conditions, the prisoner might become even more cooperative with his captors. In studying this unexpected phenomenon, Edgar Schein reported that 'Only a few men were able to avoid collaboration altogether'. Clearly, under such conditions, the apparently harmless act of making the 'trivial' statements requested by the Chinese set up increasing tension between the attitudes and behaviour of American prisoners—tension which was relieved, not by changing their behaviour to be more resistant to their captors' overtures, but by changing their attitudes to make them feel more comfortable with what they had done.

People who experience religious conversion often do so in response to changes in their circumstances which cause them to perceive religious messages in a new light. Their attitudes change because their experience of the world has changed.

The popular cliche that 'travel broadens the mind' captures the same idea: when we travel and experience cultures different from our own, this experience has an illuminating effect on our attitudes and our cages are expanded accordingly. Even people with the most appalling racial prejudice may find that it is eroded by the experience of getting to know individuals who come from the racial group which was previously detested: new experience produces new attitudes.

The point about these examples is not simply that they demonstrate the primacy of experience over attitudes; they also demonstrate the fact that we are much more likely to modify our cages in response to what we learn from our own experience, than in response to other people's attempts to change our minds through communication. We prefer to change our *own* minds in response to our own experience.

Women who have given birth to their first child often describe the experience of new motherhood as the most profound change in attitudes and values they have ever experienced. 'Nothing could have prepared me for this' is a typical response, as the new experience begins to reshape a mother's attitudes towards every aspect of her life—

often sweeping aside attitudes towards housekeeping and parenting which had previously been firmly and determinedly held.

Life-threatening illnesses and life-changing experiences (marriage, divorce, bereavement, retirement) cause many people to reassess their values and priorities and to change their minds about things which may always have seemed clear and unchangeable.

Of course, not all new experience has a cage-changing effect. One of the major themes of this book is that, even when we are confronted by new experience, we may filter perceptions of it so that it remains consistent with the existing shape and structure of the cage. We *tend* to interpret new experience in the light of the lessons learned from prior experience.

So the relationship between attitudes and behaviour does not imply that new experience will always lead to new patterns of behaviour and, in turn, new attitudes. *Some* new experience will produce new attitudes; some won't. But everything we know about the cage suggests that people are much more likely to change their minds when they learn from a new experience than when a message cajoles them or puts pressure on them to change. (There is still an important role for communication in the process of behaviour change and attitude change, and we examine that role a little later in the section 'What is the role of communication in all this?')

A teenage boy is notoriously reluctant about personal hygiene. His mother is constantly at him to shower more frequently, to use a deodorant and to take more care with his appearance. He attends an all-boys school and travels on a school bus which only carries boys from his school.

Suddenly, it is announced that the bus is to be shared with girls from a nearby girls' school. After the first couple of weeks of the new arrangement, the boy's mother notices a dramatic improvement in his personal appearance and she begins to have great difficulty in extracting him from the bathroom.

Have his attitudes changed? Who cares?

Is it really people's 'minds' that we want to change?

Our understanding of the complicated relationship between attitudes and behaviour raises an important question about the whole idea of changing people's minds: is it their 'minds' we want to change or is it really their behaviour that we want to change? Do we only talk about 'changing people's minds' because we cling to the idea that an attitude change must precede a behaviour change? If it were true that new behaviour is likely to shape new attitudes (as long as we communicate appropriately with the person who is experiencing the new behaviour), mightn't this shift the focus of our interest?

This brings us to a point of significant convergence between two approaches to the process of personal influence which, at first glance, seem quite different. One approach says that if we acknowledge that the real focus of our attention is behaviour (not attitudes), then we might as well go straight to the behaviour itself, work on that, and let the attitudes take care of themselves.

The other approach says that although we may ultimately want to change someone's attitude, we recognise that the most effective way to do this is to provide the person with some new experience from which new conclusions might be drawn and, in turn, new attitudes formed.

Either way, whether our ultimate focus happens to be on attitude change or behaviour change, we are left with the probability that changing people's behaviour will be the most productive first step. (In any case, it generally turns out to be easier to change people's behaviour than to change their minds: the fact that a change in behaviour may produce a corresponding change in attitude is something of a bonus.)

From an ethical point of view, putting the emphasis on behaviour may be something of a relief. As long as we cling to the idea that the way to change people's behaviour is to get them first to think differently, we operate in the mysterious world of 'the mind'. As long as we believe that our task is to change people's attitudes by changing their minds, we are vulnerable to the appeal of subtle and devious techniques of psychological manipulation. It is a very short step from the belief that we have to change people's minds to the idea that it is acceptable to act like 'thought police'. (The Political Correctness movement of the early 1990s attracted such hostile reactions precisely because it seemed to be trying to clean up our minds and our language ... almost regardless of how we actually behaved.)

If we focus on the other person's behaviour, our motives will be rather more obvious than if we are lurking about in the shadowy world of 'attitudes' (and, if we are smart, we will consult with the other person about what we are doing and why we are doing it). Nothing is hidden; nothing is mysterious; we all know where we stand.

Yet we persist with the idea that it is 'attitudes' or 'minds' which we wish to change. Parents talk about the need to change their children's attitudes towards table manners: what they usually mean is that they want to change the manners themselves. Road safety authorities talk about needing to change the attitudes of motorists who speed or who drink and drive: what they really want to change is their behaviour. Attitudes scarcely come into it.

When managers complain about employee attitudes, or teachers complain about the attitudes of 'today's students', they are generally expressing displeasure with some aspect of the employees' or the pupils' behaviour. They may assume that the cause of the undesirable behaviour is a set of undesirable attitudes (and they may assume, therefore, that they need to work on the attitudes), but the real problem is the behaviour.

How do we change people's behaviour?

Once we decide that it makes sense to focus on behaviour (even if we still want to think of it as a pathway to attitudes), the next question is: how do we go about changing someone's behaviour?

Any pattern of human behaviour—from driving a car to making love—is a result of the *interaction* between a person and the total environment in which that person is functioning: other people, the place, the situation, the circumstances. (The 'person' is an inextricable combination of unique inherited predispositions—genes—and the qualities and capabilities which have been shaped by all the influences on them over their lifetime.)

If we want to change the way someone behaves, therefore, we will have to change the nature of that interaction. To do that, we will have to make some change to the things that are interacting. We will either have to change the person (always a tough assignment, and sometimes almost impossible in practice), or the person's perception of their environment (easier said than done, thanks to the cage), or the environment itself.

Most times, it is far easier to start by making some change to the environment—the situation, the system, the circumstances—so the person is given the opportunity to react and respond to some new experience.

This is not to suggest that humans are mere victims of either their genes or their environment, nor pawns in some cosmic game of deterministic chess. It is simply to acknowledge that *some* aspects of our behaviour (those things we do which we could do differently) are heavily influenced by our immediate circumstances, and may be changed by changes in those circumstances. Geography, climate, peer-group influences, money, comfort, convenience, equipment, illumination levels, architecture and urban design ... these and many other factors in our social and physical environment are the kind of things which influence the way we behave. Of course, it is also true that there are basic human drives (like hunger, sex and the need for shelter) which have to be satisfied, but the way we satisfy those drives will be heavily conditioned by the environment we are in at any given time.

This is why people who are successful at influencing the behaviour of others generally start by looking for ways of changing the environment—the circumstances—in which they want people to act differently. They recognise that people tend to behave habitually (as they 'learn the ropes' associated with a particular system or a particular set of circumstances), and those habits are unlikely to be broken unless the nature of the system or the environment itself is changed.

This is why road safety authorities have long since realised that propaganda on its own is less effective than propaganda which is designed to support direct intervention in the driving environment: the introduction of random breath testing units, for example, has a much more powerful effect on drivers' behaviour (and, ultimately, on their attitudes as well) than any amount of public education about drink-driving in the absence of environmental change.

This is also why factory managers have often found that productivity increases are more likely to follow modifications in the factory environment (better lighting, air-conditioning, dust filtration, sound dampening) than the endless sending of messages about improved productivity.

It is why so many marketing companies have found that in order to get consumers to try a new product, they must distribute free samples—or create other incentives to try it—rather than simply advertising it.

All these examples point to the general proposition that *if we want people to behave differently, we must create the conditions under which it will be both easy and attractive for them to do so.* Unless we modify the environment in some way, the people who are interacting with that environment are unlikely to behave differently, regardless of how persistently we might ask them to do so.

The chief executive of a major industrial company once remarked, during a period of instability associated with a program of decentralisation: 'When we have decentralised, we will have to begin centralising again. It is only when we are reorganising that people are flexible enough to adapt to new thinking.' That may have been an extreme approach (and it produced a few nervous breakdowns along the way), but he was on the right track: changing circumstances do increase the chance of more flexible patterns of behaviour.

A manager who wanted to introduce computer technology into the workplace found that the employees concerned were very resistant to the idea. Instead of simply trying to persuade them to his point of view through communication, he offered to install a number of computers in the staff canteen, loaded with a range of intriguing games. There was nothing devious about the manager's approach: he explained exactly what he was doing and why he was doing it, and made it clear that he wanted the employees to react to his proposals on the basis of experience, rather than ignorance.

With a small amount of instruction, employees began to play computer games during their lunch break and, in the process, to familiarise themselves with computer operations. In the end, their resistance to the idea of using computers was broken down by the experience of actually operating the new machines.

You want to get someone to act differently? It is very unlikely to happen unless you do something to change the system or the environment in which they are operating.

A mother wants to encourage the members of her family to put dirty clothes in the laundry basket rather than strewing them all over their bedroom floors. She devises a system which can be easily explained but which represents a significant change in the running of the household. 'From now on,' she says, 'I will only wash clothes that are in the laundry basket. I don't mind if you leave things on your floor, but I am not going to operate in any other way. What you put in the basket will be cheerfully washed. What you leave out will be unwashed. Simple as that. You do your part, and I'll do mine.'

At first, the family might think that this is just another idle threat and may not appreciate that the system has, indeed, changed. It is crucial that she should adopt the system with the same rigidity as she expects of the others. She mustn't weaken, even if clothes pile up, unwashed. Sooner or later, everyone will decide that it is nicer to have clean clothes ... especially when all that is required is that dirty clothes should be dropped into the magic basket instead of onto the floor.

The key to attitude change is behaviour change, and the key to behaviour change is to change the system or the circumstances, after fully explaining the change and the reasons for it. It is not a sure-fire recipe, but it beats nagging, or any other strategy which relies on communication alone.

So, although we can never make absolutely general statements about the ways in which attitudes and behaviour affect each other, and although there is no 'magic formula' for changing people's behaviour, the Seventh Law of Human Communication describes our best chance of success:

> *People are more likely to change in response to a combination of new experience and communication than in response to communication alone.*

Some of the most extreme methods of changing people's

minds by modifying their behaviour were documented in the landmark book about brainwashing, *Battle for the Mind*, by William Sargant. Sargant pointed out that the process of indoctrinating political prisoners depended on first disrupting their environment to such an extent that they could no longer rely on their established framework of attitudes, values and beliefs—nor on the support of their peers.

Disorientation of prisoners has become an established strategy for interrogation by secret police in totalitarian regimes. Arrests in the dead of night; withholding of information about the nature of a charge against the prisoner; isolating the prisoner; keeping the prisoner in permanent light or permanent darkness (or altering those states unpredictably); alternately depriving the prisoner of food and then offering lavish meals; giving outlandish information which, though the prisoner would be disinclined to believe it, could not be checked against any other source. In these and other ways (including physical torture) interrogators can so disrupt the normal rhythm and pattern of a prisoner's life that they become open to suggestion.

(More recent experience in the Middle East has shown that under conditions of severe disorientation, prisoners can actually form an emotional bond with their captors because their normal frame of reference is shattered and they come to rely on the only human network to which they feel they still belong.)

William Sargant noted, however, that even attitudes which change under such harsh conditions are likely to change again when prisoners return to their normal environment. Though some people never recover from the destruction of the cage wrought by such savage treatment, others rebuild their cages in the light of subsequent experience. (The American prisoners of war in North Korea, for instance, though heavily indoctrinated with pro-communist messages, typically reverted to their original anti-communist attitudes once they were repatriated.)

Sargant documented the extraordinary forms of environmental manipulation which have been used by various religious sects and fanatics in order to induce states of near-collapse in people who are targeted for 'conversion'. Everything from the snake-handling of some American religious groups to the intense rhythmic drum-beating of voodoo cults was designed to create an atmosphere so removed from 'normal' that people caught up in it would abandon their usual perspectives.

But these are extreme cases. More benignly, the founder of the Salvation Army, William Booth, recognised that a destitute soul is more likely to listen sympathetically to the preaching of the Christian gospel on a full stomach: soup kitchens therefore became an integral part of the early ministry of the Salvation Army.

Remember when Margaret was trying to get Michael to wipe his feet (in Chapter 2)?

Like most parents, Margaret's first resort was to talking: it always seems easier to talk than to take more positive (and effective) action. But suppose she locks the door when Michael is outside and then when he tries to get in, tells him that she will unlock the door after he has wiped his feet.

This strategy involves an effective combination of a 'system change' and communication: by locking the door, Margaret has created a new set of conditions under which her message will have immediate relevance to Michael's situation: he can't get in until he wipes his feet.

Of course, doing that once probably won't solve the problem. But if she does it three or four times, a new pattern of behaviour will begin to be established (especially if Margaret reinforces the new behaviour with plenty of encouragement and praise).

That suggestion may well provoke cries of protest from some parents, who will say, 'When have I got time to go locking the door three or four times, just to train him to wipe his feet? Tell me how I can get him to do what he is told ... that's what I want to know.'

But this *is* a way of getting him to do what he is told: this approach certainly involves more short-term effort on the parent's part, but a much higher probability of permanent success. It will work better than nagging, and it is also preferable to the other obvious alternative: punishment. (Punishment may have its place in child-rearing practices, but it is usually better to look for some positive strategies for change before we resort to the negative approach—which is often simply an admission of our own failure to achieve the result we wanted.)

Which is best: to go to the trouble of locking the door three or four times to establish the new pattern, or to keep telling Michael—perhaps dozens of times—to do something which it is easier not to do? The truth is that when this pattern of behaviour has been explained, established and reinforced, Michael will be more likely to respond to similar messages in the future. The change in his behaviour is likely to produce a corresponding shift in his attitudes.

Hitler needed his rallies; Wesley needed his hymns: their messages alone were not enough.

It was Australians' experience of actually using Bank-card which changed their attitudes to credit: they did not begin using Bankcard because they had already changed their minds about credit.

Why does canned laughter on the soundtrack of a TV program encourage us to laugh at what is going on on the screen? TV program producers know that viewers are less likely to laugh when they are sitting in isolation: modifying their environment by creating the illusion of other people laughing frequently produces the desired effect.

'Plant a kiss on the Cole-face. How nice to see you.'

Margaret's father, Cole, has made one of his rare visits to see her. Michael, his only grandson, is the apple of his eye. He invariably refers to Kelly as his surprising little step-grandchild, a label which Kelly has learned to hate because she perceives—correctly—that Cole is rather uncomfortable about Margaret's status as Bill's second wife ... the idea of step-relationships vaguely bothers him.

Cole himself has been married three times but, as he himself is fond of saying, 'All my children are my own'— a line which infuriates both Margaret and Kelly every time they hear it. He is currently unmarried. He calls it 'floating' and Margaret knows that he is floating in some pretty fast currents.

Cole is the host of a long-running radio program, 'Metaphor', in which he interviews people about significant events and symbols in their lives. His audience is tiny, leading to another of his slogans, 'Never mind the width, feel the quality'. 'Metaphor' is under constant threat of being dropped, but Cole is passionate about it and talks of little else.

Bill and Michael are at the park. Kelly is at netball. Margaret is about to have a rest when Cole arrives on the doorstep unexpectedly. She makes tea and they sit on the back verandah.

'You simply wouldn't believe what the latest thing is. Security. We've all got these magic pass things which we have to insert into various slots and things to make our way about the building. Unbelievable. You simply can't get in without a pass. And we wear these all the time.' He holds up an identity card which is hanging on a chain around his neck. 'I find it easier to leave it on all the time. Easy thing to forget. Like my glasses: keep them on and you know where they are. Though that's not entirely foolproof either ... I have found myself searching for them when they were on my nose the whole time. Anyway, where was I?'

'Security. The magic cards.'

'Ah. Yes. The thing was, there were a lot of thefts going on. Quite extraordinary in a place like ours. I blame the ethnics of course—there are a lot of very strange people around the office since we've got into some of this foreign language stuff on the air. But of course you can't pin anything on anyone. And you can't say a word against any of these people, you know. The thought police are everywhere.'

'So has it worked?'

'Come again, old thing?'

'The security. Has it worked? Have the thefts stopped?'

'Well, that's the extraordinary thing. Yes, they have. But there was more to it than that, of course. There are a lot of very important people coming and going in that building every day ... to say nothing of all our tapes and archival material. There are years and years of 'Metaphor' tapes there, for a start. So there was a sort of point to it. But yes, the thieving has gone away. So far, anyway.'

'So it wasn't the ethnics after all.'

'Well, who knows. But yes, I see what you're driving at. Must have been people coming in off the street.'

'And the program is surviving. I'm afraid I don't get to hear it all that often . . . '

'Oh, surviving. Absolutely. New lease of life. But the place isn't the same. That's another thing about this security bizzo. You solve one problem. You create another. People don't move around as freely as they once did. Chewing the fat. That type of thing. It's more a case of heads down and get on with it. Funny thing. And I'll tell you something else. We're all a bit more organised than we used to be. I find I get through a lot more in a day. You don't mislay stuff like you used to . . . at least I don't. There's not the same amount of bumf drifting about. Bits of paper. Blank tapes. Things like that. It's more under control somehow. So it's an ill wind . . . '

Margaret finds herself thinking that there was probably never any theft at all. If Cole can't remember where his glasses are, he has probably mislaid an entire forest of files, over the years. But it makes a good story. Everything Cole talks about makes a good story.

'Will you stay for dinner, Dad?'

'Look, I can't. Got something on, I'm afraid. I should pop in more often. Have I missed the kids?'

On cue, Kelly comes through the door, just home from netball.

'Ah. My little step-grandchild. Goodness me. Not so little. Come and plant a kiss on the Cole-face. I'm just going. So nice to see you both.'

When Cole has gone, Margaret reflects on the striking similarity between the new security system at his office and her campaign to get Michael to wipe his feet. Locked doors have their place in the scheme of things. And any system that can get Cole organised and focused on what he is doing must have something going for it. The security aspect would be a bonus.

Every manager knows that the layout of an office—and the nature of the office systems—will have a direct effect on the work practices and productivity of the people who work there. Noise level, territorial space, privacy, visual distractions ... all such factors influence the way in which people work and *changes* in a working environment can produce dramatic improvements or deterioration in the morale of the workers and in the quality of what they do.

In other words, when our circumstances change, we may be destabilised by the change and we may have to revise our existing preconceptions and prejudices. Our cages are very strong and can withstand very considerable attacks upon them. But even the strongest cages may be disturbed by a significant set of new experiences which produce new patterns of behaviour from which new attitudes may evolve.

That is the kind of situation—applied to an entire society—described in *Reinventing Australia*. When a community is being subjected to widespread and sustained social, cultural, economic and technological change, feelings of uncertainty and anxiety are likely to occur. In turn, that feeling of instability creates a desire for new certainties and new sources of security. At a time of social dislocation, for example, people will often turn to extremist beliefs—in religion, in science, in feminism, in economics or even in astrology. When the world continues to be unpredictable, we have little alternative but to modify our cages in response to the prolonged instability of living through a period of discontinuous change.

Such a period—in the life of a community or of an individual—creates a field day for manipulators of every kind. When cages are fragile, people are vulnerable to new messages—especially those which offer the promise of a new sense of security. In the same way as we might try to change people's behaviour by deliberately changing something in their environment, so a spontaneous change in their environment may make them more willing to change.

But the opposite reaction may also occur. A boom in nostalgia often follows a period of prolonged instability, as people yearn for a return to 'the good old days' or 'traditional values' in an attempt to re-establish the comfort and security of the cage. Instability by no means guarantees an openness to new ideas: it may just as easily result in a reactionary retreat to an idealised past.

What is the role of communication in all this?

It is not simply the change in the environment that does the job, on its own: Margaret's locking the door needed to be supported by an appropriate explanation. The best long-term results come from creating new experience by creating changed circumstances while, at the same time, explaining what we are doing and what we hope to achieve. Road safety authorities do not simply install random breath-testing units around the countryside: they alert us to the fact that they are going to do so, and they explain the purpose of the strategy.

A marketing organisation does not simply distribute free samples of its product: it also distributes information about the product and follows that with an advertising campaign designed to reinforce the new attitudes which will be emerging from the new experience of using the new product.

This is why the Seventh Law of Communication states that people are more likely to change in response to a *combination* of new experiences and communication, than in response to communication alone. (Even the terrorist does not leave it to our imagination to work out what outcome he wants: the terror is combined with clear messages about the desired result.)

When we are trying to change someone's behaviour through a change in their circumstances, there are two roles for communication:

1 We need to send messages to the other person which will act as a *signpost*, identifying and explaining the changes we are proposing to make.
2 We need to use communication as *support and encouragement* for people who are adapting to the new circumstances.

What if we can't change the environment?

The Seventh Law of Human Communication emphasises that it is the *combination* of new experience and communication which is most likely to produce an enduring change in people's behaviour (and, in turn, in their attitudes). But there will be many occasions when we may want to influence other people without being able to make any of the changes to their environment which might exert a direct influence on their behaviour.

A doctor trying to modify a patient's diet, for example, has no direct control over the environment in which the patient buys or eats food.

In such cases, communication may be the only available tool. This is not a hopeless situation, but it is certainly more difficult than one in which we can introduce some environmental change as part of our strategy.

If you are trying to influence another person solely through the process of communication, there are three things to remember:

1 Base your message on some *existing* part of the other person's cage. Try to reinforce an existing attitude and relate it to your message. (Remember the cold-water washing example in Chapter 4.) Let the other person see how the behaviour you want is consistent with what they already believe.

Range Rover created an effective advertising campaign based on the slogan, 'Write your own story'. They were not persuading people to change their attitudes: they were persuading people who *already dreamed of escape* to focus those dreams on Range Rover. Their purpose was to change people's behaviour by tapping into an existing attitude.

2 Focus on the *behaviour* you want, rather than dwelling on the subject of 'attitudes'. People are much less likely

to change in response to a request for them to change their 'minds' than in response to a request to modify their behaviour—especially if it is only a relatively small modification.

The parent who asks the messy teenager to 'get your act together ... clean up your attitude ... I don't know how you can live in this mess' is very unlikely to produce a positive result. But the parent who concentrates on one aspect of the child's behaviour is more likely to succeed: 'Can we find a way of organising the books you are going to need for school tomorrow, so you won't leave any behind? Don't worry about the rest ... let's just work out a system so you can have tomorrow's books organised and ready.' Such a request focuses on a specific aspect of behaviour and bypasses any general problem associated with an underlying 'attitude'.

3 Seek a *small step* (or a series of small steps, over time) rather than a giant leap. Erosion is more effective than explosion, especially when each small step in a gradual process can be reinforced through the use of encouraging and supportive messages. (This is precisely the technique used by commercial organisations who create advertising messages to reinforce the attitudes of people who are buying their product in the hope of encouraging them to keep doing so.) Even the tiniest steps in the right direction should be reinforced through constant encouragement.

The rural education officer who is trying to persuade a farmer to experiment with heavily increased doses of superphosphate is unlikely to succeed if he attacks the farmer's attitudes: 'I don't know why you are always so resistant to change.' But if he switches his focus from the farmer's attitudes to his behaviour, he may still fail if he asks for a behaviour change which is too radical: 'Why don't you double the dose on your whole property and just see what it does to your yield next season?' He is more likely to succeed if, without raising the question of underlying attitudes, he asks the farmer to double the dose on a small, experimental paddock: 'Let's see what happens next season if you just double the dose on your small back paddock. Nothing much will be lost, but it will be a very useful experiment to see if this might work on your type of country.'

CONSULTATION: THE KEY TO MANAGING CHANGE

Some of the material in this chapter might appear to be suggesting that in order to influence other people's attitudes and behaviour, all you have to do is manipulate their environment in some way, provide a bit of encouragement and reinforcement, then sit back and watch them react, like so many rats in a laboratory.

That kind of approach would raise serious ethical questions. The underlying message of this book is that communication is most likely to be successful when it takes place in the context of personal relationships which have some inherent integrity: relationships based on a spirit of mutual respect, trust and reciprocal obligation. When it comes to influencing other people's behaviour, that message still applies.

The process of personal influence should take place in a morally sensitive climate and, indeed, is more likely to succeed when that is the case. We should be prepared to be quite frank and open about what we are doing. We should explain our motives and our goals. We should communicate as openly as we can about the changes we are making to the other person's environment.

Above all, we should consult with the people we are trying to influence *before* we design any strategies for getting things done differently.

At first glance, this may seem nonsensical. How, you may ask, are you going to influence someone to act differently if you make it transparently obvious to them that that is what you are doing? The answer is that you are even less likely to succeed if you attempt some kind of devious manipulation: there are no foolproof strategies for influencing other people, and the most effective strategies depend on achieving some degree of cooperation. (Remember that one of the 'three Rs' of communication is *relationship*.)

For example, think again about Margaret trying to get Michael to wipe his feet. Simply asking him to wipe his feet has not worked because there is no pressure on him— apart from nagging—to take the message seriously enough to act on it. But when Margaret decides that she is going to develop a strategy to influence his behaviour in the direction she wants, she should certainly discuss it with him and, in consultation with him, explain what she is going to do and how she is going to do it. 'I know you can't help forgetting about wiping your feet. But it is important for you to learn to remember because none of us like having a dirty floor to walk on. So I am going to help you remember by locking the door when you are outside. It will be a bit annoying until you get into the habit, but at least I won't get angry with you.'

Michael is only seven years old, after all, and that degree of consultation would be easy to manage. Were he older, the consultation could be even more wide-ranging, so that he might be encouraged to make his own suggestions about how to achieve Margaret's objective.

In the area of workplace change, the same principle applies. If we attempt to implement change without consulting those who are going to be affected by the change, they are likely to be more resistant to it than might otherwise be the case. Remember the factory manager who installed some computers programmed for games in the staff canteen as a means of letting the staff get used to computer operations in a non-threatening environment? His motives for putting the computers in the canteen were transparent: indeed, he explained to the staff that before any decisions were made about switching to a computer system, he wanted them to have the opportunity to 'fiddle about' with a few computers, just to see how they felt. No obligation; no commitment; just try it, and see how it goes.

Environmental modification without appropriate consultation and explanation amounts to manipulation or even exploitation. Government authorities who institute changes, for example, in the management of traffic (through such initiatives as speed cameras or random breath testing) need to go to great lengths to consult with the community and to explain to the community the nature of the problem and the reason why this particular solution is being tried. In the absence of such consultation and explanation, those initiatives would, quite correctly, be interpreted by the community as an example of 'Big Brother' at work.

People who are brought into the process of decision making about changes which affect them are much more likely to accept that the changes are necessary, and are much more likely to participate in experimental change programs to which they have contributed even if they are lukewarm about them.

In *Organisational Change by Choice*, Dexter Dunphy urges managers to adopt an open and consultative style so that employees themselves will become involved in the design of strategies for change:

> Some managers may see this as a loss of control. It *is* a redistribution of power. Our experience is, however, that systems of mutual influence operate more effectively than situations of one-way influence. It is true that the managers, owners or employers may no longer get their own way. But they seldom do so now and attempts on their part to apply coercion often result in an equally strong or more powerful countervailing force that negates their power.

None of this is to suggest that people in positions of authority (in management, or in a family) should abdicate their authority in favour of some wishy-washy process of consensual decision making by the group. Group decisions tend to be notoriously bad decisions (because no single person accepts full responsibility for them). But people in positions of authority make the best decisions when those decisions are *informed* by a process of consultation with those who will be affected by them.

The Eighth Law of Human Communication makes precisely that point:

> *People are more likely to support a change which affects them if they are consulted before the change is made.*

Why don't people listen? Sometimes it's because they weren't consulted about a change which is going to affect them and so, when we tell them about it, they say, 'First I've heard of it' and that's the end of that.

Being consulted about a decision is not the same as making the decision. Consultation is the process of involving all those who will be influenced by a change in the development of the strategies which will bring about that change. But, as Dexter Dunphy points out, the legitimacy and effectiveness of consultation depends on all of us being prepared to be influenced by it.

David, the branch manager for Croydon Bridge, is on the phone to Bill.

'I've got a pretty unhappy bunch of people up here. They've just seen Christina's missive about the new forms for the monthly returns and they're up in arms, to be frank.'

'You don't have to tell me, mate. You're the third call this morning. I didn't know anything at all about this until I saw the new forms last night, so we're all in the same boat. Which is no help at all, I realise.'

'What happened to all the hot air about consultation? Out of the window, by the looks. My people reckon this system simply won't work. They can see about ten holes in it, straight off, and they just can't understand why no one spoke to them before this was designed.'

'Reminds me of the classic about the printing shop. Did you ever hear about that one? Monumental cock-up.

Some draftsman drew the plan for a new collating machine which was to go into the printery, but he never bothered to go and look at the place for himself. Thought it was all routine. Just drew it up off the existing plans he had on file. No one told him the place had been renovated since those original plans were drawn, and there was a bloody great pillar right in the middle of the spot where the new machine was supposed to be installed. There was one heck of a row about that. Same problem. Lack of consultation. The blokes in the printery weren't amused at all. As they said, one quick phone call would have solved the whole thing.'

'That's exactly what the people up here are saying. They run the system. They know the ropes. You'd think it would be pretty fundamental to bring them in at the beginning of a process like this. You can imagine what it's done to morale. Rock bottom again. Part of the problem is that we've keyed everyone up to think that things are going to be different.'

'I know what you mean. Anyway, a spot of interesting news from home. Old King Cole came around to see Marg last weekend. She tells me he's belly-aching about their new security system. It seems he can't lose anything any more . . . so I suppose he's afraid of being found out. There is a God, after all. Anyway, I'll look into this monthly return thing and get back to you. In the meantime, you'd better tell your troops to ignore the new forms and just carry on regardless.'

'That's exactly what they've already decided to do.'

CHAPTER 7

Other Messages

Michael is playing cricket in the backyard with three of his friends. It is a hot Saturday afternoon. Bill is weeding the garden. The boys finally call the game off because of the heat and tumble inside, heading like parched travellers for the oasis of the fridge. Michael dispenses lime cordial with much hilarity. Ice blocks are taken from the freezer and added to the drinks. Television is briefly proposed and dismissed.

The boys surge into the living room. A certain amount of pushing and shoving ensues. A tumbler of lime cordial is upset and its contents splash onto the carpet. The carpet is off-white.

Bill appears at the door, having come in from the garden to investigate the whooping and yelling and to remind Michael—too late—that drinks are not to be taken into the living room.

Bill looks at the green patch on the carpet, then at Michael and his friends. Stay calm, he urges himself; these are Michael's friends. It's only a splash on the carpet. It will come out. Not very easily, though. And possibly not completely. Margaret is out shopping. I am in charge. Margaret may even have specifically mentioned keeping the boys outside with food and drinks. Almost certainly did.

'Now look,' says Bill in a voice which he hopes sounds firm, but controlled. 'I'm not angry. I just want to know what happened. Michael, you know that you're not supposed to bring drinks in here. How did this happen?'

The boys look at Bill. His face is a little red ... from the sun, or from anger? His voice sounds loud and angry, and Michael reckons he has a terrible temper sometimes. He is jabbing his finger in an angry way. Yes, this is an angry man. No doubt about it.

He's also a strange man. Although he is obviously angry, the words coming out of his mouth say, 'I'm not angry'. Best we say nothing.

There is never just one message. Whether we speak, or write, or even send non-verbal messages via so-called body language, we always send a number of messages at once. Sometimes, that package—that mixture of the things we say and how we say them—contains messages which actually contradict each other. When that happens, we set a tricky task for the listener: how to decide which messages to accept and which to reject or, more intriguingly, how to interpret the significance of the contradiction itself.

For Michael and his friends, the task of interpreting the several messages being sent simultaneously by Bill was easy. The message expressed in the words 'I'm not angry' was virtually overwhelmed by the message expressed in the look on Bill's face, the jabbing finger, the aggressive posture and the sound of his voice (almost regardless of what that voice happened to be saying).

We delude ourselves when we assume that the words we say are the most important message we send the listener. What listeners actually respond to is the total impression created by the combination of the words themselves and the way the words are 'packaged': how they are said, where they are said, when they are said and by whom they are said. If they wanted to, they may be able to 'unpack' the individual messages which contribute to the total impression they receive, but most listeners don't go to that much trouble. To them, it appears as if all those different messages are bundled together in one 'swag' and they respond to that.

Margaret and Bill are chatting, in a desultory way, about some plans to develop the garden and put in some new plants and shrubs. This conversation has been evolving, on and off, for several months. A recurring theme of Margaret's is that the colour of some of the plants Bill is proposing would clash with the pinkish colour of the house itself.

'Where did you get all this rubbish about pink flowers having to match the colour of the house?' says Bill.

'I've never said "match". You just made that up. I've only ever said they shouldn't clash. Why don't you listen?'

Think about all the ways in which Bill might have asked that question, and all the ways in which Margaret might have responded. As it happened, Bill said, 'Where did you get all this rubbish . . . ' in a light tone of voice, with no sting in the tail, and with obvious affection. His question was playful and mischievous, relaxed and non-threatening, and Margaret responded accordingly. The words, of themselves, evoked less response than the tone of voice in which they were expressed.

Had Bill been feeling tense, or had there been some unresolved conflict between him and Margaret (possibly about some other matter entirely), Margaret's reference to the clashing of colours could have triggered the same word message from Bill, but delivered in an irritated and even cranky tone of voice which would, no doubt, have evoked a very different response from Margaret.

We already know that the meaning of a message is not in the words which are spoken. Now we must face the awkward complication that the words which are spoken are only one of a number of messages to which our listeners will respond.

Pink, spiked hair, for example, can send disturbing messages of non-conformity to some listeners, but reassuring messages of rigid conformity to others. For some listeners, a speaker's pink, spiked hair will signify membership of an attractive subculture. The hair seems to say, 'Here's someone just like me; here's someone I feel comfortable with; here's someone who isn't going to threaten me or disapprove of me.'

For other listeners, though, the same hair-do will seem to be saying very different things: 'Here's someone absolutely unlike me; here's someone who makes me feel uncomfortable; here's trouble.'

In both cases, pink spiked hair is itself a message which becomes part of the package of messages—the presentation—which surrounds and supports (or perhaps even contradicts) what is being said in words.

Spiked hair, torn jeans, bow ties, double-breasted navy business suits, beards, thongs, uniforms, leather briefcases, barristers' wigs and gowns, nose rings, or any other feature of personal appearance, are all messages which will be parcelled together—along with the other messages in the package—by the listener.

This is why young people are given such specific advice

about how they should dress when going for a job interview: clean your shoes, because clean shoes are a message; have your hair well groomed because well-groomed hair is a message; dress neatly because the neatness of your clothes is a message.

Personal appearance is an obvious 'message', but almost any aspect of a communication encounter may find its way into the message pack. For instance:

The words themselves
The tone of voice (pitch, volume, timbre)
The rate of speech
The pattern of speech (stress, rhythm)
Posture
Gestures and other physical mannerisms
Facial expressions
Dress, hair and other features of physical appearance
The distance between speaker and listener
Formality or informality of the setting
Physical surroundings (indoors, outdoors; public, private)
Social setting (at home, at work, at a meeting, over a drink, etc.)
Time of day
Amount of time available for the encounter (hurried, relaxed)
Level of illumination (bright light, dim lighting, darkness)
Temperature
Smells (of the people involved, and odours in the environment)
Presence or absence of physical contact between speaker and listener

And so on . . .

Glancing down the list, it comes as no surprise to realise that, when the listener interprets such a mixed assortment of messages, the words themselves may be lost in amongst all the other messages—some conscious, some unconscious; some intentional, some unintentional; some compatible with what the words are saying and some either incompatible or downright contradictory.

The most conservative interpretation of available research evidence would be to say that, in a normal conversation, spoken words account for less than half the total meaning which will be attached to the message pack. Things like facial expression, tone of voice, rate of speech, posture and gestures will account for the rest. For one thing, a typical message pack will contain many more of those 'other messages' than word messages.

It is unrealistic to try to be too precise about all this: the relative significance of verbal, vocal, visual and other ingredients in the mixture changes from situation to situation, and from person to person. But we can make a few safe generalisations . . .

Physical-contact messages

Messages which involve actual physical contact tend to be the most significant of all: a finger prodding the chest; a fist driven into the face; a kiss planted gently on the lips (or, a different message, on the cheek); a reassuring squeeze of the hand; a hug; a slap (on the back, or across the face); an arm placed around the shoulders; an arm placed around the waist; a touch on the elbow. We can't specify the precise 'meanings' which might be attached to those physical gestures on all occasions any more than we can specify the meanings which will be attached to words, but we can safely assume that whenever we touch another person's body, that person is likely to regard our touch as one of the most significant messages in the total message pack, and one of the easiest of all messages to interpret. What I *do* to you is likely to send a clearer and stronger message than what I *say* to you.

Visual messages

In our culture, we have long recognised that 'a picture is worth a thousand words', but we have not always recognised that in conversations we ourselves are the pictures. Facial expression, posture, gestures—all the things we call 'body language'—will often send more interesting signals than the words we say. 'Wasn't his face a picture?' captures the idea.

Visual messages will mean different things to different people on different occasions: somebody folding his arms *may* be signalling his desire to exclude another person, but it may also be nothing more than a sign that this is a comfortable position for his arms. (Even Freud, a connoisseur of phallic symbolism, is supposed to have conceded that sometimes, a cigar is just a cigar.) Visual messages—like all messages—will be interpreted in the context of all the other messages in the package, but their influence is often very strong.

'I know you said you were interested, but your face told me you weren't.'

'The way you were slumped in that chair, I thought you must have decided the situation was hopeless.'

'She couldn't keep her hands still the whole time she

was talking to me ... she seemed really nervous.'

'He was a shifty-looking character ... I wouldn't trust him as far as I could kick him.'

Statements like these show just how easily we read 'meanings' into visual messages. Imagine a man who looks repeatedly at his watch while you are talking to him. It would be hard not to assume that he was impatient or distracted. At the very least, you would be inclined to think that he had another pressing engagement and was running short of time. Suppose you point out to him how unnerving it is, trying to speak while he is repeatedly looking at his watch. If he says, 'Don't worry, I am listening to what you are saying, we have plenty of time ... ', would you be convinced by the words? Or would you feel that the strongest message was still the visual message?

Where visual and verbal messages are at odds with each other, the natural tendency is to respond to the visual. When a woman yawns while being spoken to, this does not necessarily mean that she is bored, or even that she is not attending closely to the speaker, but it is a hard message to ignore.

One reason why people are sometimes perplexed by seeing photographs or videotapes of themselves is that they realise they have been sending unintentional or unconscious visual messages: their facial expression, posture or gestures seem to invite interpretations which might contradict what they were actually feeling at the time. That is one of the dilemmas created by the fact that, whether we want to or not, we are always sending a whole mixture of messages simultaneously: the challenge is to ensure that those messages have some internal consistency so that, when taken together, they add up to the total impression we want to convey.

*'Why have you got that look on your face?' says Michael
to his mother.*
  'I haven't got any particular look on my face.'
  'You look angry to me.'
  'You're imagining things. I don't feel angry at all.'

What is the truth of encounters like that? Is Margaret
feeling angry and expressing it involuntarily in her face?
Is Michael feeling guilty about something and imagining that his mother looks angry because he thinks
she should be? Or is there something about Margaret's
facial expression which suggests anger to her son, quite
unjustifiably?

   We can never be sure about the answers to such questions, but we can be sure that people are scanning our
faces and our general appearance for signs of those subtle
little messages which might aid their interpretation of
what we are saying to them. (In fact, it is quite often the
words we say which they are using to aid their interpretation of the visual messages they have already picked up.)
If the look on someone's face suggests insincerity, it is the
insincerity which will be perceived and interpreted as the
primary message.

   A quirky example of the importance of visual messages
in communication comes from the field of radio broadcasting. In a medium where listeners rely entirely on what
they hear, they create their own mental pictures. Where
listeners have never seen a radio personality, they construct an 'appearance' based on the sound of the voice.
Those images may bear no relationship at all to the actual
appearance of the presenter, but they enrich the listener's

experience by adding imaginary pictures to the message pack. Recognising the value of these imaginary pictures, some radio broadcasters have gone to considerable lengths to keep their appearance hidden from their listeners (by not releasing publicity photographs of themselves, for example) so the listeners are free to create whatever visual images they feel are most compatible with the verbal and vocal messages they are hearing.

Radio listeners sometimes experience a shock of real disappointment when they discover that somebody they've been listening to for months or years looks completely different from the way they had imagined. Once the 'true' picture has been revealed, the listener's response to the verbal and vocal messages may change quite radically.

(I once worked with a radio broadcaster who tried to create his own visual images. He insisted on dressing quite formally—with tie and jacket—when he was on the air, believing that this way of dressing would have a significant effect on the way he felt and, in turn, on the way he sounded. His colleagues, in jeans and T-shirts, either did not share his conviction or else presumably wished to sound as if they were in jeans and T-shirts.)

An even more quirky example of the urge to add a visual dimension to a non-visual medium comes from John Seabrook in the *New Yorker*, quoting Microsoft's Bill Gates: 'I comb my hair every time before I send e-mail, hoping to appear attractive.'

In *The Men We Never Knew*, Daphne Rose Kingma discusses the way in which some men prefer to express their feelings through visual messages alone:

To women's great frustration, men's emotions are endlessly permutated into action. Men *do* their emotions;

they don't *say* them. Women watch these behaviors, intuit something's going on, and can only wonder what it is.

Much as women hate this behavior, because of male socialization and the immense discomfort men feel in the face of their emotions, men have almost no choice but to translate their feelings into the actions which symbolically carry their meaning. Thus we must deduce that the man doing dishes for his law student wife is saying 'I love you; I support you; you're terrific,' although he won't say the words; that the man who buys his daughter a sports car for graduation is saying he's proud of her, even though he doesn't bother to tell her; and that the man who endlessly polishes his dead son's motorcycle is grieving, although he can't talk about it with his wife.

Of course, this brings us back to the problem of the cage: men behaving in such ways assume that the 'meaning' of their actions is self-evident, but women observing those visual messages will inevitably interpret them in their own way.

Vocal Messages

The American communication researcher Albert Mehrabian undertook a series of experiments designed to test people's reactions to the sound of the human voice. The words themselves were made unintelligible through the use of an electronic filter. Mehrabian demonstrated what the parents of infants soon learn: that we can attach some degree of meaning to the sound of a voice even when it is not speaking 'proper' words.

Mehrabian concluded that 'when vocal information contradicts verbal, vocal wins out. If someone calls you "honey" in a nasty tone of voice, you are likely to feel disliked; it is also possible to say "I hate you" in a way that conveys exactly the opposite feeling.'

Why don't people listen? Another answer is that people might not appear to have listened to what we were saying because our words were overshadowed by the way we said them. A message can seem boring, urgent, amusing, poignant, tragic or routine ... all because of how it sounds. (Think of all the different meanings you can express in the statement, 'What will we do now?', just by altering your tone of voice, your rate of speech and the emphasis you place on different words.)

People who think they have 'softened the blow' by saying something harsh or negative in a gentle way may find they have succeeded even more than they intended. It is possible to decline an invitation so gently, for example, that the listener may think you are actually undecided. People who lack assertiveness are constantly finding that their 'no' seems to have been interpreted as 'yes'.

One manager, faced with the daunting task of having to retrench someone, handled the interview so delicately that the employee was left feeling confused about whether he was being retrenched at all. The whole tone of the discussion was so warm and supportive that he believed there was still some hope of another job being found for him, even though there was nothing in the words to justify that hope. In the end, another manager had to explain the situation to him unambiguously, by matching the tone of voice to the message of the words themselves.

So how important are the words?

In this analysis of a rough hierarchy of the messages which make up the total package, we have not even touched on many of the other elements listed on page 251—particularly those involving the physical and social setting in which communication is taking place. But think of the meaning which you give to a message conveyed by someone standing very close to you, compared with the meaning you might give to the same message delivered from a 'safe' distance; or the significance you might unconsciously attach to the distance between a speaker's lectern and the audience. (Consider how your response to a lecturer may vary according to whether you are sitting at the front or the back of a lecture room, or the effect on your perception of a speaker's authority if the lectern is raised—as in a church pulpit or the stage of a school assembly hall.)

And what does candlelight say? Of course, it may say many things: 'We're having a blackout'; 'Isn't this romantic?'; 'Is he too poor or mean to turn on the light?'; 'My wrinkles are less obvious in soft lighting'. But a conversation which takes place by candlelight is likely to be interpreted differently from the same conversation taking place in broad daylight. Words exchanged in a noisy, crowded room may evoke a quite different response from the same words being exchanged over an intimate cup of coffee.

The more we appreciate the complexity of the message pack, the more we come to realise a curious fact: most of us pay a great deal of attention to the choice of words we are going to say, but very little attention to all the other messages which 'package' the words. Yet those 'other messages' will attract at least as much attention and evoke at least as much meaning from the listener as the messages in the words we actually say.

Because most of us grow up with the idea that words are the most important messages, we are inclined to resist the suggestion that we should pay equal attention to the way we package the words—things like body language, tone of voice, or the careful creation of a suitable setting for an important encounter. We are inclined to think of words as being the 'meat' of what we want to say, and the other messages as mere accompaniments.

But since it is likely that the words will account for less than half of the meaning which people will attach to the message pack we send them, wouldn't it be prudent to give at least as much thought to how we are going to say something as to what we are going to say?

Wouldn't it be a good idea to tape-record ourselves occasionally and play the tape back so that we can hear how our vocal messages might strike other people? Shouldn't we turn the family videotape recorder on ourselves, from time to time, so we can see the kind of visual messages we are sending when we interact with other people? Wouldn't it be a good idea—especially when we are facing a particularly significant encounter—to practise speaking out loud, so that we can hear how we *sound*, as well as carefully preparing the words we are going to say? Wouldn't speaking to the mirror—just occasionally—be a useful check on some of the messages which we might unconsciously or unintentionally be sending through facial expressions, and which might be interfering with our verbal or vocal messages?

There is not much point in complaining that people don't listen to us when, in reality, we may be sending

messages in an off-hand manner, or when the message in
how we sound may not match the intensity of the message
in what we say or when, for some other reason, our listeners may be distracted from our words by all those
'other messages' ... which leads us to the Ninth Law of
Human Communication:

> **The message in what is said will be interpreted in
> the light of how, when, where and by whom it is
> said.**

In his book *Steps to an Ecology of Mind*, Gregory Bateson
offers this dialogue between a father and his daughter,
talking about the relationship between words and other
messages:

Daughter: Daddy, why cannot people just *say* 'I am not
cross at you' and let it go at that?

Father: Ah, now we are getting to the real problem.
The point is that the messages which we
exchange in gestures are really not the same as
any translation of those gestures into words.

Daughter: I don't understand.

Father: I mean—that no amount of telling somebody in mere words that one is or is not
angry is the same as what one might tell
them by gesture or tone of voice.

Daughter: But, Daddy, you cannot have words without
some tone of voice, can you? Even if somebody uses as little tone as he can, the other
people will hear that he is holding himself
back—and that will be a sort of tone, won't
it?

Father: Yes—I suppose so. After all . . . the French-
man can say something special by *stopping*
his gestures.

Although our words are capable of being swamped by other
messages in the total message pack we send the listener, there
are nevertheless some circumstances in which the words
themselves are crucial. For many people, no other messages
can compensate for our failure to *say* 'I'm sorry' when we
are in the wrong: acting apologetically, or doing something
nice 'to make up for it', will rarely satisfy a person who desperately needs to hear those actual words, 'I'm sorry'.

'I love you' can be a similarly crucial word message,
which no other symbolic messages can quite replace.

*Margaret is feeling depressed. She has made great progress
in her relationship with Kelly, but it has all seemed like
very hard work. She has needed Bill to be more supportive—even to notice how much progress she has made—
but he has been busier than ever at work and, by the time
he comes home, he is ready to flop in front of TV.*

*Driven by her determination to succeed at her new job,
by her desire to repair all the damage in her relationship
with Kelly, by her need to stay close to Michael and to
protect him from some of the lingering tensions between
her and Kelly—to say nothing of her wish to keep the
house looking nice and to cling to some of the standards
she inherited from her own mother—Margaret is feeling
deeply fatigued and more than a little neglected.*

*Against all her instincts, she lashes out at Bill. 'Do you
have any idea what goes on in this house? Do you ever
stop to think how the dinner miraculously appears on the
table each night? Do you realise just how much sweat—*

real sweat—has gone into getting Kelly back on an even keel? Does it ever occur to you that the bedroom is a mess when you leave in the mornings and yet it is always tidy when you get home? Does that ever register?'

Feeling foolish, Margaret begins to sob, releasing resentments and frustrations which have been building up for weeks.

Bill looks at her warily, reaches out and takes her hand. She rests her head on his shoulder and gives a shuddery sigh.

'I know it has been rough for you, over Kelly. I haven't been much help. I realise that. Things have been hectic at work and, well . . . I'm sorry.'

'Bill. The worst thing is, I can't remember the last time you told me you loved me. I say it nearly every night when we're falling asleep. Do you ever hear me? You never say anything. What am I supposed to think?'

*Bill is shocked. 'Why do you think I am working so hard? Why do you think we have a joint cheque account for my pay, but your own account for your pay? Why do you think I take you out for dinner? Why do you suppose I changed that wretched registration sticker on your car? Why do you think I mow the lawn every bloody week? Do you think **I** care whether the grass is long or short? Isn't it obvious that I love you?'*

To Margaret, Bill's commitment to his job feels like something which distracts him from her, not something which expresses his love for her. It seems to her that he enjoys mowing the lawn and that it's anything but an act of love. She wants the *words*.

But generalisations are dangerous, even here. Plenty of relationships have run into difficulties because one partner or the other was ready enough to *say* 'I love you', but the other partner had come to regard those words as hollow because of the absence of supporting evidence.

'You *say* you love me. Well *show* me that you love me.'

It's the total impression—the total package—that triggers the response. In such cases, the words are not superfluous, but neither are they sufficient. Most times, the listener needs the words *and* the rest of the message pack in order to make sense of what's going on.

Even the eloquence of body language is not always enough on its own: we interpret what we see in the light of what we hear but we also interpret what we hear in the light of what we see. In *Unmasking the Face*, Ekman and Friesen quote an ancient Chinese proverb: 'Watch out for the man whose stomach doesn't move when he laughs.'

THE MESSAGE IN THE MEDIUM

A couple of teenage boys are loitering outside a video store late at night. A security guard, dressed like a policeman, strolls up to them and suggests that they might like to move on. He makes no threats, issues no orders and claims no special authority. As soon as he speaks, the boys start to move away, breaking into a trot as they reach the street corner.

Which message evoked such a willing response? Was it the words, 'Would you fellas like to move on, huh?' Was it the calm tone of voice? Was it the lateness of the hour and the ambiguous circumstances in which the boys found themselves? Was it the smell of garlic on the guard's breath? Was it the sight of an official uniform which, in the dim light, could well have been that of a police officer?

If it was the uniform that did the trick (and it can be no accident that so many security guards are dressed like police), was the uniformed guard a message, or was he the medium through which the message was sent?

A headmaster sits in his spartan office, interviewing the parents of a troublesome boy. The desk is small, undistinguished and bare, except for a blank sheet of paper and a freshly sharpened pencil. The chairs are straight-backed, and not upholstered. There is one bookcase, with a glass door. A single academic certificate hangs on the wall, with no other pictures of any kind. The headmaster's manner is formal, but not particularly threatening. The boy's offence is minor and the head shows every sign of being sympathetic. Yet the parents are feeling decidedly intimidated. Afterwards, they discuss how cold and forbidding the headmaster's office had seemed. Was the office itself a message, or was it a medium through which other messages reached the parents?

An employee has done something to upset her supervisor. Both are senior people in the organisation and they have had what seemed to be a close working relationship over a number of years. The latest incident seemed to the employee to be trivial and was certainly a matter over which she felt she had no control. She receives a handwritten note from her supervisor, expressing disappointment and some anger at what has happened. The employee is distressed by what is in the note, but she is even more distressed by the fact that her supervisor, who is located on the same floor, chose to write her a note rather than speaking to her, face to face. Was the written note a medium for what the supervisor wanted to say, or was the note itself a message?

In each case, the distinction between message and medium is hard to draw. Yes, a letter is a medium of communication, in the sense that it is a channel through which messages are sent. But, in the case of the employee and her supervisor, wasn't the sending of the letter itself a message? Yes, a security guard is like a medium of communication—again, a channel through which messages are sent—but isn't the uniformed guard himself a message as well? Yes, a room is just the setting for a meeting, but can you separate what the room itself is saying from what is being said in the room?

What about the human voice? We speak of the *medium* of speech, as opposed to the medium of writing, yet speech is laden with tone-of-voice messages (as well as word messages) and, in any case, the decision to speak to someone—rather than write—is itself a message.

When Marshall McLuhan published *Understanding Media: The Extensions of Man* in 1964, his opening chapter was titled, 'The Medium is the Message'. It was typical of McLuhan's style that he overstated the case, but at least that statement (which became McLuhan's trademark) encourages us to think about something which might otherwise escape our attention: each medium has its own characteristics which exert such a strong influence on the message pack that the medium itself acts like a message.

People have mannerisms and particular ways of expressing themselves which affect our perception of what they say, and so do all the different media of communication.

Quite apart from their contribution to the total impression received by the listener, the media also influence the way we design our messages.

Print demands that we express ourselves in one way; speech in another. Telephones and fax machines exert their own subtle influences on the way we handle our exchanges with each other.

Take a look at the words on this page. Forget, for a moment, what they are saying, and look at them as a pattern of letters and words arranged in a certain way. The arrangement is intensely logical. The words are ordered in a careful sequence: straight lines, one after the other, right down the page. There is an *inherent* rationality about the written word which is not present to anything like the same extent in the ebb and flow of a personal conversation.

In order to 'break into' the messages on this page, you must submit yourself to the rigorous discipline of print. You must go to the top left-hand corner of the page, start with the first word, then proceed from left to right along each line, returning to the beginning of the next line in order to work your way down the page, line by line. It is an unremitting process and it imposes its character on the messages which are exchanged via the written word.

This doesn't prevent us from saying highly emotional and even passionate things in print. (Nor does it prevent us from being irrational when we write.) But it does mean that, when we choose the medium of print, we play by the rules of the medium. For a start, we will have to say everything we want to say in words alone. (The embellishments of handwriting allow us some non-verbal 'extras'—as do different types and styles of print—but none of this approaches the subtlety of messages exchanged in a face-to-face conversation.)

What does it do to our thought processes when we develop the skill—over many years—of expressing thoughts in the essentially rational medium of print? Might we attach too much significance to the words themselves? Might we be inclined to think in 'straight lines' (and is that why Edward de Bono has made a handsome living out of trying to help us to think laterally?). Might we come to admire rationality to an excessive degree? Might we come to expect things (or even want things) to happen in a logical way? Once we have absorbed the logic of the medium, do we become the kind of people who say 'I'll believe it when I see it in black-and-white'? Or the kind of people who warn against 'reading between the lines' (when, in other media, 'between the lines' may well be where we find some of the most useful messages)? Does long-term exposure to the impersonal written word encourage us to believe that the meaning is *in* the word?

When someone says 'he talks like a book', it is rarely meant as a compliment. What it is usually intended to suggest is that 'he doesn't understand the difference between speaking and writing' and that, in particular, he is speaking in such a formal and pedantic way that it actually becomes difficult to follow what he is trying to say.

'She writes exactly as she speaks' makes precisely the same point in reverse. Many readers find it difficult to handle messages in the written word which have not been designed to fit the character of the written medium. Rambling, chatty or barely coherent messages may work well in the oral medium of conversation. They may even seem witty and entertaining. But, in written form, the same words may lose all their sparkle.

Transcripts of extemporaneous talks or discussions reveal this media difference starkly—sometimes to the alarm of speakers who subsequently read what they had said. 'Was I really so ungrammatical? Did I really repeat myself that much?' Yet, at the time, the audience may have been entranced.

In his introduction to *Culture of Complaint*, Robert Hughes thanked his editors for 'their encouragement, enthusiasm and hard work in turning the spoken word into the word on the page'. That 'hard work' is a good sign: if the lectures on which Hughes's book was based worked well *as lectures*, they would certainly have needed heavy revision before they would work equally well as a book.

We need to prepare our messages to suit the medium we are going to use. If a lecture or speech is prepared as if for the written word, the audience is going to be in for a hard time. Having prepared each word to 'look right' on paper, speakers are generally reluctant to break free from the script. Their audiences are then treated to the unedifying experience of observing a speaker reading out those carefully wrought words. If the speaker lacks the skill to extemporise—or even to give the appearance of some spontaneity which might establish a sense of connection with the audience—this can create a very dreary listening experience. By contrast, when a speaker addresses the audience directly—making eye contact, using the idioms of the spoken word, referring to notes only occasionally—the experience for the audience is of a different order.

'Wasn't that a boring lecture?' says a listener who might

actually have found the very same material quite riveting in print.

Differences between the character—or 'mannerisms'—of the media of print and speech are typical of the differences which exist between all communication media. Think about the effect on a conversation of being conducted by telephone, rather than face to face. The telephone is now such a routine medium for most of us that it is easy to overlook some of the ways in which it influences the quality and style of communication.

On the telephone, there is a more formal separation of the role of speaker and listener, from moment to moment, simply because all messages are lost when we speak simultaneously. For some people, the phone depersonalises the conversation; for others, it feels even more intimate than face-to-face conversation. (Teenagers' romances often move ahead more rapidly when they discover the intimacy of the telephone.) Some people find the telephone an intimidating medium and report that they 'can't wait to get off the phone'; others can talk for hours in a relaxed and confident manner.

Like all the indirect and non-personal media of communication, though, the telephone eliminates a large number of messages which could otherwise be exchanged if we were speaking to each other directly. The phone offers vocal as well as verbal messages, but the elimination of visual messages makes it easier to conceal our true feelings from each other on the phone; easier to deceive each other; easier to be 'phoney'.

Receiving a telephone call is a different experience from receiving a letter or a personal visit. As with all other media, the decision to use the telephone is itself a message.

There are times when, even with the best will in the world, Margaret finds it very hard to respond enthusiastically to Bill's rather hearty approach to communication. She knows he means well. She knows that he has been trying harder ... especially since Kelly's crisis.

It's hard for her to put her finger on it, but when Bill wants everything to be OK, he talks as if everything is OK ... as if his family should reassure him even if it means bending the truth. Sometimes he asks the kids if things are going well at school, and his tone leaves them in no doubt that everything had better be fine. Margaret still hasn't found a way of raising this with Bill, because she can see how hurtful it could be to mention it straight out. Bill would be amazed to find that, just when he thinks he's doing his communication duty, the other members of his family are rolling their eyes and wondering why he bothers to go through the motions.

When he's in that mood, the kids don't feel as if they can say what they might want to say, and they know that Bill isn't really listening. He doesn't like things to seem heavy, even when they are.

Take Bill's routine greeting when he comes home. If Margaret is home first, she can virtually guarantee that Bill will say, as he kisses her on the cheek and sweeps into the bedroom to change his clothes, 'How was your day?'

Several times, Margaret has started to answer that question as if Bill might mean what he says, but Bill's offhand response has made it clear that this is not what he wants to hear. Margaret's problems at the office are an unwelcome topic when Bill himself is looking for a bit of sympathy and support after a hard day at his own office.

But today is different. Margaret seizes the opportunity to sit at the kitchen table and write a little list of her woes, with suggestions about what Bill might do to help her out. She seals her missive in an envelope and waits for his arrival, anticipating the scene in her head.

Bill bounces through the back door, looking even more cheerful than usual. He'll be expecting the rest of us to be more cheerful than usual, as well, Margaret says to herself, already doubting the wisdom of her strategy.

'How was your day?' she hears Bill say to Michael. It isn't a question.

'Not so hot. Paul got me into trouble again, and Miss Dalton said . . . '

'Don't worry about it, Mike. Bigger fish to fry.' Bill tousles Michael's hair and Michael smiles uncertainly, trying to work out what his father means about the fish.

*Bill comes into the kitchen. 'How was **your** day?' He kisses Margaret and is about to move away when she hands him her envelope.*

'What's this?'

'My answer.'

'Your answer to what?'

'The question you asked me.' Margaret is being gentle, keeping a note of whimsy in her voice. She wants to make a serious point, but she doesn't want a row.

'I didn't ask you a question. What are you talking about?' Bill is suspicious.

'Just now. You asked me how was my day. This is my answer. Sit down and read it. Would you like a drink?'

'Sounds as if I'll need one.' Bill is deflated, but more puzzled than cross. He opens the envelope, frowns, then

laughs out loud. 'OK. You win. I get it. Sorry.'

It would be hard not to love him, Margaret says to herself.

Margaret deliberately switched media in order to send a quite different message to Bill. Realising that in the home-coming ritual, Bill has a particular mind-set, Margaret understood that messages sent through the normal medium for that situation—speech—would not attract the attention which she wanted them to receive. So she employed the written word and achieved the desired result.

Why don't people listen? They may not listen because the medium might be incompatible with the message we are trying to send, or inappropriate to the circumstances in which we are trying to communicate.

Why don't people listen? They may not listen because the message in the medium might have overpowered the message in the words. They might not listen because they were unresponsive to the medium, even though they might have responded to the same message if it had reached them via a different medium.

In many business organisations, for example, employees learn to ignore the large number of written messages which reach them, on the grounds that 'if I really need to know something, someone will tell me about it' ... meaning that someone will *say something* about it. Managers operating in that kind of corporate culture may be intensely frustrated by the feeling that people are not attending to their messages. Indeed, when they hear the complaint that 'this organisation has a communication problem', they may be enraged: 'How can people say there is a communication problem when we keep them so well-informed about what is going on?' The answer is that the messages are overshadowed by the medium: the medium of print is perceived as being inappropriate (too impersonal, perhaps; or too routine) and so the messages themselves are virtually ignored.

In a survey of Australian employees' reactions to various forms of corporate communication, T.J. and S.M. Larkin found that, overwhelmingly, employees prefer to receive information in the context of person-to-person discussion. Videos, company newspapers and other forms of communication were generally dismissed: the Larkins found fewer than 10 per cent of Australian employees expressing satisfaction with information received through company newspapers, and less than 1 per cent expressing satisfaction with information conveyed via corporate videos. In the light of their research, the Larkins' overwhelming recommendation is that managers who wish to communicate with employees are better using face-to-face encounters, rather than relying on impersonal media.

The same general conclusion emerged from a 1980 study of *The Communication Climate in Australian Organisations* (published by the Australian Institute of Management) in which the quality and extent of personal contact between employees and their managers was consistently identified as the most significant factor influencing employees' attitudes towards the quality of communication in their organisations. The report on that study noted that 'increased automation and the development of sophisticated communication systems seem to pose distinct threats to the communication climate', and employees distinguished clearly between 'information' (of which there was generally far too much) and 'communication' (of which there was generally far too little).

It's no wonder, therefore, that managers are being encouraged to put more emphasis on the concept of 'management by walking around'. It is the time and effort devoted to the establishment of personal contact which creates a climate in which communication will occur more easily and more effectively. Even the occasional use of non-personal media will be more effective when it happens in the context of a flow of personal messages through the medium of personal contact. In the absence of that personal contact, people will feel they are being 'fobbed off' with data in place of communication.

In schools, similarly, communication works best when the staff—from the principal down—place strong emphasis on establishing *personal* contact with as many students as possible and allowing the channel of personal relationships to develop as a communication medium. Newsletters, school magazines and other media of communication have their place, but their effectiveness is greatly enhanced when they are used in a climate which emphasises the *primacy* of person-to-person communication.

Face-to-face, person-to-person contact is the most natural way for human beings to communicate with each other and it is the only satisfactory basis for establishing personal relationships. Long-term success in communication usually demands that, sooner or later, we will spend time with each other.

Of course, there are many circumstances in which the use of non-personal media of communication will be highly desirable and highly effective. Where precision is required, for example, messages may need to be written down. Where privacy or secrecy is demanded, print may work better than any other medium. For messages of enduring significance, the permanence of the written word—whether stored on paper or electronically—is necessary. When we want to use a medium which will help us to organise our thoughts into a logical sequence, the act of writing them down (or typing them on a keyboard) may be an important part of the creative process. When we want to defuse an explosive situation or clarify a confused one, print will serve us well.

On the other hand, where a message has some immediacy or urgency about it, the telephone or fax are hard to beat. The phone or e-mail (that is, electronic mail sent directly from one computer to another) work very well for routine 'maintenance' contacts between people who have already established a personal relationship. Bill Gates, the chairman of Microsoft, describes his feelings about e-mail like this:

> E-mail is a unique communication vehicle for a lot of reasons. However e-mail is not a substitute for direct interaction . . .
>
> There are people who I have corresponded with on e-mail for months before actually meeting them—people at work and otherwise. If someone isn't saying something of interest it's easier to not respond to their mail than it is not to answer the phone. In fact, I give out my home phone number to almost no one but my e-mail address is known very broadly. I am the only person who reads my e-mail so no one has to worry about embarrassing themselves or going around people when they send a message. Our e-mail is completely secure . . .
>
> E-mail helps out with other types of communication. It allows you to exchange a lot of information in

advance of a meeting and make the meeting far more valuable ...

E-mail is not a good way to get mad at someone since you can't interact. You can send friendly messages very easily since those are harder to misinterpret.

Gates's reference to e-mail allowing us 'to exchange a lot of information in advance of a meeting' illustrates a crucial point about the use of non-personal media in communication: all such media are more effective when they are used in the context of an established *personal* relationship, or as an overture to personal contact. The written word (whether on paper or a screen) is particularly valuable as a preparation for a meeting or a record of a meeting, but it is no substitute for a meeting.

The media paradox

Am I communicating with you now? There's no way of knowing because, although I am writing these words in the hope of sharing meaning with you, this book is actually keeping us apart. Oh, I realise we are unlikely ever to meet face-to-face, so the book is the best we can do. But how do I know which bits you didn't understand, or which themes might have struck a more responsive chord if only we'd had the opportunity to explore them together? (Come to think of it, there's something odd about choosing a book as the medium for presenting ideas on the subject of communication.)

Whenever we use any medium apart from face-to-face conversation, we come up against another of the great paradoxes of communication: every mechanical or electronic medium—from the handwritten letter to the videophone—seems to put us in touch with each other but, at the same time, keeps us apart. As the media of communication become more efficient in a technical sense, they offer us more and more ways of staying away from each other.

When we speak on the phone, we are obviously making voice contact with each other, but we are settling for a less complete opportunity for communication than when we speak personally to each other. The phone has linked us but it has also come between us.

Notice that Bill Gates remarked that 'e-mail is not a substitute for direct interaction'.

Whatever virtues the non-direct, non-personal media of communication may have, it is obvious that the most *comprehensive* medium of communication is face-to-face personal contact. One way of dealing with the media paradox, therefore, is to resolve that we should generally try to communicate in person, except where the messages which we want to send would actually work better in another medium, or where the pressures of time and distance make face-to-face contact hard to achieve.

A good rule of thumb: make sure you have a reason to justify *not* being face-to-face with someone when you need to communicate.

THE HAZARDS OF CLEVER TECHNOLOGY

The electronic media of communication are so efficient, quick, convenient and precise in the way they transmit and receive data that some people ascribe particular 'power' to them and even assume that they may be more effective than personal communication.

It is easy to be seduced by the dazzling prospect of 'cruising the information super-highway' and, as the computer-based revolution in information technology gathers momentum, the power of the new media to impress us with their technological brilliance will only increase. So it is important to remind ourselves that, as human beings, each new development in mechanical or electronic media technology is just another device to keep us apart. Interactive television, computer networks or even video-phones may be a big improvement on earlier technologies, but the messages they deliver are still thinner than those you and I can share in a real-world, same-place conversation.

Personal relationships remain a more powerful source of influence than communication via any of the non-personal media: those who spend most money communicating via the mass media—the advertisers—know that their marketing efforts would be even more effective if only they could afford to have regular face-to-face encounters with each of their customers. (Ask Amway.)

But because the non-personal media of communication are becoming so attractive and so easy to use, they create some hazards for us in our thinking about communication.

For a start, *we are in danger of thinking of machines as being better communicators than people.*

This problem is being brought into sharp relief by the extraordinary capacity and sophistication of new communications technology, but it is by no means a new problem. In 1967, George Miller, an American academic psychologist and communication systems researcher, wrote an essay called 'The Human Link in Communication Systems', in which he said this:

It is quite clear that man is a miserable component in a communication system. He has a narrow bandwidth, a high noise level, is expensive to maintain, and sleeps eight hours out of every twenty-four. Even though we can't eliminate him completely, it is certainly a wise practice to replace him whenever we can ... Our society has already made the first steps towards eliminating human bottlenecks from communication systems, and the years ahead are sure to bring many more.

'Eliminating human bottlenecks from communication systems' indeed! Miller's approach is to assume that communication *is* the system of transferring data, so he naturally finds that machines can do that better than people can. If we allow ourselves to fall for the trap of confusing communication with data transfer (that is, the sending and receiving of messages rather than the sharing of meaning) then Miller's approach is justified: of course machines can do the data-transfer job better than we can, at least for some of the message pack.

But if we allow ourselves to equate the transfer of information with the process of communication, we will not only come to think of machines as being 'better' than people; we will also threaten our sense of what it means to be a community. Because machines are very good at doing what they do, many of us will be so satisfied by their performance that we may lose sight of the hazardous consequences for a society where machines replace more and more of the communication functions previously performed by people.

In his book *Megatrends*, John Naisbitt coins the phrase 'high-tech, high-touch' to alert us to the fact that, as human beings, we need to compensate ourselves for our increasing reliance on technology by paying extra attention to our human contacts. Customers of a bank, for example, need particularly warm and personal service whenever they make face-to-face or telephone contact with members of the bank's staff, simply because so many of their transactions are now conducted via impersonal technology (such as automatic telling machines). Similarly, a retail store which is highly automated and committed to self-service must offer its customers correspondingly high levels of personal service in those circumstances where a customer is confused, in need of guidance, or wishes to make a complaint.

It has become a widespread fear in contemporary society that we are losing our sense of belonging to a community and, as a result, our sense of mutual obligation (and therefore our moral fibre itself) is in decline. People who perceive a close connection between 'community' and 'morality' are tapping into ancient wisdom. It is that sense of belonging to each other—having connections with each other—which makes us inclined to be more responsible towards each other. Being part of a community encourages us to take the needs of other members of the community into account, and even to discharge our responsibilities to listen to each other. (After all, we tend to behave better towards someone today when we know we are likely to meet them again tomorrow.)

The dubious idea that sophisticated communications technology will somehow enhance our relationships with each other may tempt us to pay less attention to the need to preserve our role as members of local communities. Unless we are careful, our love affair with electronic communications media may accelerate the present trend towards fragmentation of the neighbourhood and isolation of the individual.

There is no need to suppress our excitement about the technological miracles which will create the mega-communities to which we will all belong in the future. But we should be thinking about developing strategies to ensure that our personal relationships are not neglected along the way. We'd better watch that our ability to communicate is not diminished by our growing dependence on technology which is—paradoxically—supposed to make us better communicators.

What will happen, for example, to our levels of patience in our relationships with each other when we have been conditioned by high-speed communications technology to expect instant answers to our questions and instant solutions to our problems? What will happen to our sensitivity to each other when we are conditioned by machines to expect that, whenever we wish to say something, the machine is always ready to receive our message? What will happen to our need for periods of reflective detachment when there is a continuous flow of attractive information coming to us via the electronic media of communication? What will happen to the art of conversation if, in response to the seductive pleasures of 'virtual reality', we find each other rather less entrancing than we find our machines?

Contemporary communications technology creates the *illusion* of personal contact, and even the illusion of belonging to a community: Marshall McLuhan spoke of an emerging 'global village'. But the global village is a fraud: most of the things which constitute village life are denied to the electronically linked 'villagers' of mega-communities. When the emphasis is on information transfer rather than relationships, the life of the village becomes meaningless: shared data is no substitute for the sense of shared identity and mutual obligation which come from shared experience.

The fact that people *say* that they feel emotionally involved in the computer networks to which they belong—or that they derive a sense of 'community' from listening to talk-back radio, or that TV soap operas are the equivalent of neighbourhood gossip—only emphasises the problem. The more efficient and attractive and non-personal media of communication become, the more we will be tempted to isolate ourselves from *real* communities and to reduce the effort we are prepared to make to establish and maintain networks of close personal relationships with each other.

The so-called 'power' of the media of communication is not in their power to influence us by what they say: it is in their power to *change the way we live* and to encourage us to confuse machine-based information transfer with human communication.

In his book, *Amusing Ourselves to Death*, Neil Postman succinctly expressed the impact of all new media of communication on our way of life:

Introduce the alphabet to a culture and you change its cognitive habits, its social relations, its notions of community, history and religion. Introduce the printing press with movable type, and you do the same. Introduce speed-of-light transmission of images and you make a cultural revolution.

Another hazard arising from increasingly sophisticated communications technology is that, as we become more dependent on machines for the sending and receiving of information, *we may dramatically increase our capacity to receive messages while, correspondingly, reducing our capacity to interpret them.*

People already speak of 'information overload': what they mean is that they are being called upon to process so much information that their capacity to sift it, evaluate it and interpret it is being diminished. As we have access to more and more information, we feel ourselves under pressure to 'know' more and more: it is already true that people feel themselves obliged to be well-informed about an extraordinary range of worldwide current affairs and to be knowledgeable about events in other countries which have no obvious relevance to their own lives or circumstances.

If we continue to increase the rate at which we receive information via ever-expanding communications technology, we may find that our moral clarity—our capacity for making judgments—is actually dulled by the sheer number of messages we are expected to attend to, and the sheer number of concerns we are expected to have. If we feel obliged to worry about events which do not touch us, or to have opinions about situations in which we are not involved, we may finally lose our capacity for deciding what is important and what is relevant. This hazard was well expressed by George Gilder in *Life after Television* when, echoing T.S. Eliot, he asked:

Where is the wisdom we have lost in knowledge?
Where is the knowledge we have lost in information?
Where is the information we have lost in data?

None of this is to suggest that we should turn our backs

on new communications technology, nor that we should be reluctant to harness the new machines to do the things which they are so brilliant at doing. But, as we come to rely on machines to do more and more bits of the communication process for us, we shall have to put even more emphasis on those bits of the process which we are going to continue to do for ourselves.

We must teach our children, in particular, to master the miraculous machines of the future, but not to be mastered by them. The media they use for communication will inevitably shape and style the way they communicate—as our media have shaped and styled us. As the media at our disposal become more diverse and more efficient, our effectiveness as *human* communicators will depend on keeping the machines in their place.

Perhaps we need to remind ourselves that 'user friendly' is a nonsensical expression, because it implies the existence of human emotions in a machine which is devoid of emotion. Machines may be easy or difficult to use, but they are neither friendly nor unfriendly. Love doesn't reside in machines, nor do courage, integrity, fidelity or morality; nor do patience, generosity or tolerance. Yet these are the very things on which our performance as communicators depends.

Why don't people listen? Unless we are watchful, another answer to that question may emerge in the future: they don't listen to each other because they have grown too accustomed to the voice of the machine.

CHAPTER 8

What about your own cage?

Margaret is battling to meet a client's deadline. She is coordinating some artwork and typesetting for an advertisement and, as well, she is preparing an agenda for the meeting at which the material will be presented. The client's office is forty minutes away and the meeting is due to start in an hour. Still no sign of the advertisement.

Margaret has the uneasy feeling that she is not getting the degree of support and cooperation given to some of the other account directors and she can't help wondering whether she is the victim of someone's deliberate campaign to clip her wings. She can guess who. Things were certainly easier before she was promoted.

Her assistant rushes in with the ad, wrongly assembled. Margaret looks at it. She is exasperated.

'That's all round the wrong way. The headline is supposed to be underneath the illustration, not on top like that.'

'But you told the layout artist to balance it differently from the last ad. We all thought you wanted the picture in the middle.'

'What I said was that the last ad was unbalanced because the picture was too small for the headline.'

'Well, you didn't actually say that. We thought you were more worried about the position than the size.'

'Look, it was perfectly clear at the last meeting. **All** the ads in this campaign follow the same formula: picture, then headline, then copy. Everyone knows that. I was complaining about the balance within that formula. It's a dreadful picture anyway. I can't imagine why anyone would have seriously proposed using it. Dreadful.'

'But you didn't criticise the picture at the meeting. We could see you weren't happy, but you only mentioned the balance.'

'Well, there wasn't much time, but I thought I'd said something about it. Anyway, there isn't time now, either . . . get them to fix it and send it over to the client a.s.a.p. I can talk about some other things until it arrives.'

'How do you mean, "fix it"? Do you want to use this picture or not? Will we just move the headline or change the picture as well?'

'Oh . . . I'll have to live with the picture, I guess. Just move the headline.'

Driving to the meeting, Margaret reflects on this mis-understanding which is becoming typical of her life at the agency. Yes, she does feel more negative about that picture than she had expressed at the meeting. She remembers, now, that the layout artist was being very aggressive and she knew he had been criticising her to other people in the agency. She was letting her personal taste cloud her professional judgment, he said. Ha! That was great, coming from him.

So she was feeling rather defensive and, yes, perhaps her own views were less clear than she thought they were. Perhaps she was confusing her feelings about the layout with her feelings about the artist. She could have created the wrong impression by trying too hard to stay calm and matter of fact. The whole mood of the meeting seemed *to be against her, so she was probably not as focused as she should have been.*

Clients are certainly easier than colleagues, she thinks, as she turns into the client's car park. She turns off the engine and glances at the clock. Five minutes early. Amazing.

Savouring a few moments of unexpected peace, Margaret finds herself dwelling on a scrap of an old song she heard on the radio this morning: '... but the words got in the way'. The agency's creative director often says the same thing: 'The words can easily get in the way of a good idea.'

Somehow, that seems to connect with a crack her father is fond of making about people who speak for a living (himself excepted, of course). He varies it according to his target: 'A politician/economist/clergyman is someone who approaches every question with an open mouth.' It is one of Cole's favourite lines.

Margaret is acutely conscious of a dangerous—and widening—gap between what is going on in her head and what comes out of her mouth. Why does she suddenly find it so hard to say what she means? Why does she keep saying things which don't sound right, even to her? It's almost as if there are two languages ... one for thinking and one for talking.

We are understandably reluctant to admit that we don't always say what we mean. We are ready to complain that other people don't listen to us, but we are not so ready to face the possibility that we may not have said what we intended to say; we may not have expressed our feelings quite as clearly as we felt them; we may not even have been sure what our true feelings were on the matter.

In such cases, we shouldn't really be surprised when we feel dissatisfied with the responses we are getting from someone else: on reflection, we may feel that we didn't give them much to go on. The message may have been such a poor, inadequate or misleading expression of our ideas that we could hardly expect anyone else to make more of it than they did. After all, no one has access to our minds except us: if we don't do a very good job of telling other people what's going on in our minds, we can hardly blame them for failing to respond in the way we would like.

When we see ourselves on videotape or hear an audio recording of something we said, it can be a sobering experience. In fact, teachers of communication skills report that one of the best ways to get someone to improve their performance is to put them through the experience of seeing and/or hearing themselves. Quite commonly, people who observe themselves in a communication encounter find that they have not expressed themselves as well or as clearly as they thought they had. Sometimes they say things like, 'Do I really sound like that?' or 'Now I know what my wife means when she says I have "that look" on my face—I do look a bit fierce when I'm concentrating, don't I?'

More to the point, people who are able to review their own performance as communicators frequently feel that what they actually said—quite apart from how they said it—was not the best possible way of expressing their thoughts: 'It was much clearer in my head than it sounded on that tape.'

Even without the benefit of an audio or video tape to let us see or hear ourselves as others do, most of us have the occasional experience of realising that we are not doing a very good job of saying what we mean: emotions may be running high and we may be losing control of ourselves, or the subject might be a difficult one to discuss, or we may be conscious of being distracted by the pressure of time or by something else going on in our minds.

At such times, we have almost certainly failed to give the listener a sufficiently clear picture of our thoughts to produce the kind of response we wanted. If we then fail to communicate, it will be through no fault on the listener's part: even the most zealous listener can't be expected to be a mind-reader when we have let ourselves down by creating a message which did not even satisfy us.

Perhaps you have had the unnerving experience of coming across a letter you had written to someone years ago and being not quite able to see the point of the letter. You must have been trying to say something; it must have seemed clear to you at the time. But now, coming to it fresh, you can't easily grasp what was going on in your head at the time.

People who develop the habit of drafting important letters or reports, then letting a few days pass before re-reading the draft, almost always end up making significant improvements to the messages they have written, simply because they are giving themselves a second chance at expressing what they are really trying to say. Putting thoughts into words is a big challenge for most of us: we shouldn't be surprised when we get it wrong, but our attempts at communication would obviously be more successful if we could get it right.

The need to listen to ourselves

Throughout this book, we have been concentrating on the need to listen with patience, with courage, with generosity and with a willingness to accept the legitimacy of others' views, even when we don't agree with them. Perhaps the time has come to remind ourselves that we owe all that to ourselves, as well. Perhaps it wouldn't be a bad idea to re-read Chapter 5 with a different perspective: what about the need for us to pay ourselves the compliment of listening to our *own* thoughts, feelings and ideas?

In precisely the same way as our willingness to listen to others will fuel their self-esteem and reassure them that they are taken seriously as persons entitled to an opinion, so we need to give the appropriate attention to what is going on in our own cages. It is true that communication with other people is a clarifying and reassuring experience for us—we learn a lot about who we are from our relationships with other people and from their reactions to us—but it shouldn't stop there. We don't learn all we need to know about ourselves— our strengths and weaknesses, our highs and lows, our desires and aspirations—from others. We also need to introspect; to explore our own cages; to take time to be alone with our thoughts and feelings so that, when the time comes to speak, we are more likely to be sure of what we want to say.

The idea of communicating with yourself raises some tricky philosophical issues which we are not going to discuss here (such as: Who is the real 'self'? How can you communicate with yourself when there is only one of you?). In practical terms, 'communicating with yourself' is just a way of referring to the process of reflection and meditation upon the self. It is a process of taking yourself seriously (not, of course, to the point of not being able to laugh at yourself), in precisely the same way as you take others seriously. When we spend time listening to ourselves and becoming more attuned to our own attitudes and values, we become clearer in our thinking and more effective as communicators. When we take ourselves more seriously, others are likely to follow suit!

People with low self-esteem—and people who are out of touch with their own feelings—generally find that other people take them less seriously than they would like. If I am not interested in me, why should anyone else be? If I don't listen to my own thoughts, why should anyone else listen to me? If I don't take the business of expressing myself seriously, why should anyone else be expected to bother responding to what I say?

'Everybody loves a lover' is a piece of folklore which captures the idea that, when we are feeling good about ourselves (such as when we are in love), others are more likely to attend to us. Similarly, the Christian injunction 'Love your neighbour as yourself' implies that charity, kindness and respect towards others depends upon having a healthy level of self-respect: we have to feel positive about ourselves to be able to take a positive interest in others.

None of this is intended to promote narcissism: it is simply to acknowledge that, unless we develop a proper interest in what is going on inside us, we are likely to become victims of the power of other people's cages. We need feedback from ourselves, as well as from others. We need to extend to ourselves the same kind of courtesy we give to others. Just as insecurity in a relationship inhibits communication between us and others, so insecurity within ourselves will inhibit our ability to stay closely in touch with our own thoughts and feelings.

There are all kinds of cliches and metaphors to cover

the process we are describing: 'Listen to your heart'; 'Always let your conscience be your guide'; 'Know yourself'; 'Be true to yourself'; 'Tune into your own wavelength'. What they are all saying is that, in order to function with personal integrity, we need to spend time in reflective detachment, observing ourselves as it were, and keeping in touch with what is going on in our own cages. What is equally true is that in order to sustain successful personal relationships, we have to present ourselves as we are.

The need to be who we really are

In listening to others, our greatest challenge is to accept what we hear. The same is true of the process of listening to ourselves: the first step towards becoming the kind of person I want to be is to understand *and accept* the truth about myself as I am.

This is not to suggest that we ought to be complacent about things we don't like about ourselves, nor that we should simply learn to live with things we would rather change. But it is crucial to our mental health that we should learn to recognise and accept how we are *now*. That is the starting point for any changes we may want to make. Indeed, one of the paradoxes of human development is that, until we learn to accept what we are, we are unlikely to change. That is the basis of organisations such as Alcoholics Anonymous: accept the truth about yourself first; then, and only then, can you begin to move on. And it is why judges and magistrates look for some sign of remorse in the prisoner when determining a sentence: until we face the truth about who we are and what we have done, there is no possibility of rehabilitation.

As long as we hide from the truth about ourselves—as long as we pretend to be something we are not—we will become locked into a role we create for ourselves. As long as we act like a certain kind of person in order to please someone else (rather than because that's who we really are), our growth towards maturity will be stunted. As long as we conceal our true self from ourselves (and therefore from others) our entire approach to communication will be flawed because the messages we send will be inaccurate representations of who we really are, and what we really think.

The person who is denying feelings of anger in herself, for example, will be sending entirely false messages to the person with whom she is angry and her relationship with that person will be based on deception—however well-meaning it might be.

Similarly, the person who denies his taste in music or food or literature in order to please someone else or to meet some social expectation, will be trapped in a way of talking which doesn't ring true for him and which may not ring true even for those he is trying to impress. While the 'pose' may ultimately become the reality, that leaves open the question of what might have happened to the 'real' tastes and preferences which were denied along the way.

Of course, people may want to *modify* their tastes and preferences, but that's another matter. Some people will actively seek to learn more about food or wine or music which they do not understand or appreciate—and they may well come to appreciate them as a result of that process—but the beginning of any maturing or development which involves the growth of the person lies in accepting who they really are, now; not pretending that they are already what they hope to become.

Suppose a person is so keen to get a job that her enthusiasm blinds her to her unsuitability for that type of work and leads her to misrepresent herself at the job interview. Suppose she is an introvert who dislikes dealing with the public, but the job she is offered requires a lot of customer contact: the aftermath will be stress and conflict as she comes to realise that this is the wrong job for her, and her employer comes to realise that she is not really as she seemed to be at the interview. Were she to continue to misrepresent herself, vague feelings of frustration and discontent may ultimately build into bitterness and aggression directed, quite unfairly, at the customers.

It is one thing to be able to see ourselves as others see us; it is quite another to be able to see ourselves as we are. It is certainly important—and useful—to know how our cage looks from outside, but, in the end, the most important reference-points for understanding ourselves will be those we discover from our exploration of the cage on the inside. It is only when we have come to terms with who we really are that we can take full responsibility for ourselves and begin the exciting journey of moving on from self-discovery to self-fulfilment.

How might we set about getting to know ourselves better so that—in communication, as in other aspects of our lives—we can be who we really are?

A good place to start is by examining any gaps which exist—as they do in most of us—between our attitudes and our behaviour. What examples can we find of differences between what we say and what we do? Are they significant? Do we wish we acted more in accordance with what we say, or do we feel quite happy with the way we behave, but wish we could be more consistent in what we say? Should we be more assertive in expressing our views, so that people can react to us as we really are?

Are there aspects of our behaviour which create tension in us because we know we are sending 'false signals' about our real attitudes or values? Are we true to our innermost feelings when we express affection, or when we withhold it? Are we frank with ourselves about our fears or uncertainties?

Are we conforming to other people's behaviour which, if we were true to ourselves, we would not copy? Are we persisting with relationships which make us feel uncomfortable and which seem to distort our sense of who we are?

Part of the process of self-examination and reflection involves examining the priorities expressed in what we do to see if our behaviour expresses the priorities we think we have. How much of our time do we devote to activities which we later come to resent, or of which we feel ashamed? Do we often find ourselves regretting that we have not been able to spend more time on other activities? Do we spend enough time with the people whom we judge to be important in our lives? Do we allow other activities to crowd out time which we would rather devote to personal relationships?

While we are exploring the truth about our priorities, we will also begin to explore what our values are: What do we really want out of life? What is our attitude to marriage or parenthood? Are we the kind of mother or father we want to be; the kind of son or daughter, brother or sister, we want to be? What is our moral framework: do we have strong views about what is right and wrong, and do we find ourselves acting in ways which contradict those views?

What do we want to be able to say of ourselves when

we reach the end of our lives? Are we doing the things which will lead us to be able to say what we want to say, at the end? Do we have a sense of obligations not fulfilled? Of creative impulses not yet expressed? Of ambitions not yet achieved? Of potential not yet realised?

Constructive self-examination involves being open to all kinds of questions about ourselves, our motives, our goals and our life's direction. This does not have to be a grand journey of exploration: it is more likely to involve a series of small investigations which take place gradually as we devote regular little periods of time to listening to ourselves. Most importantly, the process of self-exploration should be undertaken in a spirit of acceptance.

The challenge of accepting what we learn about ourselves is not an easy one. For a start, the more we explore our own cages, the more we will find some unexpected inconsistencies, ambiguities, complications and contradictions. If I think *this*, how can I think *that* as well? Doesn't one attitude contradict the other?

Such questions are bound to arise because it is part of the human condition to live with inconsistencies and contradictions. Yes, it is true that I believe in the idea of free will; and yes, it is true that I also believe we are driven to do some things which seem to be beyond our control.

Perhaps I believe that I should only eat 'healthy' food yet I also believe that 'a bit of what you fancy does you good'. Isn't that a logical contradiction? So what? Whoever said that my cage had to consist of logically compatible bars? Whoever said that my frame of reference would be entirely rational? What rule of life says that I have to be a consistent person who can't tolerate some ambiguities and complications in my world view?

Many people find that their attitudes towards religion

are of this kind: they want to have the faith to believe in a god, or in an afterlife, but there is constant tension between faith and doubt (and isn't doubt the very essence of faith?). Many people experience the same kind of tension in their most intimate loving relationships: how can a person who is loved with intense passion suddenly seem to be such an irritating person? Easy: that is the way of human beings. That is the complicated kind of people we are, and that is why our cages are such subtle and ever-shifting structures.

How can I find one of my children so attractive and one so unattractive, when I love them both equally? How can I feel that my overseas trip is the most important thing in my life, yet be dying to come home almost as soon as I have gone away? How can I feel so unsure of myself at forty when I was so sure of myself at thirty?

Questions like these simply emphasise the importance of learning to accept the irrationality of much of what we will discover about ourselves. We don't have to like everything we find in our own cages—any more than we like what we find in other people's—but we do have to accept that what we find is what is truly there. Self-acceptance is a necessary part of self-knowledge.

Why don't people listen? We have already seen that one answer is that people don't listen to us because they know we are not listening to them. Another answer may well be that people don't listen to us because they know we have not been listening to ourselves: they don't attend because they sense a lack of integrity in what we are saying, and they know—perhaps intuitively—that our messages are mere contrivances.

The joy of communication comes from the freedom to relate to another person with openness, frankness, honesty and integrity. How can we be open to others if we have not first been open to ourselves?

The need to resolve internal conflict

Although most of us are destined to live with ambiguities and contradictions built into our cages, that is a quite different thing from finding that we are in a state of active internal conflict. Most of us can live with some contradictory attitudes without experiencing any particular turmoil as a result. Internal conflict, on the other hand, can be a source of damaging tension.

Conflict between the *real* me and the me I am *pretending* to be, for example, can be very debilitating. 'Living a lie' is an uncomfortable position for most of us to sustain for very long. In the end, the internal conflict is likely to erupt in the form of conflict in our relationships with other people.

It is a safe assumption that some of our most deep-seated and enduring conflicts are not between us and others, but within ourselves. A wife is deeply disappointed in her husband's achievements, yet she still loves him and continues to believe that he could have 'made something' of himself. Her unresolved conflict between her love and her disappointment may generate tensions which permeate their whole relationship. Never revealing the conflict to him, and never allowing him the opportunity to reveal *his* ambitions and *his* priorities, she spends years needling and criticising him over trifles so that he ultimately doubts her love and comes to feel that he is nothing more than an irritation to her.

People who are experiencing the tension of inner conflict are already in an adversarial frame of mind whenever they enter into a discussion with someone else. The lack of resolution of their internal conflict disposes them to be argumentative.

A conflict between someone who holds one view and someone else who holds a different view can be resolved in a reasonably straightforward manner. But when one of the parties to the dispute is in a state of internal conflict as well, the matter is far less simple: it is hard for most of us to prevent a state of internal conflict from sparking conflict with another person.

'Are you premenstrual by any chance?' Bill is trying to be sympathetic.

*Margaret is not amused. 'Do you have the faintest idea how infuriating it is when you say that? You think I'm some kind of animal, do you? At the mercy of my hormones . . . not able to deal with my bodily functions like an adult . . . **do** you?'*

'No, of course not. But . . . '

'Don't "but" me, Bill. I'm not premenstrual, by the way. I take it you think I'm being unreasonable in some way. Right? I'll give you unreasonable: when you accuse me of being premenstrual, I feel murderous, if you want to know.'

'Sorry.'

'It's OK. I did jump on you from a great height, I'm afraid. Just tired. Sorry.'

'Can I start again? I was telling you about Christina's latest tantrum. She has decided that we're all too steeped in public service traditions and she wants us all to go off and do management courses in the private sector. Cross-pollination she calls it.'

'*Just like the birds and bees. So, she wants to pack you all off to some secluded resort. She'll tag along, too, no doubt. She's welcome. Anyway, she's probably right. You probably are all a bit inbred.*'

Margaret is sounding tense and her voice is rising again.

Bill treads warily. '*OK, don't get worked up about it. Whose side are you on, anyway?*'

'*Oh, that'll be the next thing . . . I'll be accused of standing up for the sisterhood. Is that it?*

'*Hey, Marg. Come on. We've had a row every night this week.*' *Bill puts a tentative arm around his wife's shoulders but she shrugs him off.* '*What is it?*' *he persists.*

Margaret stands there, glaring at him. '*I'd hate to be in Christina's position. All you smug men, just waiting for her to make one false move. If she stumbles, you'll cheer. I can just imagine. Anyway, I've got work to do.*'

Margaret goes to the study, turns on the computer and begins to work her way through a pile of meeting reports which have been banking up for several weeks.

Two hours later, Bill puts his head around the door to say goodnight. '*No one's waiting for you to make a false move, are they?*'

Margaret picks up her pen and tosses it at him, only half in jest. She follows him to the bedroom and suddenly throws her arms around him.

'*Hey . . . what's this?*' *Bill tries to tilt her head up to meet his gaze, but she buries her face in his chest.*

'*Of course they're waiting for me to stumble. Of course they are. It's the most chauvinistic office I've ever worked in . . . and the most competitive. There's a queue of people waiting for my job, and the Grey Eminence would give it to any of them without a second's hesitation. One false move. That's all it will take.*'

'It's not working out as well as you'd hoped.'

'Oh, the work is terrific and the clients are nice. But the back-stabbing at the agency ... your place sounds like heaven by comparison.'

'You feel really insecure? I mean, is it a real worry for you?'

'Yep. **Really** insecure. It's like a tightrope every day.'

'I didn't realise it was as bad as this.'

'I thought I was handling it. But this week ... well, you've seen how I am ... I guess I'm not handling it. But I'm glad I've admitted it. I think I am, anyway.'

'You know what I'd do?'

'Bill. Don't. Men always want to act. It's enough that you know, and you understand. You do understand, don't you?'

'I think I do. The constant stress must be awful. I'm sure it's nothing like Christina, by the way. She's pushing us all day ... no wonder people are getting a bit toey. But you're not like that. All I was going to say was, you don't **have** to stay there. You can call it quits whenever you like. Take a break. Find something else. Go part-time. You've got all those options. It's not worth sticking at it if we **all** have to suffer. No. That wasn't well put. I mean, why should you have to suffer all this, just for a job? Anyway, to be truthful, we do all suffer, and that isn't fair to you, either. You don't want Kelly and Michael thinking you're cranky with them when it's really nothing to do with them at all.'

'I'm sure I can handle it. Part-time would be better, but let's give it a bit more time.'

'OK by me. Just one condition. You're only allowed to get cranky with me when you're cranky with **me**.'

Unless we are prepared to come to terms with our own internal conflicts, we will often find ourselves behaving quite inappropriately, simply because we are being affected by the tension of unresolved conflict. When we hear ourselves saying things which we know to be uncharacteristic of us, this may be a sign of a struggle going on inside us.

A man caught in a love triangle, unable to resolve the internal conflict which he feels, may begin to act aggressively towards both his partners. He may even resort to the words of the old song, 'You made me love you', as a means of affixing blame on one or both of the women with whom he has become involved. He may find himself getting into more and more frequent arguments over more and more trivial matters simply because his own seething inner turmoil has not been confronted and dealt with.

In extreme cases, people may express their internal conflict through psychosomatic illness, letting the body develop other symptoms to express the underlying tension, so that attention can be diverted from the conflict itself.

Vandalism and other forms of delinquency sometimes turn out to be examples of internal conflict which has been channelled into antisocial behaviour rather than dealt with at its source. Anger about unemployment, the lack of a stable home life, or rejection by a sexual partner can lead people to act with aggression towards entirely unrelated targets, simply because the real nature of the underlying tension has not been explored.

How many parents have suffered outbursts of aggression from their teenage offspring where, simply because of a lack of understanding of the nature of inner conflict, unfocused aggression is directed towards the nearest available person?

All such responses, while understandable, are unhealthy because they are signs that the people concerned are out of touch with what is really going on inside them and are responding to internal conflict by projecting it onto external targets.

But the problem of internal conflict is just one example of the general problem which arises when we lose touch with who we really are, and when we fail to deal with tensions between what is going on inside our cages and what we wish was going on (or what we want other people to think is going on). Such tension is bound to erode the quality of communciation in our personal relationships. When we are not being true to ourselves, the chances of maintaining integrity in our relationships with other people are seriously diminished.

When we are disappointed, why not admit that to ourselves? When we are angry, why not acknowledge the anger, investigate where it came from and consider how it might be dealt with? When we are confused or uncertain, why not accept that in ourselves and not push ourselves into a position where we will appear more confident than we actually feel?

Deliberate distortions or misrepresentations of our attitudes are damaging enough to our performance as communicators, but distortions and misrepresentations which occur because we are out of touch with our own internal states are even more damaging.

A cautionary note: although it is desirable to keep closely in touch with our own evolving sense of who we are—and, in particular, to be alert to inner conflicts which may destabilise us—this does not mean that we have to *share* all of our innermost thoughts with anyone else. Confronting and dealing with our own anger or jealousy or disappointment is necessary for our mental health, but that does not mean that we always have to express those feelings to anyone else—even including the people who we might judge to have been the cause of our emotional difficulties. Being angry with someone does not always mean that we should display that anger: it is essential to accept and deal with the anger in ourselves and, sometimes, it is appropriate to reveal to that person just how angry we feel. But sometimes it is not appropriate: sometimes, our sensitivity to the feelings of others, or our respect for them as persons, may mean that it would be better (for us as well as for them) to deal with the anger in private (or even by whacking a golf ball).

Some people find that letters written in anger are better left unposted. The writing of the letter can be a helpful way of accepting, focusing and dealing with the anger but, in the end, it may seem to be unnecessary to do more than deal with it internally: sending it to its 'target' may do more harm than good. But the *most* damaging thing would be not to be in touch with that anger—not to deal with it—and have it erupt in inappropriate ways which might affect our relationship with someone else altogether.

The need to listen to ourselves, to explore our own cages, and to speak and act as if we are who we really are is so fundamental to our ability to communicate that it is expressed in the Tenth Law of Human Communication:

Lack of self-knowledge and an unwillingness to resolve our own internal conflicts make it harder for us to communicate with other people.

The implication of that, of course, is that if we want to become better communicators—and if we want people to listen to us—we must get to know ourselves better. We must take time to introspect. We must be prepared to entertain our own ideas, as well as other people's. Sometimes, it might even be helpful to talk to ourselves.

Learning to say what we mean

Even when we are in touch with our own thoughts and feelings, there remains the problem of trying to express what we want to say in a message which accurately captures what is going on in our minds.

This is actually a problem of translation: when we try to 'say what we mean' we are moving from the language of *meanings* to the language of *messages*. We are moving from the language of thoughts and feelings (which is an internal, high-speed, invisible/inaudible and complex language) to the language of symbols (which is an external, low-speed, visible/audible and relatively simple language).

So 'saying what you mean' is not as simple as it sounds. The translation from the language of thoughts and feelings to the language of symbols (such as words) is at least as complicated as the translation from one cultural language (such as French) into another (such as English). There are many words which work satisfactorily in the language of one culture because they stand for something which has 'meaning' in the culture of that language, but which might not be transferable to the language of another culture. Slang and other idiomatic expressions are sometimes locked in one language to the extent that the task of translation may defeat us utterly.

(How do you say 'stirring the possum' in French? Was the Argentinian writer Jorge Luis Borges right when he said that the subtlety of meaning which lies behind the word 'machismo' simply cannot be expressed in one English word because there is no one, equivalent notion in English culture?)

The difficulty which many people experience in saying what they mean is rather like that. We can experience complex thoughts, intense emotions and vivid images in the conceptual language of the mind, yet find it almost impossible to translate those thoughts and feelings into symbols which accurately represent them. 'I know what I want to say, but I'm having trouble putting it into words' is the typical statement of someone who is making heavy weather of the translation process.

When people sit down to write a letter of condolence, for example, they often find themselves disappointed at the gap which exists between the intensity of the emotions they are trying to convey and the relative paucity of the message on the page. Some thoughts are so fleeting or ephemeral that we scarcely dare to make the attempt to capture them in symbolic form, because we know—even before we start—that we are going to fail.

For people who think in visual rather than verbal terms, the task of translating thoughts into words is even harder. Some people report that they can 'imagine' smells—like a bunch of violets—but they find it almost impossible to express in words what is going on in their minds. The response to music may be keenly felt, but very difficult to verbalise.

This brings us back to the problem we originally explored in Chapter 2: because words don't actually contain meaning, we can only use them to give each other hints about the meanings which are in our minds. Because words are not much more than 'linguistic hints'—rough-and-ready translations from the language of thoughts and feelings—we should perhaps be more patient with each other's attempts to say what we mean. Meanings may be vividly clear to us in the confines of our own minds, but the tragedy of human communication is that, unless we are creative artists who have the ability to move easily from the concepts to the symbols, we are always going to be frustrated by the gap between thought and language.

In Chapter 5, we touched on the differences between the rate of speech and the rate of thinking. This poses another problem for the process of translating from conceptual to symbolic language: considering that, even when we think in terms of words, we are probably thinking about four or five times faster than we can speak, it is no wonder that we often experience something which feels like a bottleneck when we try to say what we mean.

Unfortunately, there is no magic formula that would allow us to unlock the secrets of conceptual language so that other people can have direct access to what is going on in our minds. We are stuck with the problem of having to translate into symbolic language whenever we want to communicate. But there are some disciplines which might help us to get a little closer to the ideal of saying what we mean.

For a start, we need to acknowledge that words *are* a translation of thoughts, and so we need to take more time and more care with the translation process. We need to remind ourselves that the first rush of words may not capture what we have been trying to say. When we write, we would do well to work with drafts which can be rewritten. Even when we are going to speak, we would do well to pause briefly to consider whether what we are intending to say will actually express the thought which is in our minds. It is often better and safer to express our ideas in a number of different ways in the hope that one version of the message will come closest to expressing our thoughts (and one version of the message might have more chance than others of striking a responsive chord in our audience). Even in those few seconds when we are dialling a phone number, we can mentally rehearse what we plan to say in order to test whether it will actually express what we mean to say.

We must also remember that the listener has to rely on the message pack and has no other way of knowing what we are thinking. We have to create messages in the full knowledge that they will be cast adrift from the thought which brought them into being. Those who listen to what we say cannot know what meanings lie behind our messages: we have to imagine how those messages will sound to someone who does not know the conceptual language from which they sprang.

All of this should make us hungry both for playback and for feedback. It is only when people begin to tell us what *they* heard us say, and how they responded to what they heard, that we can begin to have confidence in the competence of our own translations.

Next time you feel like saying to someone, 'Why don't you say what you mean!', remember that the truthful response may well be, 'I'm trying to, but it isn't easy'. When serious matters are at stake, it rarely is.

THE OTHER USES OF LANGUAGE

The urge to communicate is an almost universal urge, but it is often quite different from the urge to speak.

It is true that, when we communicate with someone, we need to translate our thoughts into symbolic language (speaking, writing, body language), but it is certainly not true that, whenever we employ any of these forms of language, we necessarily want to communicate. In fact, there are many occasions when we use language for reasons which have almost nothing to do with communication.

Language as excluder

Our experience tells us that people sometimes use language as a code to *prevent* the sharing of meaning. The very same language which helps us to reveal our meaning to some people may simultaneously conceal it from others ... and it often seems to be done deliberately.

This is presumably why jargon evolves in the language of professional groups or other technical specialists. The very words which are supposed to facilitate communication between members of the group appear to be designed to exclude outsiders from understanding what is being said: the language works like a barrier to entry of the group.

The same phenomenon appears in the school playground where children often develop codes and secret words which they will gleefully use in their communication with each other in the full knowledge of the fact that they are concealing their meaning from those not 'in the know'. In the world of espionage and secret intelligence services, the use of codes is a fundamental requirement of the communication process. Codes allow secret—that is, exclusive—communication. But codes are simply a special case of language systems as a whole: all languages are 'codes'.

On a larger scale, the motivation to exclude others from our culture is presumably what produces regional dialects and, indeed, entire languages which serve as a repository of one culture while simultaneously concealing the mysteries of that culture from outsiders.

Noam Chomsky has theorised that there is a 'deep structure' which is common to virtually all languages and which is acquired innately. He suggests that it is this genetic acquisition of 'deep structure' that allows infants to master the complexities of a language like English at such an early age and with such remarkable facility.

(This is a controversial point, of course. It might be argued, on the contrary, that children are taught language more intensively and extensively than they are taught anything else. With parents and other people speaking incessantly around them for twelve months or more before they begin to master the language, a case could be mounted for suggesting that humans are actually quite slow to acquire speech.)

But if we accept Chomsky's hypothesis about 'deep structure', the really fascinating thing about the evolution of language is still the fact that, all over the world, we develop *different* languages which are impenetrable to people who live outside each linguistic community. French is a wonderful language for French people to use when they are communicating with each other, but it is equally effective at excluding the Germans and the English from an appreciation of what is being said. (The French even have an academy to keep their language—

their cultural code—pure and distinct from other languages.)

In his monumental book *After Babel,* George Steiner explores the puzzle of why there are thousands of mutually incomprehensible tongues spoken on this small planet. Steiner believes that the problem of exclusive language arises out of the deep instinct for privacy and territory. People have, in their own language, an immense body of shared secrecy. Steiner therefore argues that a major purpose of language is not to tell things but to hide them from outsiders. To quote Steiner: 'Languages conceal and internalise more, perhaps, than they convey outwardly.'

He makes the point that, in a society of rigid class distinctions, accents and dialects serve both as a code for mutual recognition ('accent is worn like a coat of arms') and an instrument of exclusion. The subtle inflection in the pronunciation of a particular word can fix a socio-cultural gulf between speaker and listener.

Steiner claims that it is the dual functions of language—to communicate and to exclude—that makes the task of translation so difficult, because many of the subtleties of meaning expressed in particular languages, dialects, codes, accents and argot are *deliberately* obscure and may therefore be hidden from the person who is trying to translate them into another language. So language itself is rather like a 'cultural cage'.

The slang of teenagers is a commonplace example of Steiner's theory. While groups of teenagers evolve their own speech idioms and expressions apparently to communicate more effectively with each other, they are simultaneously ensuring that others (such as teenagers from other gangs, adults, and especially parents) cannot readily grasp what is being said within their community of shared meanings.

Learning a language is like learning a culture. Learning the words is the easy and, in some ways, least significant part of the process. Translation is not primarily about words at all; it is primarily about culture.

Here's what Jorge Luis Borges has to say about the cultural difficulties of translation: 'We do not consider English and Spanish as compounded of sets of easily interchangeable synonyms; they are two quite different ways of looking at the world, each with a nature of its own.'

Even if Chomsky were right and we had an innate sense of the deep structure of language, we have certainly demonstrated that we are strongly resistant to any genetic disposition towards homogeneous language. Our ancient and primitive need for separate cultural identity smothers our common linguistic structure with unique vocabularies, and we are left with linguistic chasms which divide our world more effectively than any geographical, political or economic factors. The concept of a universal language (like Esperanto) hasn't a hope: it runs counter to our deep need for cultural privacy.

The truth is that language keeps us apart from each other at least as efficiently as it keeps us together. Within a culture, within a town, within an office or even within a family, the very language that helps us to communicate also helps us to avoid communication.

So, one of the many reasons why people don't listen to us is that they may simply be unable to penetrate the language we have used. They may not be able to translate what we have said (in our teenage slang, our computer-speak, our legalese or our religious jargon) because we have, consciously or unconsciously, spoken in a language which reflects our culture, our group or our training—but not theirs.

There is much more to language than communication (in the same way as there is much more to communication than language). We should not assume that language exists purely to help us to communicate: it is equally valuable as a means of ensuring that we have concealed our meaning from those who do not inhabit the same 'tribal ground' as we do.

Why don't people listen? There are many occasions when they don't listen because—whether we intended to or not—we have simply made it too hard for them by using langauge in an uncommunicative way.

It is easy to see how other people's cages protect them from our messages and filter what we say. Perhaps we should be more alert to the filtering and distorting effect of our own cages on the messages we *send*: messages have to pass through the bars of our own cages before they even reach the cages of those who listen.

Language as self-expression

Because we rely so heavily on the use of language in communication, we sometimes forget that another important function of language is to allow us to express how we feel, or what we are thinking ... even when there is no possibility of sharing our meaning with someone else (or no need to do so). In other words, language sometimes allows us to 'let off steam', or 'get something off our chest', in circumstances where there is no motivation whatsoever to *share* such feelings.

When we use language to communicate, our message

is an offering to the other person: when we use language as a form of self-expression, no offering is involved. There are times when speaking or writing is the equivalent of baking a cake which we intend only to eat ourselves.

Most of us are constantly torn between our need for privacy and our need for community: while we are social creatures who need the stimulation, support and comfort of relationships with other people, we are also individuals who need solitude and opportunities for quiet reflection, self-examination and pure self-indulgence. The same language serves both our need for privacy and our need for community, but it functions very differently according to which need it is serving.

When our most urgent need is to clarify our own thoughts or to get in touch with our own feelings, language will do that for us. We may choose to use it in the silent discourses of the mind, or by putting our thoughts on paper. We may even choose to speak out loud to another person, but without really intending to communicate—to share meaning—with that other person. In both cases, language helps us to express what we are feeling and, in the process, to come to understand our feelings better.

When we use language as a form of self-expression, speaking or writing becomes a creative act just like the creative act of an artist painting a picture, a sculptor shaping a piece of marble or a composer writing a symphony. For most creative artists, the purpose of the exercise is to express some inner experience and, in the process, to clarify or capture the experience. Of course, the results of creative acts sometimes become works of art which are appreciated by many other people (some of whom will read 'meaning' into them), but it is rarely the primary purpose of creative artists to communicate. They are less in the business of sharing than of self-expression.

In precisely the same way, most of us—lacking the creative skills of an artist or a poet or a composer—will often feel the need to express ourselves without necessarily wanting to communicate with other people. In such cases, language is the medium we use for self-expression, but it is important to recognise that our use of language in such cases does not commit us to the process of communication—even when we may happen to be expressing ourselves to another person.

In fact, it is sometimes hurtful to involve another person in our attempts to clarify our own feelings—especially when they concern that other person.

For example, a terminally ill patient is seeking comfort from her family and friends. Most of all, she wants people to accept the imminence of her death; to be open about it; to face it with her. Yet, well-meaning visitors keep saying things like this:

'You'll be OK.'

'You'll pull through ... you'll soon be back to your old self again.'

'Try not to think about it.'

The effect of such messages is to make the patient feel stifled, isolated and excluded. In trying to express sympathy, the visitors manage only to reveal their own reluctance to come to terms with the reality of her situation.

There is a simple test for deciding whether, when we want to say something, we are responding to the urge to communicate or the urge merely to express ourselves. If we know that we will feel better for having said what we are going to say (regardless of the reactions of another person), then we are using language as self-expression. But if we know that our primary concern is with the response of the other person (because we actually want to share thoughts or feelings with that person), then we are in the business of communication.

Both uses of language are equally valid, but we can get ourselves into a mess if we don't understand the difference between them.

The picture is further confused, of course, because the support of other people can be quite helpful even when we are using language as a means of self-expression, rather than communication. To have someone else listen to us in a supportive way can add a therapeutic and clarifying dimension to our use of language as a means of self-expression—but that is still a very different thing from using language as a means of communication. The sympathetic attention of another person under those conditions has more in common with the audience attending to a symphony, or a person gazing at a painting, than with an active participant in a communication encounter.

When we are in self-expression mode, it can be irritating to have someone trying too hard to grasp what we are saying, or asking us to express ourselves more clearly. Like creative artists who are oblivious to the reactions of other people to their work, our use of language as self-expression is a private, self-directed activity. It is nice when other people agree to help us to achieve our purpose but, in the end, our purpose has nothing to do with them. Sometimes, we prefer *inactive* listeners.

Personal relationships are made easier when we can recognise in each other the signs that language is being used purely for self-expression, and that communication is not on the agenda. Letting other people express their own thoughts or feelings freely is a generous and supportive thing to do. Where they are simply trying to clarify or relieve feelings within themselves, it is actually less generous to participate fully in the encounter and to treat it as if it is communication.

A person who is consumed by fury, for example, may be just as happy to express it in a monologue (or even a soliloquy) as to have to discuss it with someone else. We have already remarked that many people have regretted posting letters written in anger when they would have been better advised to confine themselves to self-expression. Similarly, people who are hurt or confused may need to 'talk it out' without needing much in the way of feedback.

Margaret has resigned from her job at the advertising agency. She is perplexed by the range of contradictory emotions she is experiencing: relief, anger, disappointment, pride, resentment, gratitude to Bill . . . and a surprising ache of sadness. She is embarrassed by the intensity of her own feelings and she is working hard at keeping them under control during her last couple of weeks at the office.

Encouraged by her friend Kate, she has already put out a feeler for a senior job in another agency and received an enthusiastic offer, but she is aware of something like grief which she has to get out of her system before she can throw herself wholeheartedly into the idea of a fresh start.

This job meant so much to her. The promotion was such a thrill. The challenge was so big and so . . . welcome. And she handled it well. She knew that. The clients were appreciative. Even the Grey Eminence acknowledged that. But the pressure . . . the sense of open disloyalty among her colleagues . . . knowing that they wanted her to fail. Partly being a woman. No doubt about it. But partly . . . well, just the way they are. The worst thing was feeling that it could be contagious . . . that the competition inside the agency could become more important than dealing with clients. It was already starting to happen . . . she could feel it.

Two nights after she has submitted her resignation to a predictably impassive Grey Eminence, Margaret suggests that she and Bill go out for supper. They drive to the restaurant in silence and then, after a while, Margaret begins to talk. Bill has never heard her like this before: savage; sharp; cruel in her judgments about the agency and its morality. She is furious with the key player in the game of office politics. There's a hint of some sexual tension as well—and not pleasant, by the sound of it: the constant pressure of the most childishly chauvinistic remarks which always end up making her feel weak or vulnerable because they always make her angry . . . all the stuff she's been so determined to ignore. Even the Grey Eminence daring to suggest that she might wear 'something special' to a meeting with a new client, while the creative team turn up in T-shirts and dirty joggers.

Mostly, she is staring into her coffee but occasionally she looks at Bill, not for a reaction but for a focus.

At first, he asks questions. Interested. Sympathetic. Ready to share her disappointment or her anger. But she doesn't want to clarify. She just wants to talk.

Bill realises that he is not really part of this moment. He is there, but not there; needed, but not involved. As he senses his role more clearly, he drifts a little, watching her but not fully concentrating. When she pauses, he remains silent. He nods. He touches her hand.

It takes a full hour. She has said it all and is spent. She looks at him in a different way, engaging him.

'Does that all make sense?' she asks, but doesn't need to know. He nods anyway.

'You're a nice man. You know that? Let's go home . . . '

CHAPTER 9

How to Encourage Good Listening

People listen to us when
they know that we will always listen
to them;
        and when they know that what we say is a
        response to our understanding of them.

They listen to us when
they sense that we are in touch with
our own feelings;
        and when our message has the integrity
        of coming from someone who believes it
        themselves.

They listen to us when
they can see the relevance of what we are
saying to their own situation,
their own values, their own aspirations;
        and when they feel comfortable
        about making a response.

They listen to us when
all the messages in what we say and
how we say it are consistent with
each other;

and when the message comes to them
through the channel of an established
personal relationship.

They listen to us when
it is clear that we have taken their
feelings into account;
>   and when we don't ask for too much
>   agreement at once.

They listen to us when
they have learned to trust us;
>   and when they have the security of
>   knowing that each encounter is a
>   stepping stone to the next.

But people *don't* listen to us because
they know we don't listen to them;
>   or because they sense that we don't
>   even listen to ourselves.

They *don't* listen to us because what
we are saying doesn't appear to have
any relevance to their own situation;
>   or because we used a 'trigger word'
>   which set off a chain reaction of
>   private thoughts.

They *don't* listen to us because what
we are saying represents an attack
on their cage;
>   or because they were expecting us to say

something quite different, and so that's
what they thought we said.

They *don't* listen to us because we
talked about us, not them;
> or because they couldn't see what they
> could do about what we were saying.

They *don't* listen to us because we just
said what we thought, and left it at that;
> or because what we said was overwhelmed
> by the message in how we said it.

They *don't* listen to us because they
haven't learned to trust us;
> or because they feel intimidated or
> insecure when they are with us.

A man once gave a lecture about music, in which he
concentrated on the idea that all musical instruments
make distinctive sounds and that each demands of its
player a particular style and a particular skill.

As the lecture drew to a close, he opened a trunk on
the platform beside him, and announced that he was
going to demonstrate the different sounds of the different
instruments. 'I will begin with the rich and powerful
sound of the trumpet,' he announced.

With that, he reached into the trunk, withdrew a
violin, pressed it to his lips and blew. Nothing happened.
The audience stirred uneasily.

'I seem not to have brought my trumpet, but I do want
you to hear the sound of the trumpet, so I'll just try a
little harder to get the sound I want out of this violin.'

He blew again, and again. He became red-faced with his blowing. Still nothing happened.

The audience laughed. 'You are crazy,' they shouted.

(But was he any more crazy than the person who thinks you can get a response from someone else just because you want one?)

The Ten Laws
of Human
Communication

1 It's not what our message does to the listener, but what the listener does with our message, that determines our success as communicators.

Chapter 1, page 25

2 Listeners generally interpret messages in ways which make them feel comfortable and secure.

Chapter 3, page 88

3 When people's attitudes are attacked head-on, they are likely to defend those attitudes and, in the process, to reinforce them.

Chapter 4, page 103

4 People pay most attention to messages which are relevant to their own circumstances and point of view.

Chapter 4, page 114

5 People who feel insecure in a relationship are unlikely to be good listeners.

Chapter 4, page 127

6 People are more likely to listen to us if we also listen to them.

Chapter 5, page 157

7 People are more likely to change in response to a combination of new experience and communication than in response to communication alone.

Chapter 6, page 226

8 People are more likely to support a change which affects them if they are consulted before the change is made.

Chapter 6, page 242

9 The message in what is said will be interpreted in the light of how, when, where and by whom it is said.

Chapter 7, page 261

10 Lack of self-knowledge and an unwillingness to resolve our own internal conflicts make it harder for us to communicate with other people.

Chapter 8, page 309

Bibliography

Adams, G.R. (1977) 'Physical attractiveness research', *Human Development*, 20, pp. 217–39

Allen, J.P.B. and Paul Van Buren (eds.) (1971) *Chomsky: Selected Readings*, London: Oxford University Press

Argyle, Michael (1967) *The Psychology of Interpersonal Behaviour*, Harmondsworth: Penguin

Barrett, William (1961) *Irrational Man*, London: Heinemann

Bateson, Gregory (1987) *Steps to an Ecology of Mind*, Northvale: Jason Aronson

Benn, Stanley I. (1967) 'Freedom and Persuasion', *The Australian Journal of Philosophy*, Vol. 45, No. 3

Berlo, David K. (1960) *The Process of Communication*, New York: Holt, Reinhart and Winston

Berne, Eric (1967) *Games People Play*, Harmondsworth: Penguin

Bernhardt, Karl S. (1970) *Being a Parent*, Toronto: University of Toronto Press

Bolton, Robert (1979) *People Skills*, Englewood Cliffs: Prentice-Hall

Borges, Jorge Luis (1971) *The Aleph and Other Stories*, London: Jonathan Cape

Carnevale, Peter and Dean Pruitt (1992) 'Negotiation

and Mediation', *Annual Review of Psychology* 43, pp. 531–82

Carpenter, Edmund (1976) *Oh, What a Blow That Phantom Gave Me!*, St Albans: Paladin

Chalmers, A.F. (1982) *What is this thing called science?*, St Lucia: University of Queensland Press

Cherry, Colin (1966) *On Human Communication*, Cambridge, Mass: M I T Press

Cialdini, Robert B. (1985) *Influence: Science and Practice*, Glenview: Scott, Foresman

Cronkhite, Gary (1969) *Persuasion: Speech and Behavioural Change*, Indianapolis: Bobbs-Merill

Dawkins, Richard (1982) *The Extended Phenotype*, Oxford: Oxford University Press

DeVito, Joseph A. (1974) *Communication: Concepts and Processes*, New Jersey: Prentice-Hall

Donovan, R.J. (1991) 'Public Health Advertising', *Health Promotion Journal of Australia*, Vol. 1, No. 1, pp. 40–5

Dowrick, Stephanie (1991) *Intimacy and Solitude*, Melbourne: Heinemann

Duck, Steve (1981) *Human Relationships*, London: SAGE Publications

Dunphy, Dexter (1981) *Organisational Change by Choice*, Sydney: McGraw-Hill

Eakins, B.W. and R.G. Eakins (1978) *Sex Differences in Human Communication*, Boston: Houghton, Mifflin Co

Efran, M.G. and E.W.J. Patterson (1976) The Politics of Appearance, Unpublished manuscript, University of Toronto. Quoted in Robert B. Cialdini, *Op cit.*

Ehrenberg, Andrew (1974) 'Repetitive Advertising and

the Consumer', *Journal of Advertising Research*, Vol. 14, No. 2, pp. 25–34

Ekman, Paul and Wallace Friesen (1975) *Unmasking the Face: A guide to Recognizing Emotions from Facial Clues*, Englewood Cliffs: Prentice-Hall

Eysenck, Hans and Michael (1981) *Mindwatching*, London: Michael Joseph

Fabun, Don (1970) *Communication: The Transfer of Meaning*, Glencoe: Free Press

Festinger, Leon (1957) *A Theory of Cognitive Dissonance*, Stanford: Stanford University Press

—— (1964) 'Behavioural Support for Opinion Change', *Public Opinion Quarterly*, Vol. 28, No. 3, pp. 404–17

Fishbein, Martin (1971) 'Attitude and the Prediction of Behaviour', in Kerry Thomas (ed.), *Attitudes and Behaviour*, Harmondsworth: Penguin

Fisher, Roger and William Ury (1981) *Getting to Yes: Negotiating agreements without giving in*, London: Hutchinson

Gerbner, George (1972) 'Communication and Social Environment', in *Communication: A Scientifiic American Book*, San Francisco: W. H. Freeman

—— (ed) (1983) 'Ferment in the Field: Communication scholars address critical issues and research tasks of the discipline', *Journal of Communication*, Vol. 33, No. 3

Gilder, George (1992) *Life After Television*, New York: W. W. Norton

Ginott, Haim G. (1970) *Between Parent and Child*, London: Pan

Grahame, Kenneth (1908) *The Wind in the Willows*, London: Methuen, republished by Methuen Children's Books (1980)

Gumpert, Gary and Robert Cathcart (1979) *Inter/Media*, New York: Oxford University Press

Haskins, Jack B. (1964) 'Factual Recall as a Measure of Advertising Effectiveness', *Journal of Advertising Research*, Vol. 4, No. 1, pp. 2–8

Hayes, Lyn (1993) 'Gender and Communication: Power as an influencing factor in gender and communication', *Australian Communication Review*, Vol. 14, No. 4, pp. 47–61

Hillmer, Frederick G. (1989) *New Games, New Rules*, Sydney: Angus & Robertson

Horne, Donald (1964) *The Lucky Country: Australia in the Sixties*, Ringwood: Penguin

Hovland, Carl I. and Irving L. Janis (eds.) (1959) *Personality and Persuasability*. New Haven: Yale University Press

Hughes, Robert (1983) *Culture of Complaint*, New York: Oxford University Press

Ignatieff, Michael (1984) *The Needs of Strangers*, London: The Hogarth Press

Johnson, David W. (1981) *Reaching Out*, Englewood Cliffs: Prentice-Hall

Joyce, Timothy (1980) 'What do we know about how advertising works?' in S. Broadbent (ed.), *Market Researchers Look at Advertising*, Amsterdam: European Society for Opinion and Marketing Research

Kenny, Peter (1980) 'The fourth monkey: "swap no meanings"' (Review of J. Williamson's *Decoding Advertisements*), *Media Information Australia*, 17

Kingma, Daphne Rose (1993) *The Men We Never Knew*, Sydney: Millennium

Klapper, Joseph T. (1960) *The Effects of Mass Communication*, New York: Free Press

Knickerbocker, H.R. (1939) 'Diagnosing the Dictators', *Hearst's International-Cosmopolitan*, reprinted in William McGuire and R. .F C. Hull (eds.), (1980) *C. G. Jung Speaking: Interview and Encounters*, London: Picador

Krippendorff, Klaus (1989) 'The Ethics of Constructing Communication', in Brenda Dervin et al (eds.), *Rethinking Communication Vol 1: Paradigm Issues*, Newbury Park: SAGE Publications

Larkin, T.J. & S.M. (1994) *Communicating Change*, New York: McGraw-Hill

Larson, Charles U. (1973) *Persuasion: Reception and Responsibility*, Belmont: Wadsworth

Leonard, Elmore (1993) *Pronto*, London: Viking

Lin, Nan (1973) *The Study of Human Communication*, New York: Bobbs-Merrill

Littlefield, Lyn et al (1993) 'A model for resolving conflict: Some theoretical, empirical and practical implications', *Australian Psychologist*, Vol. 28, No. 2, pp. 80–5

Mackay, Hugh (1980) *The Communication Climate in Australian Organisations*, Sydney: Australian Institute of Management

—— (1985) The Illusion of the Global Village, *Transactions of the Menzies Foundation*, 9, pp. 141–4

—— (1991) The Ethics of the Reinforcement Effect, Unpublished manuscript, Macquarie University

—— (1993) *Reinventing Australia*, Sydney: Angus & Robertson

McLuhan, Marshall (1962) *The Gutenberg Galaxy*, London: Routledge and Kegan Paul

—— (1964) *Understanding Media: The Extensions of Man*, London: Routledge and Kegan Paul

Mehrabian, Albert (1968) 'Communication Without Words', *Psychology Today*, Reprinted in Joseph A. DeVito (ed.), *Op cit*

Miller, George (1970) *The Psychology of Communication*, Harmondsworth: Penguin

Miller, Jonathan (1971) *McLuhan*, London: Fontana

Naisbitt, John (1984) *Megatrends*, London: Futura

Nicholls, Ralph G. (1961) 'Do We Know How to Listen?' *The Speech Teacher*, 10, pp. 118–24, Reprinted in Joseph A. DeVito (ed.) *Op cit*

Nierenberg, G.I. and H.H. Calero (1973) *Meta-Talk*, New York: Simon & Schuster

Nuttin, J.M. (1974) *The Illusion of Attitude Change*, London: Academic Press

O'Keefe, Daniel J. (1990) *Persuasion: Theory and Research*, Newbury Park: SAGE Publications

Olsen, James M. and Mark P. Zanna (1993) 'Attitudes and Attitude Change', *Annual Review of Psychology* 44, pp. 117–54

Pace, R.W. and R.R. Boren (1973) *The Human Transaction*, Glenview: Scott, Foresman

Pease, Alan (1985) *Body Language*, Sydney: Pease Training Corporation

Penman, Robyn (1993) 'Conversation is the common theme: Understanding talk and text', *Australian Journal of Communication*, Vol. 20 (3), pp. 30–43

Postman, Neil (1986) *Amusing Ourselves to Death*, London: Heinemann

Rogers, Carl R. (1967) *On Becoming a Person*, London: Constable

—— (1977) *On Personal Power*, New York: Delacorte Press

Rogers, Carl R. and F.J. Roethlisberger (1952) 'Barriers and Gateways to Communication', *Harvard Business Review*, reprinted in November–December 1991

Sargant, William (1959) *Battle for the Mind*, London: Pan

Schein, E. (1956) 'The Chinese indoctrination program for prisoners of war: A study of attempted "brainwashing"', *Psychiatry*, 19, pp. 149–72

Schramm, Wilbur (ed.) (1963) *The Science of Human Communication*, New York: Basic Books

Schramm, Wilbur et al. (1961) *Television in the Lives of Our Children*, London: Oxford University Press

Schwartz, Tony (1973) *The Responsive Chord*, New York: Anchor Press/Doubleday

Seabrook, John (1994) 'The E-Mail from Bill [Gates]', *New Yorker*, 10 January

Searle, John R. (1969) *Speech Acts*, London: Cambridge University Press

Steiner, George (1975) *After Babel*, New York: Oxford University Press

Stewart, J. E. (1980) 'Defendant's attractiveness as a factor in the outcome of trials', *Journal of Applied Social Psychology*, 10, pp. 348–61

Weaver, Carl H. (1972) *Human Listening*, New York: Bobbs-Merrill

Wertheim, Eleanor et al. (1992) *I win, you win: How to have fewer conflicts, better solutions, and more satisfying relationships*, Melbourne: Penguin

Whittaker, James O. (1964) 'Cognitive dissonance and the effectiveness of persuasive communications', *Public Opinion Quarterly*, Vol. 28, No. 4

Williamson, Judith (1978) *Decoding Advertisements*, London: Marion Boyars

Wilson, James Q. (1993) *The Moral Sense*, New York: Free Press

Winn, Marie (1978) *The Plug-in Drug*, New York: Viking/Bantam

Winter, Gibson (1958) *Love and Conflict: New Patterns in Family Life*, New York: Doubleday

Wood, Christine and John Davidson (1993) 'Conflict resolution in the family: A PET evaluation study', *Australian Psychologist*, Vol. 28, No. 2, pp. 100–4

INDEX

Index

Hugh Mackay
Generations

*Provocative, illuminating, compelling . . . above all, a
convincing and reassuring explanation of the generation
gaps between the Baby Boomers, their parents and their
children.*

In *Generations*, Hugh Mackay devotes his analytical skills to
the task of exploring the attitudes, values and outlook of
three generations of contemporary Australians.

In the process, he examines how all of us are shaped by
the social, cultural and economic influences on our
childhood and adolescence, and he explains why these
three generations are, in effect, the product of three different
Australias.

Mackay's analysis will change the way you think about inter-
generational differences and conflicts. As he says in the
Introduction to this important book: 'It will have served its
purpose if, seeing themselves reflected in these pages,
members of those generations find it a little easier to
understand themselves and each other.'

Hugh Mackay
House Guest

*'I came at six o'clock tonight, and I will leave at six o'clock
on Sunday evening. It won't be unpleasant for you. Just
some questions. Some tests. Some observations. This is
merely a survey; an information-gathering exercise. No harm
will come to you, of course.'*

Max enters Alice's life with a simple knock on the door one
Friday evening. Once inside her apartment, Max's seemingly
innocent market research survey becomes an intense
psychological drama in which Alice must confront some
tough questions about her past, and some unpalatable
truths about herself.

Tense and unnerving, *House Guest* is an extraordinarily
skilled novel, both original in its conception and frighteningly
astute in its observation of the innermost workings of the
human psyche.

Praise for Hugh Mckay's first novel, *Little Lies*:

'accomplished, highly readable and blackly funny'
CANBERRA TIMES

'deftly and adroitly managed;
AUSTRALIAN BOOK REVIEW

'At last an Australian has created an original novel'
SUNDAY MAIL

Hugh Mackay
Little Lies

From Australia's foremost social commentator comes a novel of deception and intrigue, told in three voices. Three voices, three stories . . . but who can you trust?

Cole's story:
Modesty and humility don't get you far in this business, I'm afraid. No, let me be more candid: modesty and humility can be great assets, as long as you don't let them stand in the way of your ambition . . . and I never did.

Georgina's story:
I sometimes wonder whether Cole is actually the sort of man who needs the tension of having two women after him at once . . . it seemed to keep him under control, in a funny kind of way.

Keith's story:
What do you make of Cole's extraordinary behaviour at the cemetery? Blood on his hands? Would you say? You wouldn't. Neither would I. Too melodramatic. Way off the mark. Truth would be nastier than that.

Little Lies is a brilliantly controlled, blackly funny novel from the bestselling author of *Reinventing Australia* and *The Good Listener*.